It's all about
thinking

It's all about
thinking

Collaborating to Support All Learners

IN MATHEMATICS AND SCIENCE

FAYE BROWNLIE, CAROLE FULLERTON,
AND LEYTON SCHNELLERT

PORTAGE & MAIN PRESS

Portage & Main Press gratefully acknowledges the financial support of the Province of Manitoba through the Department of Culture, Heritage, Tourism & Sport and the Manitoba Book Publishing Tax Credit, and the Government of Canada through the Canada Book Fund (CBF) for our publishing activities.

PERMISSION ACKNOWLEDGMENT
The publisher has made every effort to acknowledge all sources that have been used in this book and would be grateful if any errors or omissions were pointed out so they may be corrected in subsequent editions. The following illustrations are identified by figure number.

Figure 12.9: © CHINA DAILY/Reuters/Corbis

Figure 12.13: © OSMAN ORSAL/Reuters/Corbis

Figure 9.1, Figure 9.6, and Figure 12.3: VAN DE WALLE, JOHN A.; LOVIN, ANN H., TEACHING STUDENT-CENTERED MATHEMATICS: GRADES 5-8, 1st Edition, ©2006. Reprinted by permission of Pearson Education, Inc., Upper Saddle River, NJ.

Figure 11.1: Addison Wesley MATH MAKES SENSE 6, Morrow, Peggy; Don Jones, and Bryn Keyes, © 2006, page 173, Pearson Education Canada and "reprinted with permission by Pearson Canada Inc."

Printed and bound in Canada by Friesens
Cover and interior design by Relish Design Studio Ltd.

LIBRARY AND ARCHIVES CANADA CATALOGUING IN PUBLICATION

Brownlie, Faye
    It's all about thinking : collaborating to support all learners in mathematics and science / Faye Brownlie, Carole Fullerton and Leyton Schnellert.

Includes bibliographical references and index.
Issued also in electronic format.
ISBN 978-1-55379-269-7

    1. Critical thinking. 2. Mathematics--Study and teaching (Elementary). 3. Mathematics--Study and teaching (Secondary). 4. Science--Study and teaching (Elementary). 5. Science--Study and teaching (Secondary).
I. Fullerton, Carole II. Schnellert, Leyton III. Title.

LB2395.35.B77 2011   370.15'2   C2011-903149-3

PORTAGE & MAIN PRESS

100-318 McDermot Ave.
Winnipeg, MB Canada R3A 0A2
Email: books@portageandmainpress.com
Toll-free: 1-800-667-9673
Fax-free: 1-866-734-8477

www.pandmpress.com

FSC
www.fsc.org
MIX
Paper from
responsible sources
FSC® C016245

Dedication

To all those learners who have pushed our thinking and encouraged us to share with others.

Acknowledgments

In the first book of our series *It's All About Thinking*, teachers in the curriculum areas of English, social studies, and humanities opened the doors of their classrooms to us. In this second book of the series, we explore the application of similar approaches to the content areas of mathematics and science, and extend our thanks to the teachers in math and science classrooms who also believe that thinking skills are at the heart of the work they do with students.

Special thanks to: Mindy Casselman, Lori Davis, Jeremy Ellis, Starleigh Grass, Kristi Johnston, Catherine Ludwig, Susan Schleppe, Tracy Snipstead, Nicole Vander Wal, Katie Wagner and Nicole Widdess.

FAYE BROWNLIE has worked in staff development with teachers, schools, and districts across Canada, the US, and internationally. She recently completed multi-year projects in BC: the Leadership for Learning Academy, the DART (District Assessment of Learning Team) Consortium, and the Early Primary Reading Assessment Consortium; and in Latvia: the Reading and Writing for Critical Thinking Project. Faye continues to teach one day a week in the Richmond School District in BC. She has co-authored many books for teachers.

CAROLE FULLERTON (formerly Saundry) has taught in elementary and secondary classrooms in BC and Ontario in both English and French. A passionate mathematician, Carole has given presentations at Canadian, US, and international conferences on mathematical thinking, visualizing, and reasoning. In her work with teachers, she promotes a teaching through problem-solving approach to mathematics learning, using the Big Math Idea (backwards design) as a framework for supporting diversity and facilitating assessment for learning.

LEYTON SCHNELLERT is an assistant professor at The University of British Columbia-Okanagan. His research and teaching focus on teacher inquiry, learning theory, and supporting diverse learners. He has been a middle, junior high, and secondary school classroom teacher, and a learning resource teacher for K–12. He continues collaboratively plan, teach, and reflect with colleagues and students through research and consulting activities. On most Fridays, he can be found co-teaching in a BC or Yukon grade 4-12 classroom exploring responsive instruction and meaningful and engaging learning experiences for diverse groups of students.

Table of Contents

Introduction

More and more frequently we are being asked about twenty-first-century learning and personalized learning. One interpretation of personalized learning seems to be the notion of devising *individual* learning pathways as opposed to developing *independent*, self-directed learners. This interpretation has teachers wondering about the future of classrooms and the learning communities that we have worked so hard to create. In fact, one administrator posed the question, "How does what you do fit in with personalized learning? Do you think you'll still have jobs?" We smiled because we believe that what we do *is* personalized learning.

We strive to prepare all learners with the skills to lead successful and happy lives. When following a personalized learning path, learners acquire the behaviours and capacities that characterize the twenty-first-century learner: the ability to problem-solve in creative ways, to think critically, to communicate and make sense of media, to collaborate and work in teams, to develop cross-cultural understandings as well as social responsibility, self-regulation, and self-reflection. It *is* all about thinking. What better set of skills to equip students with—so that they might be successful in a future we can only just imagine?

These capacities develop over time and require rich experiences that actively encourage wonderment and open-ended inquiry. Meaning-making is only possible in a "thought-full" and safe learning community. Although the competencies are for students to develop, they are ours to clarify and promote through purposeful curriculum design, framed by common principles and personalized to address the learning needs of a specific group of learners.

How do we, as educators, develop the capacity to work in this way? We believe that we do it best through collaboration. Working together allows us to move beyond the limits of our own experience, to weave our thinking together with that of another, and to work together in co-planning, co-teaching, and co-assessing. Michael Fullan, in *All Systems Go* (2010), describes this as "collective capacity," which he believes enables ordinary people to accomplish extraordinary things. He elaborates: "Collective capacity generates the emotional commitment and the technical expertise that no amount of individual capacity working alone can come close to matching." Not only is it more effective to work with others, it's more fun too!

Chapter 1

Meeting the Needs of All Learners

Nothing can be taught unless it has the potential of making sense to the learner, and learning itself is nothing but the endeavour to make sense. (Frank Smith 1978)

Teaching is complex and intriguing. Each semester and each school year begins a new journey, often toward a familiar destination but never along the same route. It is the learners who determine our route, who cause us to revise our travel plans and detour toward unexpected surprises, to hurry through known territory, and to linger longer in other areas. It is the learners who help us visit known sights with fresh eyes and expand our horizons. It is the learners who engage with our curriculum, who engage and develop because of our relationship with them, who make teaching worthwhile. Today's learners are more diverse than they have ever been. They hold the promise of tomorrow, and they are today's challenge.

Who Are the Learners?

Today's classrooms are diverse. Yet students have *always* had different learning styles and different rates of learning. In the past, to address different learning needs, students were often segregated based on their differences. Students who learned at a slower pace were placed in a class with similar students. Students who had learning difficulties or disabilities may have been placed in a separate class. Students who had difficulty with impulse control and behaviour management could have been in yet a different class. Sometimes, these classes were in the home school of the student; sometimes they were not. Sometimes the placement was for part of a day; sometimes it was a full-time placement. One of the challenges was deciding who was in and who was out. The intent was to better address the learning needs of all students and leave the teacher with a more homogeneous and, thus, more teachable group, but classroom teachers recognized that diversity still remained in their classes. There were still students who learned differently and at different rates.

In recent years, other groups of students have added to the diversity in our classrooms. One emerging group is made up of students whose first language is not English, those who may be learning English as a second, a third, or even a fourth language. In the past, more students tended to share a common first language and a common culture. Canada's 2006 Census data show that one in five Canadians is born abroad, the highest foreign-born population since the Depression. Canada is now home to citizens from 200 different countries who still speak 150 different languages. Children from all these countries arrive in our schools (Statistics Canada 2006). Within this group, there is wide disparity. Some of the students have attended schools, but some have not. Some students have been living in refugee camps for several years and might even have been born there. The experience of just entering a school building is new to them.

Another group of students whose unique learning needs are becoming more recognized are Aboriginal learners. From 1951 to 2001, Canada's population doubled; in the same 50 years, the Aboriginal population increased seven times. Although the Aboriginal population makes up 3.5 per cent of the population in Canada, 30 per cent of Aboriginal children live in homes receiving welfare; this figure is 50 per cent in British Columbia, and 80 per cent in both Manitoba and Saskatchewan (Calvin Helin, Rural Schools Conference, Vancouver, BC, October 2008). Across Canada, there is great disparity between the graduation rates of Aboriginal and non-Aboriginal populations. In BC, 80 per cent of non-Aboriginal students graduate from secondary school but only 48 per cent of Aboriginal students graduate. Across Canada, 71.5 per cent of non-Aboriginals graduate from secondary school, but only 57.7 per cent of Aboriginals graduate from secondary school. Failure to finish secondary school correlates with poorer health and lower economic prosperity. We are failing this group of students. They, too, must be recognized and included in our discussions of diversity.

Finally, children of poverty make up a third group of diverse students. They often go hungry; they lack the background experiences that align easily with the curriculum; and they feel disenfranchised. To help break the cycle of poverty, they, too, need access to a quality curriculum. According to Mary Ellen Turpel-Lafond, British Columbia's Representative for Children and Youth, a recent study in that province found that children whose families were receiving welfare were more likely to become involved in crime than they were to graduate (Making Connections Conference, Richmond, BC, November 2008). This research and the research of Doug Willms suggest that this trend can be broken if students form attachments with adults at school, if they learn meaningful pro-social behaviour, and if they have access to equality in their school curriculum; that is, if they are exposed to and can access the same high-quality content and courses as their peers (Willms 2002).

As a consequence of policies of inclusion and of recognition that all students have the right to be educated in the least restrictive environment and to be with their peers, all these students are now found in regular classrooms. We believe that all students belong in regular classrooms, engaged in high-quality, thoughtful learning experiences with their peers while pursuing a complex, meaningful curriculum. We begin our planning with all students in mind and with the conviction that our planning for a full range of learner strengths and styles means that more students will have opportunities to be successful more of the time, and that fewer adaptations and modifications will be required for students with special needs. This is the essence of Universal Design for Learning, which is discussed in more detail in chapter 4.

Today's classrooms present a challenge: How do we best address the wide range of learners' needs—academic, social, and emotional? How do we build a community of learners who, as a result of working together, are more individually able than they would have been working alone? How do we prepare our students to be the best they can be in a complex, ever-changing world? What can we do in the classroom to make a difference for *all* learners? To answer some of the questions, we turn to the research.

What Makes a Difference for Adolescent Learners in Math and Science?

What helps adolescents learn more effectively? What can we do to better meet their needs? Linda Darling-Hammond and an impressive list of co-authors (David Pearson, Brigid Barron, and Alan Schoenfeld) provide a research-based summary in their book *Powerful Learning: What We Know about Teaching for Understanding* (2008). The authors outline three principles of learning that influence and inform effective teaching:

1. Students come to the classroom with prior knowledge that must be addressed if teaching is to be effective.
2. Students need to organize and use knowledge conceptually if they are to apply it beyond the classroom.
3. Students learn more effectively if they understand how they learn and how to manage their own learning.

Each of these research-based principles describes the authors' beliefs about students—students as thinkers, students as learners, and students as creators of knowledge. The principles affirm that students have the power to direct their own learning and to mediate and reflect on their own thinking and learning. This mindset is foundational to planning the kind of instruction that deepens learning for all students, which is the most important outcome of education, regardless of subject area or grade level. Empowering students to be critical thinkers and problem-solvers is the critical role of schools.

So how do teachers translate principles into practice? Darling-Hammond, Pearson, Barron, and Schoenfeld are respected members of the education research communities in literacy, science, and mathematics. Their pooled expertise and common beliefs about students as thinkers have led to the elaboration of seven common classroom practices aimed at deepening understanding across subject areas (also see *How People Learn* by Bransford, Brown, and Cocking 2000). Effective teachers use these practices to engage students in meaningful learning—learning that promotes thinking and problem solving.

Seven Common Classroom Practices

1. Create meaningful and ambiguous tasks that reflect how knowledge is used in the field.

Meaningful Tasks

In mathematics and science, teachers provide instruction focused on the content of their discipline: cell biology, the Pythagorean theorem, electricity, ecosystems, area and volume. Traditionally, these content-focused lessons were teacher-directed, involving minimal engagement from students who were asked to memorize and apply the necessary procedure or set of skills. Today, math and science teachers recognize that students' success depends on much more than procedural knowledge, on more even than the application of skills and procedures. For students to achieve proficiency in math and science they must also acquire deep understanding of the concepts, competence in relevant strategies, and a disposition to persist at problem solving.

To internalize important ideas, adolescent learners need to engage with mathematical and scientific content through meaningful tasks. The tasks should be rich, open-ended, with many possible solutions or many possible solution methods, and they should engage students in developing the important understandings about mathematics and science. Consider the following question which provides a rich task for students:

How much forest has to be removed to construct a four-lane highway 15 km long?

In solving this problem, students have to estimate the width of one lane of a highway, perhaps using the referents of car widths or parking spaces, and make adjustments for highway shoulders and medians in order to calculate the total area of forest that would have to be removed to accommodate a four-lane highway. The process of visualizing the highway and its impact on the surrounding forest will involve the students in a great deal of conversation, measuring, and reasoning, all the while making connections to prior knowledge. The students might make personal referents or points of comparison—for example, "the width of a car is about the same as 3 adult school chairs pushed together like the back seat of our van" or "my driveway is about 8 snow-shovel widths across, and that's about the same width as a lane of traffic." Such a process allows them to make important personal connections to the concepts covered. By solving this problem with partners or in groups, students simulate the real work of mathematicians.

By contrast, consider this task:

Find the area of this rectangle.

15 km

In essence, students doing this task will arrive at the same result as those doing the "forest and highway" task, but all the richness and the open-endedness in methodology are stripped away—and with them all the potential for student engagement. Students have only to apply the formula for finding the area of a rectangle, a memorized procedure, which means that, in using this type of task, teachers have no way to assess their students' understanding of mathematical concepts.

Ambiguous Tasks

The authors of *Powerful Learning* also note that ambiguity is a necessary element of worthwhile tasks. Effective teachers of math and science do not avoid complexity in the tasks they present to their students; rather, they foster struggle and promote risk-taking in their classrooms. Deep learning comes from dealing with the challenge of problematic situations in a safe learning environment. The responsibility of teachers is to craft or select problematic situations from within their discipline; it is the responsibility of students to engage in and think critically about solving these problems. To be truly prepared for an ever-changing world, students need to have well-developed problem-solving capacity and the ability to reason. When the problems in math and science are ambiguous and meaningful, the solution is not immediately evident. It is this dissonance that engages students in "hard fun," a term coined by students to describe tasks that are fun *by virtue of* their complexity, as referenced in the work of Seymour Papert. Seymour Papert first coined this term in 2002 in an article for the *Bangor Daily News*. (Bangor, Maine). His subsequent articles and research include the term, which is well-known in technological circles, particularly around robotics.

Consider the following problems:

What can you find out about the pine beetle infestation? How should the problem be addressed?

Imagine what a box holding 24 chocolates might look like. Design the box for the most economical production.

In both cases, the student must define the task, apply a solution strategy, determine the result, and justify it. There are many possible ways to approach each problem and many solutions, which makes the problems truly muddy and complex learning situations. Learners crave this kind of thinking, the kind we use to resolve the uncertain, the ill-defined, the complex tasks — or problems — that we face each day. What better way to prepare students for the real world than to present them with opportunities to engage with important content in challenging ways?

Connecting to the Field

Mastering both the content and the thinking processes of these disciplines demands that students learn what it means to behave — and think — like mathematicians and scientists. Students must learn the thinking skills required within the context of each discipline.

In valuing and creating "thought-full" students in our math and science classrooms, teachers are working to promote strategies and dispositions for thinking in the content areas. In the 2006 *Common Curriculum Framework for K–9 Mathematics* from the Western and Northern Canadian Protocol (WNCP) for collaboration in education, these strategies and dispositions are made explicit. That framework includes "The Mathematical Processes," a list of seven ways in which students are expected to engage with content and master the learning outcomes for math:

1. communication
2. connections
3. predicting (mental math, estimation)
4. reasoning
5. visualizing
6. problem-solving
7. technology

The *National Science Education Standards* (NSES) describe the activities and thinking processes used by scientists who are seeking to expand human knowledge of the natural world (NRC 1996). In the NSES, the outcomes of science learning contained in the content standards are summarized as the development of the scientifically literate student (NRC 1996, 22). Scientific literacy means that a person can:

- ask and propose answers to questions
- describe, explain, and predict
- read with understanding a range of articles about science
- identify issues
- express positions
- evaluate scientific information and the methods used to generate it
- pose and evaluate arguments based on evidence

By modelling for students how to think like scientists and mathematicians, teachers as mentors show what goes on in their minds as they inquire, problem-solve, and make meaning out of learning situations in their disciplines. They demonstrate connection-making and reasoning behaviours as they engage with the content they present to students. After all, if these are the ways in which mathematicians and scientists think while problem solving, how better to engage students in the content so that they capture the essence of the concepts presented?

In math and science, using processes as meaning-making strategies supports students in developing and consolidating the enduring understandings from the content presented. These behaviours reflect how knowledge is used in the field—and what is valued within the realm of problem solving in the sciences and mathematics.

2. Engage students in active learning so that they will apply and test what they know

Active Learning in Math and Science

Active learning means that students will learn math by doing math, that is, by problem solving and reasoning, estimating and predicting, and by generalizing, modelling, and constructing. Active learning means that students will learn science by experimenting and testing hypotheses, by examining data and observing living things. The major part of a math or science lesson should be devoted to active explorations of important concepts—using manipulatives to model and solve algebraic equations; using a magnifying glass and sketchbook to observe, sketch, and predict changes in the cell structure of a living organism given different reagents. These shared explorations are the raw learning opportunities, the foundation for conversation and meaning-making. They can rarely be understood, owned, or interpreted if only read from a book.

Collaborative Learning

To build their repertoire of thinking strategies and develop content knowledge, students need opportunities to work both alone and in collaboration with others. Instructional strategies that enable students to problem-solve together and to construct understandings of the content in context help move students beyond the limits of their own experience. Paired and group structures are effective in helping students link their learning with that of other students, frame questions for experts and for research, and dig more deeply as they socially construct their knowledge and understandings of math and science concepts. The mathematical and scientific processes of communication and connection-making are promoted in collaborative learning situations based in the context of the discipline.

3. Draw connections to students' prior knowledge and experiences

Students come to middle and secondary school with a range of experiences, aptitudes, and background knowledge. For all of them, their learning has been acquired in different classrooms with different teachers; for some of them, the learning has taken place in other countries or in other languages; the learning may have been hands-on and connected, or it may have been rote and procedural.

Van de Walle and Lovin (2006) speak to these connected experiences and their impact on learning. They note that deep understanding depends on networks of connected experiences and that, for students to achieve conceptual understanding, they must access prior knowledge, recognize its value, and apply it to new learning. They go on to say that the lack of connection to prior knowledge limits success for students who struggle, which makes it crucial for teachers to activate and validate prior experience in all students, and to support adolescent learners in making and maintaining connections to what they already know within the realm of the discipline.

When working with text, we have elaborated three types of connections that students make while reading—text-to-text, text-to-self, and text-to-world (also see Harvey and Goudvis 2000; Tovani 2000). In math and science, these connections can be customized to fit the discipline and thereby help students to focus their thinking. Consider how we might focus students' thinking and activate prior knowledge by asking them to read a piece of text about kinetic molecular theory (the theory that describes the movement of molecules) and to make science-to-self, science-to-world, and science-to-science connections in the margin of the text itself. This can also happen in conversation with a partner—for example, during or after watching a YouTube clip that shows a sped-up example of the water cycle or when examining specimens under a microscope. The nature and complexity of those connections give teachers valuable formative assessment information; a lack of connections or less-developed connections would signal the need for some targeted instruction.

Although we want students to acknowledge the importance of mathematics and science in their lives (math-to-self connections) as well as the omnipresence of mathematics and science and their usefulness in the world (science-to-world connections), we recognize that the deepest mathematical and scientific thinkers are those who can identify and describe math-to-math connections or science-to-science connections. We want students who can make connections to concepts learned in elementary school (e.g., multiplication using a rectangular array or area model) and advanced, abstract concepts like the multiplication of polynomials taught in secondary school. The simple fact is that these concepts are intimately connected. If more students had opportunities to make math-to-math and science-to-science connections, mathematical and scientific meaning-making would become the norm rather than the exception in classrooms.

In carefully constructed lesson sequences, teachers of math and science create opportunities to promote connection-making, tying each new lesson's big idea to the enduring understandings of the previous one, if not the entire unit. In this way, students focus on the important things to know, and they learn to sort out how such essential understandings fit within the web of knowledge for the discipline. This is a critical learning activity for students.

4. Assess student understanding in order to scaffold the learning process step-by-step

When students do not make or maintain connections, when they fail to grasp a central idea, when they persist in applying misconceptions, we need to assess why and work out ways of addressing the issue. Diagnostic assessment tools, whether formal or informal, can provide invaluable data for planning lessons and lesson sequences for whole groups, small groups, or individuals, based on their needs. A careful investigation of students' understanding is the first step. Asking a few key questions before teaching can provide a wealth of assessment data and focus instruction.

Consider these sentence stems:

What do you know about — Pythagoras? triangles? integers? biomes?

What do you know so far about — how human traits are passed down? force and motion?

What are important things to know about — graphing data? environmental adaptation?

These questions might be posed at the beginning of a unit or at the start of a lesson. After student responses are collected and analyzed, teachers can use the background knowledge and prior learning students already possess to plan their instruction.

Students may have gaps in their understanding of math and science concepts that impede success. We are learning that targeted instruction in these areas supports student progress. Consider the grade 8 math curriculum. To be able to successfully manipulate ratio and rate problems, students in grade 8 must have mastered and understood the concept of equivalent fractions. For those who lack this particular skill, a targeted mini-lesson on equivalent fractions, *and their connection to this new content*, will help them apply this information to problems of ratio and rate. Having these background skills is important, obviously, but a student's understanding that these mathematical ideas are linked within the web of numeracy is critical. Mathematicians know that equivalent fractions and ratios are an essential math-to-math connection.

Although a diagnostic assessment can point to areas of need before the new topic is introduced, it can also help to assess what has already been mastered within that topic. For students who already have a solid understanding of the impact of acid rain on an ecosystem, there is little reason to pursue that topic; rather, there is an opportunity to explore it in more depth, making science-to-science connections to the effects of disease on the human body. Approaching teaching in this way offers opportunities to build a shared knowledge base and extend the learning for those who need more.

Scaffold the Learning Process

Some students require more time and more specific teaching in order to achieve the specific curricular outcomes. Allow some additional time and specific teaching either in the regular class or in after-hour tutorials; the greater needs of some students might require intensive additional programming. In many middle schools and secondary schools, students view the resource centre as the place to get help with their homework. For some of them, however, this outreach is often just for "getting through stuff" rather than building and increasing relevant skills, such as how to synthesize the key ideas and concepts. To narrow the achievement gap for such students, teachers should create structures to help students learn and develop critical skills that they can then apply independently. Solutions might range from an additional course to a tutorial, but the focus should be on increasing thinking and reasoning capacities, not just on completing assignments. This attitude to assignments is epidemic; too many students say, "Don't ask me to think about this, just tell me the formula!" Teachers and tutors should not overlook the learning potential in targeted instruction or in supporting a learner in the process of deconstructing an assignment into its essential components so that the embedded concepts can be better understood as a whole.

5. Assess student learning continuously and adapt teaching to student needs

Continuous Formative Assessment

Black and Wiliam's (1998) study of formative assessment practices for the Assessment Research Group clarifies how teachers are changing their assessment practices to emphasize formative assessment. With formative assessment, teachers use the information gained from classroom work, daily assignments, interviews, conferences, and snapshots of student performance to guide their teaching and their students' learning. This assessment is called assessment *for* learning. Its main purpose is to guide instruction and inform learning.

Adapt Instruction to Student Needs

We consider the following questions when we look at how assessment informs instruction from a teaching perspective:

- *What can my students do?*
- *What is missing?* or *What do they still need to learn?*
- *What do I need to teach?*

- *Is my teaching making a difference?*
- *If not, what do I need to teach now?*
- *Do I teach in a different way, or move on?*

With formative assessment, students become more aware of the expectations for learning and therefore more involved in giving feedback to one another and in self-evaluating their progress toward these expectations. Involving students in formative assessment has been shown to increase student learning and raise achievement.

We know that student learning is greatly enhanced when teachers focus on student metacognition and goal-setting. We consider the following questions when we look at how assessment informs learning from a student's perspective:

- *What am I able to do, considering the criteria for success?*
- *What is missing?* or *What do I need to learn?*
- *What is my plan for learning?*
- *Who can help me?*

Adapt Resources to Student Needs

Richard Allington (2001) posed the question "How can you learn from texts you can't read?" This is a common concern. Far too often, math and science classrooms provide everyone with the same textbook. All students are expected, first, to be interested in it, then to be able to read it. However, the readability of many textbooks—particularly in math and science—is far beyond the reading capacity of our students. Subject-specific vocabulary and a mixture of symbols, graphs, equations, and charts combine to make reading-for-meaning in math and science a subject-specific task that requires explicit instruction.

That said, students can learn the content when it is presented with accessible text and when students are armed with specific strategies for reading that text. Content expressed in accessible text can build students' background knowledge and allow them to tackle more challenging text. But this is a Catch-22 situation. If teachers themselves are tied to one text for all students—or if all information and activities come from a single math or science text, we limit content learning for a large group of students. We prefer to use a textbook as a scaffold for some learning but not as the core source for all learning.

In both mathematics and the sciences, there is a return to teachers working outside a traditional text, engaging students in explorations and investigations that are embedded in students' experience. These learning tasks are connected to students' contexts and grow out of their questions—which encourages students to personalize the math and science inquiry. Mathematical investigations of the competitiveness of cell phone plans or a science inquiry into the acidity of water in local parks provide learning situations in which students engage with different kinds of texts (brochures, websites, newspapers) that further engage them by connecting the math and science exploration in a meaningful context. More students become involved in learning when the learning is not defined by the textbook but by the students themselves.

6. Provide clear standards, constant feedback, and opportunities for work

Clear Standards

Effective teachers have high expectations for their students. They set clear standards for student success and involve their students in crafting the criteria for assignments. They provide exemplars of high-quality work for their students to deconstruct and analyze so that each learner understands what success in creating a lab report, a theoretical proof, or a piece of reflective writing looks like.

More importantly, teachers of science and math embody thinkers in their discipline. They model for their students what it means to think like a mathematician or a scientist. They demonstrate a disposition of inquiry and allow their students to struggle. They problem-solve and think aloud in front of their students so that the students can witness an expert at work—accessing background knowledge, considering and trying out more than one line of thinking or one strategy, posing questions—then reflect on and analyze their thinking to see what was relevant and helpful. Such teaching behaviours validate student curiosity and perseverance and demonstrate teacher expectations that all students will behave in this way while engaged in investigations of math and science concepts.

Feedback and Self-Monitoring

The artistry in teaching for understanding involves asking the right questions—questions that promote thinking and move the learning forward. Sometimes the questions help direct a whole class discussion with the aim of highlighting important relationships or big ideas; for example:

> *So I hear you saying, Christine, that you believe global warming can be stemmed by human action. Do the rest of you agree?*

At other times, the prompts provided by teachers come in the form of feedback to students, developing their understandings about a topic.

> *I see you've constructed a rectangular array as a model for this polynomial expression. How are those ideas connected?*

> *Why do you think these organisms are symbiotic?*

> *What is your hypothesis?*

Questions of this type are intended to support connection-making and elicit reflection on the part of the student.

Teachers have an important role to play in giving feedback and probing student thinking, but knowing what to ask at the right time can be challenging.

Van de Walle and Lovin (2006) outline three questions that teachers should ask to support students in working through a task. These questions are generic enough to be used in just about any learning situation, because they probe the process, the reasoning, and the connection-making:

1. *What are you doing?*
2. *Why are you doing it?*
3. *How does it help you?*

Try the following classic problem-solving task. While you solve it, pause and ask yourself the three questions. How do they help you to be more metacognitive? What do you notice yourself doing while you problem-solve?

A tree frog is climbing up a tree 20 m tall. By day he climbs 4 m. At night, he falls down 2 m.

How many days will it take the frog to reach the top of the tree? How do you know?

The three questions above guide students in thinking *about* their thinking *while* they are thinking; notably, used often enough, these questions become part of students' internal script for learning, and support their ability to self-monitor their learning behaviours.

From the research in assessment for learning (AFL), the three descriptive feedback questions are:

1. *What's working?*
2. *What's not?*
3. *What's next?*

These questions are another way to frame a conversation between a teacher and a student, or between two students, or when a student is engaged in personal reflection. Such questions move the learning forward. (See a more in-depth discussion of these questions in chapter 3).

Providing Opportunities for Work

Effective teachers of math and science recognize the need for meaningful practice in their disciplines, for the consolidation of concepts and skills. In a classroom where "doing math" or "doing science" is the work of students, teachers have multiple opportunities to give feedback, to monitor student progress, and to adapt where needed. For example, after a large-group debriefing about tundra, asking students to identify and examine the features of two or more biomes *of their choice* helps them to apply thinking skills and science knowledge.

Writing in Math and Science

In math and science classes, students need the opportunity to write intensively, to write *connected text*—that is, text that requires them to generate ideas and to link these ideas through writing. Writing helps them clarify their thinking and hold their thinking, whether on paper or on the computer, while they reflect on it and polish it, alone and with others. Students need to write to make sense of the content they are engaging with. Writing, not rote copying or filling in quick answers to someone else's questions, is a constructive, meaning-making process. The *Principles and Standards for School Mathematics* (2000), developed by the National Council of Teachers of Mathematics (NCTM), promote the use of writing in math class as a means of consolidating ideas, but also as an effective assessment tool for evaluating content-based understandings. The *National Science Education Standards* (1996) <www.nap.edu/openbook.php?record_id=4962> make similar claims, encouraging teachers to teach students *how* to write in their discipline as a means of expressing concepts, reviewing information, summarizing data, constructing a reasoned argument, and responding to critical comments.

7. Encouraging strategic and metacognitive thinking, so that students learn to evaluate and guide their own learning

As Wilhelm, Baker, and Dube (2001) remind us, the explicit teaching of reading comprehension strategies is important only when the strategies help students construct personally meaningful understandings—they are not strategies for their own sake. Students need to work with and learn effective reading, writing, and thinking strategies in all areas of the curriculum. Researchers such as Lenz and Deshler (2004) have found that students often do not generalize these thinking skills across units of study, let alone across subjects and contexts. Thus, the explicit teaching of these strategies has to happen in many settings and as part of the criteria for what successful thinkers and learners are expected to do and get better at. Students need to be taught how to make sense of all their different texts—labs in science classes, recipes in home economics, primary sources in history, maps in geography, problems and applications in mathematics, poems in English, images in art, and so on.

Gradual Release of Responsibility

Effective instruction for reading in the content areas follows a pattern called the "gradual release of responsibility" (Pearson and Gallagher 1983), which includes:

- model
- guided practice
- independent practice
- independent application

This gradual release of responsibility supports all learners in becoming better readers of text in math and science, and follows an instructional flow:

- First, the teacher models the thinking of how to make meaning from the text. This includes setting a purpose for students' reading, often in relation to a learning task. To introduce helpful ways to work with text they usually "think aloud," verbalizing for students how to determine, sort, and compare relevant information and ideas.

- Then, opportunities are provided for students to think aloud with partners or in small groups, giving one another feedback on how they are working through their thinking. The teacher supports and coaches this phase.

- Then, the students begin to work with the strategy or approach independently, still within the established framework for teaching and learning.

- Ultimately, the teacher looks for independent application of what has been taught. For this to happen, opportunities need to exist beyond the day's assignment, for the students to demonstrate—without teacher guidance—their independent use of the strategy for making meaning out of text, be that a mathematics problem or the application of a math concept or instructions for an experiment in a science lab.

Most importantly, students need opportunities to monitor their use of thinking strategies in gradual release and to make links between how and why they are used in different tasks and settings. (This and other key instructional principles are explained further in the next sections.)

Metacognitive Thinking and Motivation

Motivation affects engagement, the key to all learning. Motivation is often directly related to the quality of the relationship that a student has with the teacher. It is also related to the student's sense of voice and choice in the classroom. When all control seems to exist other than within the student, students may have difficulty maintaining their motivation for learning. For example, some approaches that inherently have more choice built in include inquiry learning, teaching with and to multiple intelligences, open-ended teaching, investigations, and experimentation.

These approaches, while becoming more prevalent in social studies, language arts, and humanities instruction, are still considered by some to be incongruous with math and science teaching. Direct instruction as the dominant or only pathway to content delivery can contribute to a student's feeling of lack of control over the learning in these subject areas.

In the NCTM's *Principles and Standards for School Mathematics* (2000), the importance of motivation in learning is made explicit:

> Learning with understanding also helps students become autonomous learners. Students learn more and better when they take control of their own learning. When challenged with appropriately chosen tasks, students can become confident in their ability to tackle difficult problems, eager to figure things out on their own, flexible in exploring mathematical ideas, and willing to persevere when tasks are challenging. <standards.nctm.org/document/chapter2/learn.htm>

Midway through a unit with her Science 8 classes, Sandra McAuley asked the students to figure out what the "big idea" was. After discussion in small groups, then with the whole class, the students determined the big idea was that "cells are the building blocks of life." Then she invited them to look at the curriculum's three key learning outcomes—plant vs. animal cell, organelles and functions, and the process of osmosis/diffusion as a means of transportation within and in/out of cells. As they moved toward the end of the unit, she told them that they could do whatever they wanted to demonstrate their learning. She had students making movies and PowerPoint presentations, building cell models, writing papers, and creating an electronic display board. Interestingly, there was a marked discrepancy between her two classes in their initial reaction. One class excitedly started generating ideas, getting into groups, talking, and planning. They were motivated and engaged. The second class was quieter, more reserved, and not quite sure what to do. It took them more than one class to transition from "waiting to be given an assignment with exact steps to follow" to "synthesizing their understandings and taking control of their own learning."

Within any of these instructional approaches, having opportunities to set personal goals and to be involved in self-assessment makes a difference in student learning. As Sandra saw with her two classes, students' willingness to set personal goals and become more self-directed requires the teacher's gradual release of responsibility while offering needed levels of support. It is so much more than the general, broad questions—*What do you want to learn?* or *How do you want to learn this?*

Inviting students to be metacognitive about their thinking and learning in math and science helps them to internalize how to think and learn in these fields. When asked, Eric Jones' Biology 11 students reported:

> Thinking and working like a scientist has changed my thinking because most of the time any work that I do is just about finding the right answer. Working this way is more about starting with a question and working to the best of your ability.

> Even if you mess up, you're left with the results, which usually tell you something even if that something is only what you could do better next time. I find this a much better way to work.

> Your answers must reflect all your steps and even a failed experiment is a learning experience.

> You should talk in group work as much as possible to make sure everyone is working in the same direction.

> [This approach] has changed my thinking because I am more open to other opinions.

> [This approach] has changed my thinking because I feel more challenged to go deeper.

Building opportunities for students to assess their own thinking and learning against shared criteria is one of the most effective ways to help students develop skills in metacognition—that is, thinking about their own thinking and learning. As students learn to use metacognition, they begin to make and monitor personalized plans for their growth. When students examine their progress and explore the depth of their learning (*What do I really understand about algebra? What is really important to know about matter changing states? What connections can I make between reasoning in algebra and in other areas of math?*), they personalize their own learning pathways. As teachers provide support and feedback to students, the students become greater agents of their own learning. This leads them to self-direct and to self-regulate, or monitor, their own learning.

Integrating Technology into Math and Science

Though this is not included in the Darling-Hammond et al. (2008) research, it is evident in other research (e.g., *Reading Next* 2004, 2006) that integrating technology into classroom learning can better support students as they process, personalize, and transform their learning. Looking at international assessments in science and mathematics, it is clear that students struggle to achieve deep learning (Scardamalia and Bereiter 2008). Deep learning implies a progressive process, using the understandings gained from inquiry to formulate new problems and questions that could not have been formulated before (Bereiter and Scardamalia 1993; Hakkarainen and Sintonen 2002). Technology offers students opportunities to work with and represent concepts and relationships in new and evolving ways. For instance, over the course of a science unit on space, students can input and arrange information in a variety of ways to help them both process and synthesize this information. They can create a scene, a set of categories, or a narrative sequence using visual tools. Using technology in this way requires students to hold and work with key information in relation to a schema. Web 2.0 tools (with which students can share and comment on each other's thinking and representations) offer students ways to interactively compare, relate, and create knowledge. By commenting on blogs or participating in online chats, one person's views can be linked to other views and can be integrated into higher-level principles that can only be arrived at through collaboration.

In the mathematics classroom, technology plays a critical role. Not only is the use of calculators accepted, but learning to use a calculator appropriately and critically has become part of the curriculum from the elementary grades. Graphing calculators at the upper secondary level are changing how students visualize and gain deeper understanding of functions and relations. Data analysis tools—both hand-held and online—allow students to manipulate information in dynamic ways, comparing attributes of data to make inferences and generalizations. Applets and flash animations can be used to model important mathematical concepts like the multiplication of fractions, to easily perform a probabilistic experiment, or to visualize the derivation of the volume of a sphere.

Thus, technology can be a tool to make thinking visible and to enhance thinking where students create multiple forms of representation and co-construct interpretations and representations (Scardamalia and Bereiter 2008).

Transformative Learning Experiences

Technology is more than a tool to manipulate ideas; it is a tool to enhance thinking. Online communication tools like blogs, wikis, and podcasts give students opportunities to exchange and shape their ideas around a topic or issue. Online collaborative tools like <bubbl.us>, a web application for brainstorming online, provide a forum to share and collectively organize details and main ideas. Presentation tools like Prezi, a web-based application for both building and sharing a presentation, give students ways to present their synthesis of ideas to a wide audience.

Picture Cam, a 13-year-old, sitting on the couch with his laptop, watching videos online on the Discovery Channel. He is researching the construction of the great pyramids of Giza for an assignment. He has viewed four different segments thus far and has explored a range of ideas, including the possibility that the pyramids were created by aliens. While he listens, he is typing up the report that he is required to write about this ages-old mystery—and he is chatting with his friend Cassidy at the same time. Many of today's learners, like Cam, are smoothly integrating technology into their learning outside the classroom. It is time we caught up with them, inside the classroom.

Meeting the Needs

So what do effective teachers do? What works in classrooms? These are our four key beliefs:

1. Teachers need a mental model of effective learning

A mental model of effective learning works as a lens through which information is viewed—new strategies, new programs, new curricula, new assessment tools, and new mandates. Teachers use their mental model to describe to others—and to themselves when planning and reflecting—what they value in learning and what works in their classrooms. They use their model to examine information to see how it fits with their beliefs. If it doesn't, they either discard the new information or rework it in order to make it fit.

Consider, for example, a teacher working to implement a new math curriculum, working hard to figure out how to include all her learners, to help them to make meaning of the important math concepts, while engaging them in real-world experiences. A colleague volunteers to share a "foolproof" new math program with her—one that comes complete with levelled workbooks for every student and ready-made tests to match. Although the classroom teacher appreciates the varying levels provided, she does not feel comfortable with the "fill-in-the-blanks" format of the booklets. She sees the workbooks as reducing the mathematics to rote procedural knowledge alone, valuing only correct answers and not conceptual understanding. She wants her students to be "reason-ers," not calculators. Nor do the ready-made tests match her view of assessment of mathematical competence—conceptual understanding supported by reasoning and strategic thinking.

She knows that, to truly assess what her students know and can do, she must structure tasks and frame questions that are connected to key concepts and mathematical processes. The assessments have to match what her students are learning, not the page they are on. She declines the "foolproof" help, wanting to use her teacher voice and her knowledge of her students to create effective programming for them.

2. Open-ended strategies support all learners

Purposeful, constructive activities that teachers engage their students in will link experiences with the content of the curriculum and prepare them to construct their own understandings. When planning instruction, teachers take into consideration the learners in their class and the curriculum expectations in order to design strategic learning sequences that will assist the learners in moving from their current learning place to another learning place as described in the curriculum. This requires knowing the learner, knowing the curriculum, and knowing how best to facilitate the learning.

To help students construct their personal understandings, we divide our strategies into three categories, based on their purpose:

1. Connecting
2. Processing
3. Transforming and personalizing

Figure 1.1 Planning open-ended strategies

Strategy Category	Strategy Purpose
Connecting	· Connect to others and to curriculum content
	· Access and activate background knowledge
	· Acquire and build background knowledge
Processing	· Interact with new ideas
	· Build understanding by adding on new information and revising former information
Transforming/Personalizing	· Show acquired information in personalized, thoughtful ways

Figure 1.1 captures our view of planning. We try to work with collaborative strategies as much as possible to capitalize on the social aspect of learning. We want all students to connect what they and others already know to the ideas and concepts they will be studying. We often start a learning sequence by asking students to predict, link, and compare key words, ideas,

images, artifacts, or relationships before engaging with new content. These are *connecting strategies*, helping students build from what they know. This might involve a simple quick-write, in which students record, draw, web, or give examples of everything they know about a particular topic related to the day's work. It might involve students tackling a problem with a partner, then have the class share out the range of ways they approached it. A simple strategy—nonetheless, it activates prior knowledge and allows teachers to help students make predictions about the day's big math or science idea and connect to key vocabulary.

Next, we use *processing strategies* to help students build the comprehension, communication, and analysis skills that they need to successfully use, link, and compare key information from the new content with what they knew previously. In science, students might be asked to record or highlight a key word from a paragraph and find three other words that provide details related to this key word. In math, they might be asked to complete a Frayer diagram, giving examples and non-examples of a key concept like exponents or linear relations. Processing strategies can be used with all kinds of texts—print, media, visual, and oral; in math, they may also include mathematical problems, learning situations, or applications of mathematical ideas; in science, they may also include experiments.

Finally, we use *personalizing/transforming strategies*. We want our students to be able to take information, to synthesize and represent it in a way that shows they have taken important, relevant ideas and understood them enough to transform them and, when possible, interpret the information in their own way. Reflective writing in the math and science classrooms, using a range of graphic organizers and conceptual frameworks, provides valuable artifacts of students' growth and deepening conceptual understanding. Creating dramatic or visual representations or using analogies and metaphors are other ways that students might demonstrate that they have personalized and synthesized their understandings.

3. Collaboration counts

We develop and choose open-ended and collaborative strategies with all the learners in mind. These strategies are open-ended in that they do not ask students to find the "right" answer but rather require students to make connections, process information and concepts, and personalize and/or transform the information and approaches in a variety of ways. They involve solving problems with more than one answer—or more than one way to arrive at that answer. Working with open-ended strategies leaves room for us to scaffold learning based on the strengths and needs of the individual students within the class. The strategies are collaborative in that they require students to share their thinking at several points along the way—both teaching and learning from one another. All ideas are welcome and understandings are refined over time. In designing instruction this way, we find that we need to make fewer adaptations and modifications for the diverse learners in our class. This allows us more time for both whole-class teaching, small-group coaching, and individual conferencing. More students are included as members of the learning community and are exposed to quality teaching rather than working on separate packages of material designed for them as individuals and/or removed from the classroom learning context. For us, a supportive classroom is one that welcomes and celebrates learners' diverse ways of thinking and is designed to encourage all of its community members as strategic thinkers.

All teachers, no matter what their role in a school is, work in exceedingly complex jobs. We believe that such complexity is decreased when we work together. Michael Fullan (2004) says that the ability to collaborate is one of the core requirements of postmodern society. He believes that, without collaborative skills and relationships, it is not possible for students to learn and to continue to learn as much as they need in life beyond the classroom. This is as true for adults as it is for students! Collaboration comes in the form of co-planning, co-assessing, or co-teaching. In all forms, teachers work together as equals, bringing their unique and complementary skills together to create a stronger whole. Hourcade and Bauwens (2003) consider no longer appropriate the traditional model of one educator teaching alone in one classroom for the entire day while trying to meet the needs of all students. Professional collaboration is the way of the future, and cooperative teaching is at the forefront of professional collaboration. Collaboration opportunities include resource teachers (e.g., special educators, librarians, instructional coaches) as well as two or more classroom teachers working together. The teaching scenarios in this book have all been developed collaboratively.

4. All students belong in the regular classroom

We begin planning with all students in mind, then build in further adaptations and modifications as necessary. As much as possible, resource teachers focus on supporting the work of the regular classroom. We consider that resource teachers include all non-enrolling teachers whose job it is to support atypical learners. These may include learning assistance teachers, special education teachers, English as an Additional Language teachers, or English as Second Dialect teachers. This does not preclude strategic tutoring outside the classroom but does change the focus of the program design.

The initial question in planning for students with special needs is not *Whom should I see? What should I do?*. It is *Let's build a class profile, set class goals, examine our lesson design, and then see who will need additional support and how this can best be given.* Whenever possible, the focus of the intervention should be in the classroom, scaffolding student learning to the curriculum content and the classroom context. Most important is that teams set shared goals for all students and work to address how teaching and learning sequences can be designed for maximum impact. Then the classroom and resource teachers think about the time they have at their disposal and their own strengths and skills, and work to build support for students accordingly. A resource teacher's role might include:

- **Team-teaching lessons**, where both teachers have interchangeable roles leading lesson sequences, checking in with small groups, creating adaptations and modifications within the sequences to scaffold specific students' learning.
- **Complementary instruction**, where each teacher takes on specific aspects of the lesson. In science, for example, one teacher prepares the sequence for content-area reading strategies and a graphic organizer, while the other finds a range of texts and resources and adapts the sequence and organizer for various students. In math class, one teacher prepares and delivers the open-ended task with a think-aloud, while the other collects and distributes manipulatives to support deep understanding of the concept.
- **Supplementary instruction**, where one teacher takes the lead in large-group instruction and the second teacher works with small groups to pre-teach, re-teach, or deepen understanding.

These and many other configurations involve planning together with the diverse needs of all learners in mind, and they involve a commitment to giving students engaging, coherent learning opportunities. Thus, working together in the regular class ensures that all students receive foundational content, modelled strategy instruction, and collaborative learning opportunities. In instances where support occurs outside the classroom, it is still with the same goals in mind.

Chapter 2

Working Together as a School

Only through sharing ideas, materials, resources, and expertise do teachers develop, survive and thrive. (Villa, Thousand, and Nevin 2004)

Teaching is a complex endeavour. Gone are the days—if they ever truly existed—when it was assumed that one teacher, working alone, could meet the needs of all learners in a classroom. We believe that together we are better, that working as a member of a team and within a school helps us grow as professionals and supports us in being the best we can be in the classroom, and in having the greatest impact on student learning.

Many teachers work with their students to develop vibrant learning communities. Over the course of the school year, they see their students begin to thrive. But making a difference in one classroom in one academic year is only the beginning. Shared efforts among teachers and across years of schooling build the potential for making a more significant impact. When teachers work together with shared goals, they help students develop understandings and strategies that can be celebrated and thus reinforced and applied in various settings. When teachers work together as interdisciplinary teams to understand their students' strengths and challenges, they develop approaches that help students connect to, process, transform, and personalize important concepts and thinking skills. Their schools become learning communities, the most important unit of change.

All Teachers, All Subjects

Over the years, we have worked with elementary, middle, and secondary school teachers and staffs to develop "thinking classrooms." We believe that every classroom should be a thinking classroom, a place where students get to

- access and use their prior knowledge
- process and make connections among ideas
- personalize and transform what they have learned

We want engaged, meaning-making, critical, and self-regulating thinkers. The behaviours developed in thinking classrooms are relevant in all disciplines and in all jobs in the world. They are used by writers, mechanics, statisticians, actors, chemists, translators, cooks, parents, taxi drivers, grocers … the list goes on.

To participate in a democratic society, citizens have to use what they know to make sense of new situations, keep their minds open to new possibilities, make decisions when considering multiple sources of information, and reflect on their beliefs and actions. We see schools and classrooms as places where students are apprenticed into this way of being in the world. We want to nurture their thinking skills, building from what they already bring us, rather than thwart their creativity and individuality. We want our students to participate in authentic learning activities that contribute to their future choices and their potential to participate in the world.

To create authentic and coherent learning opportunities for diverse classrooms, teachers benefit from working together to plan lessons and units of study. In using their combined knowledge and expertise, they can better engage and support diverse learners to simultaneously learn key concepts and develop learning strategies. Teachers focus on aligning formative assessment (assessment for learning), instruction, learning sequences, and summative assessment (assessment of learning).

How We Can Work Together to Best Meet the Needs of Diverse Learners

We believe that when teachers make time to understand and build from the learning profiles of their students, they can make a difference in the school success of those students and thus in their life opportunities. In particular, we know that when teachers use information from formative assessments to set goals, make plans, and involve students in developing specific strategies and practices, students and teachers get better at what they are doing.

Much of what we have learned comes from working with elementary, middle, and secondary staffs to develop approaches to better support their learners. To explain this work and situate it in research, we refer to the Carnegie Corporation's *Reading Next: A Vision for Action and Research in Middle and High School Literacy* (Biancarosa and Snow 2004) and the six "infrastructural improvements," or school-wide factors, that the authors recommend.

Six School-Wide Factors

1. Extended time for active learning

When you stop to think, it is just common sense that a person becomes better at something with practice. Malcolm Gladwell (2008) calls this general rule of success "the 10,000 hour rule." Ten thousand hours is the probable number of hours that any expert has spent in practice in order to develop expertise in a particular field. Reading, writing, and, yes, thinking scientifically and mathematically are skills—and you become a better reader, a better writer, and a better scientific or mathematical thinker the more you engage in, that is, practise these skills.

This is particularly true for reading and writing in the content areas. None of the powerful learning approaches described in chapter 1 could make much difference if students had no opportunities to read, to write, to analyze, and to discuss texts that could contribute to learning the subjects they study. You can see what teachers, teams, and schools value by what actually goes on in the classrooms. If we want students to become better readers, writers, and thinkers—better mathematicians and scientists—then we have to set up opportunities for them to develop and practise strategies that help them learn about increasingly complex ideas by using increasingly complex texts and engaging with increasingly complex tasks in math and science.

The *Reading Next* experts suggest that students need two to four hours of literacy-connected learning daily. Within this time, teachers are to model particular thinking skills and embed them in content-area learning. For example, teachers might choose to focus on comparing perspectives within a science unit on sustainability. They model the process by assuming first the point of view of a lumber company executive, then the opposing view of an activist member of the Sierra Club, and still another view that is in between, say, the point of view of the lumber consumer. Then, they help students practise comparing perspectives on the same or a different issue, perhaps fish-farming. As follow-up, they ask students to help decide on the criteria for assessing this particular skill, comparing perspectives, in an assignment that they will complete independently.

We believe that students in math and science classrooms should spend their time on inquiry-based tasks, exploring concepts and procedures needed for the discipline. We believe that time on task is critical, and that instructional time must be spent engaged with the complexities of mathematics or engaged with the interconnectedness of science.

Talk has an important role to play in these classrooms as well, allowing students to work together to make sense of new information, to use new vocabulary, to ask questions and clarify their developing knowledge, to consolidate their understandings. In his grade 9 science class at Burnaby South Secondary School, Kent Lui asks his students if they are up for a challenge, to do a quick-write using the terms *work*, *power*, and *energy* in a scientific context. This is his way of making a quick assessment of what the students already know about the scientific meaning of common words, and of providing a focus for today's lesson. The students write enthusiastically for three minutes; when they share their stories, it becomes evident that they do not yet know how these words are used in the sciences. Kent then shares his own quick-write, a story of Bob pushing against an immovable door, using several images of sport and yoga and asking the questions: *Is this work? Is energy being used? Is power being used?* His students work with partners to discuss each scenario, using the terms *energy, power,* and *work.* The lesson proceeds as Kent builds a chart on his tablet (a technology where what one person writes is projected and the class can see what has been written) with the headings WHAT?, SO WHAT?, THEN WHAT?—with these three terms in the left column. An experiment determining personal power follows, and the students discuss and record observations and thinking in the chart. The lesson concludes with another quick-write, again using *energy, work,* and *power* in a scientific context. The learning is obvious—the task has been complex and goal-directed, and talk has been woven throughout the lesson.

The teacher's role in these situations is to model the processes of inquiry, problem-solving, and reasoning as they are used in mathematics and the sciences while also modelling and teaching students how to think about the content, using strategies specific to these disciplines (Smith and Wilhelm 2006; Wilhelm 2007). To help them reason and make connections, teachers may ask their students to read a graph of a linear function and to describe the relationship they see, drawing parallels between the slope and y-intercept of the line and the kind of growth and constants included in the corresponding table of values. As teachers model this kind of math-to-math connection with a think-aloud, they support students in incorporating this strategy into their repertoire; in turn, they teach not only the important algebraic content but also the art of thinking.

We believe that students can develop these thinking skills while they are learning the content of math and science. The two go hand in hand. They need the thinking skills to access and explore the concepts at the heart of the discipline. In order to help develop numeracy and scientific literacy, students need extended time to engage in reading, writing, and thinking activities throughout a unit of study. Experts agree that such activities help students think deeply about concepts and issues by exploring and developing a range of approaches and perspectives (Alvermann 2001; Smith and Wilhelm 2006).

Unfortunately, in North American math classrooms, the quality and content of classroom lessons is not what we might desire. In their international study of teaching mathematics as a cultural activity, James Stigler and James Hiebert examined teaching practices in the United States, Germany, and Japan at the middle school level. (Canada was involved in the international assessment, but was not mentioned in Stigler and Hiebert's study.) The cultural script for instructional practice in U.S. classrooms comprised taking up homework, demonstrating procedures, having students practise procedures, reviewing procedures, and providing definitions (Stigler and Hiebert 2009, 42–45). Hardly "thought-full" work. In Japan, by contrast, lessons began with a review of concepts addressed in the previous day's lesson, followed by the presentation of the problem for the day and an invitation to extend that task (if needed), individual work time on the problem, then group work, and finally a teacher-led summary of the key concepts reached by individuals and groups as they worked through the task. The Japanese instructional practice, focused on reasoning and thinking, is strikingly different, one which we believe has the potential to increase the type and number of mathematicians we inspire in our middle schools and secondary schools. The Japanese math classroom is a thinking classroom.

2. Professional development

Ongoing professional development significantly helps teachers reflect on their students' learning profiles, uncover trends of strength and challenge within the class or the grade, and design a plan that incorporates approaches that build student engagement and lead to active, strategic, and self-regulated learning. Effective professional development must continue over time for teachers to develop, explore, and integrate ideas and practices that support the development of their students' thinking. One-time workshops are out. Working together over time to understand and support students and their learning is in!

We know that sustained, collaborative, inquiry-based professional development can help teachers develop new understandings and approaches. For individual schools and school districts to make a difference in student learning, the best approach is to set up ongoing professional development activities in which teachers learn collaboratively (Butler and Schnellert 2008).

The *Reading Next* panel advocates professional development activities that include "opportunities to implement and reflect upon new ideas … and help school personnel create and maintain a team-oriented approach to improving instruction and structures that promote better adolescent literacy" (p. 20). The National Council of Teachers of Mathematics (NCTM) envisions an ideal continuous learning cycle for teachers, asking us to "imagine that all mathematics teachers continue to learn new mathematics content and keep current on education research. They collaborate on problems of mathematics teaching and regularly visit one another's classrooms to learn from, and critique, colleagues' teaching" (p. 368). The *National Science Education Standards* (NSES) echo this notion, emphasizing that professional development for science teachers—especially given the dynamic, evolution of their content—must likewise be a continuous lifelong process. They continue to discourage technical training for science teachers but instead encourage "opportunities for intellectual professional growth," those in which the art of thinking are emphasized over content in isolation (pp. 56–57).

To promote collaborative learning communities in math and science, we need to meet often and with intention. These are opportunities where teachers use what they know about their students, the content of the curriculum, and research in order to plan, try out, and reflect upon approaches that they helped choose, create, and adapt. Research and research-based methods and approaches are offered as possibilities to be explored in relation to other factors. One example of this is the "lesson study" model, a frame for developing high-quality lessons and "thought-full" teaching practices through research-grounded conversation and collaborative planning, as described by Stigler and Hiebert (2009). Drawn from Japanese math classrooms, this compelling model has the power to transform the quality of teaching. Essentially, a team of four teachers meets to co-plan a lesson, using research-based methods and approaches and their collective expertise. One teacher volunteers to teach the lesson, the others observe, then they all deconstruct the lesson and refine it together. Next, the process is repeated in another teacher's classroom. Reflecting together on the teaching and the impact of the teaching on all learners becomes a powerful agent of change.

This model does not suggest that a generic approach (i.e., an instructional strategy) will work the same way in different classrooms. Instead, teachers need opportunities to look at formative assessment information, set goals together, and select, plan, or adapt related ideas and approaches. When professional development activities also offer repeated opportunities for teachers to work together to reflect on how things are going, they are better able to make the curriculum more accessible while building students' reading, writing, and thinking skills (see also Butler and Schnellert 2008).

3. Ongoing formative and summative assessment of student learning and programs

When our formative and summative assessment activities are linked to the content and strategies we teach, we can reflect on whether or not our teaching is making a difference for our students by examining student progress against criteria. Without assessment information that focuses on key thinking skills, it is difficult to support student learning or to examine the effect of particular pedagogical approaches. When we see our students successfully learning and developing the thinking skills that we have been working on, we can target new thinking skills. When we see that things are not progressing as expected, we plan and re-teach in new ways to help students develop the thinking skills we have been working on. Paying careful attention to our students' work helps us to be very specific in our goal-setting and to focus our planning and teaching on helping all students move forward in their learning.

Within the units we teach, we include our students in examining or developing the criteria used for assessing their learning. Summative assessments should allow students to show what they have learned about the key content of a discipline and the skills they have developed over the course of a unit. When we focus our assessments on the most important concepts and the related thinking skills that we have targeted, the focus of instruction shifts from teachers covering content to students making meaning and developing deep understandings. (In chapter 3, we discuss formative and summative assessments in greater detail, particularly how we can use them to support all students in their learning.)

Teaching teams and schools should engage collaboratively in cycles of assessing, planning, goal-setting, doing, reflecting, and adjusting (Schnellert, Butler, and Higginson 2008). They then can use meaningful data from formative assessment at the school level, such as a fall performance-based assessment of reading, writing and/or numeracy (see chapter 3) to set grade- or school-wide long-term goals that are specific to the students. A teaching team focused on one grade might set one shared goal for student learning (e.g., determining importance; communicating more than one way to solve a math problem), and the individual teachers might set another more class-specific goal (e.g., making connections).

Performance-based assessments are often used formatively in the fall to target thinking skills, then summatively in the spring to gauge student progress. They help schools track the students' improvement, and they provide the teaching staff with specific information to help plan future professional development activities and to consider what additional goals might be set mid-year or for the next year.

Both types of assessment are meaningful at multiple levels. Teachers can use them to assess individual progress toward learning-centred goals for individuals, classes, grades, and schools. They can use them to plan appropriate supports for students and teachers. When we use formative assessments as descriptive feedback for our teaching, we teach more responsively. When we look at formative assessments, we ask ourselves: *What is working? What is not working?* and *What is the plan?*

Summative assessments provide information about what individual students have internalized and can do independently. The information that these assessments provide differs from that provided through formative assessments. The information provides a synthesis of the number or percentage of students achieving at different levels related to specific school, grade, and classroom goals. Grade-specific or school-wide assessments that are administered in the early spring provide teaching teams and schools with evidence of students' progress (which is useful for establishing school goals for the fall); they also provide data that classroom teachers use in developing their instructional goals and descriptive feedback to students for the remainder of the spring term.

One of the most important things that we have learned is that teachers and students are integral to making assessments meaningful and useful. Whenever possible, teachers and students need opportunities to reflect on assessments so that meaningful classroom and school decisions can be made.

4. Teacher teams

The *Reading Next* (2004, 2006) panel of experts point out that as students get older and move from primary to junior/intermediate to middle and, finally, to the secondary years, they have to relate to more and more teachers as their curriculum evolves into distinct disciplines. Students' experiences of schooling may end up fractured and confusing at an age when they crave interrelatedness. Does your school's structure support coordinated instruction? Are there interdisciplinary teams? Teachers do not have to teach in similar styles to coordinate what they do and to reinforce key concepts, thinking skills and approaches. Adolescents bring rich literacy, math, and science practices and understandings into their later years of schooling because, in earlier grades, these were often integrated across content areas, lessons, and units. Yet, as students move into discrete subject areas, they often do not tap into their prior knowledge or full skill sets. They face our common challenges in learning—those of applying and adapting what we know and are newly capable of doing to new or different settings and situations.

Teachers working in teams can identify the thinking skills that students need in order to expand or develop their knowledge or understanding. By coordinating their efforts, teachers can visualize how shared goals for shared students can be refined in their specific subject classes. While teamwork promotes higher collegiality and staff communication across disciplines, it also helps ensure that the students do not receive conflicting messages about learning—nor fall between the cracks from class to class.

The importance of collaborating should not be underestimated. Working together to develop community-minded classrooms, where all kinds of learning styles are not only welcome but celebrated, takes flexibility and planning. We have worked with a number of schools that have focused their energies on designing learning experiences both to help students develop targeted thinking skills and to invite them to use their prior knowledge, interests, and talents as a way to connect to and personalize new content. You will see several of these examples in chapters 5 to 12.

At Heritage Park Secondary in Mission, BC, librarian Kristi Johnston's collaboration with subject-area teachers on student research is quietly moving throughout the school (chapter 8). The collaboration between Carole Fullerton and Catherine Ludwig in a grade 5/6 math class (chapter 11) put into practice a school-wide emphasis on teaching the skill of making inferences. The teachers in both situations worked together to develop and share ideas for increasing student engagement and learning. Working together helped sustain their belief in their innovations, and sharing their expertise made their units of study more accessible for more students, thereby increasing the learning for all students.

Embedded within these co-planned units are key criteria or, using Hourcade's and Bauwens' terminology, "high standards" (2003). We set the expectation that all students can learn and improve from wherever they start. From these expectations, teachers target their teaching while personalizing the experience for students by having them work toward the criteria and receive descriptive feedback.

Grade-wide teaching teams can make a significant difference in student learning. Teachers who meet regularly as teams increase coherence for students moving from class to class and help them make connections across subject areas.

At Alpha Secondary in Burnaby, all grade 8 students are taught in pods, that is they share the same science and math teacher and the same social studies and English teacher. Bryn Williams and Jayshree Rana each teach grade 8 science and math. They co-plan their lessons and frequently combine their science or math classes to co-teach. They find that both they and their students benefit from the dual perspectives they present in the lessons using their combined expertise—Bryn's in math, Jayshree's in science. Working together in this way enables them to constantly refine their practice and to address their shared goal of increasing their use of assessment for learning strategies.

In classrooms where teachers work together—learning resource teachers and classroom teachers co-teaching, coaches and classroom teachers working together, two classroom teachers combining their classes—we see more students getting support when they need it. In collaborative classrooms, inclusion is not a special education model, it is a school model, and it is different from pull-out-focused models of support. The emphasis is on designing learning experiences so that more students have more success in each individual classroom. As professionals, we want to constantly examine and refine our practice. By working together, we discover what does and does not work and can adapt our instruction in real time. When collaborative teaching is ongoing (i.e., when teachers work together weekly), we always build in 5 to 15 minutes to debrief, to determine how a lesson went, and to plan ahead. We have found that collaborative problem-solving and teaching result in new ideas, new or better units of study, and a feeling of connection with colleagues. Working together, teachers can develop lessons and activities that reach more learners. Most importantly, we design learning sequences that better engage our students while we become more strategic in our teaching.

5. Leadership

Many an initiative lives or dies based on the support of a principal or superintendent who fulfills a key responsibility—that of instructional leader. Their participation in the school community is crucial. They must visit classrooms and know what is going on in there! Collaborating with teachers in their classrooms, covering a teacher's class so that he or she can co-teach or co-plan with a colleague, and sitting in on grade-wide planning meetings are ways that administrators can help teachers as they work together to improve student learning. A leader in education has to keep up-to-date with practice and research by attending professional development activities with staff and taking part in professional book clubs. Principals who teach or co-teach a class and who publicly share their own process of revising and integrating their planning with instruction and formative and summative assessment support the development of the school as a learning community. The practice of principals promoting and participating in teacher learning and development activities has a more profound impact on student learning than any other practice (Robinson 2007). To develop collaborative, community-minded classes that are focused on learning, school leaders need to participate in staff learning communities. Both formal and informal leaders play a key role in modelling learning.

Similarly, teacher-leaders must take a collaborative, learning-centred approach to professional development and curricular innovation. Numeracy coaches, consultants, and department heads follow the same approach; they model and contribute to a culture of professional learning. Working in this way honours a range of teacher philosophies and styles. We recommend that leaders openly share what they are learning and how they are developing their own practices. Within this context, more opportunities arise for educators to collaboratively establish instructional goals as colleagues, allowing for each professional to have input.

6. A comprehensive and coordinated literacy program

The authors of *Reading Next* (2004, 2006) say that the first five "infrastructural improvements," or school-wide factors, should be part of a school's comprehensive and coordinated literacy program. We think these ideas apply to all school-wide teaching and professional development that situates students to become thinkers. Extended time for developing students' capacities as scientists and mathematicians requires teachers to build purposeful and authentic activities into their units of study. Cross-curricular teams are needed in order to make thinking skills a priority across classrooms. Targeting a few thinking skills based on formative assessment information allows students and teachers to focus on developing and integrating them into content learning. Deep content learning is possible when these strategies are used.

Coming together regularly to share information and plans and to problem-solve is the behaviour of a learning community—that is, one that values all members as well as their efforts and questions. Developing a vision and goals for students and a range of approaches that support student learning must be a shared process. A comprehensive plan informed by research must be developed and refined over time. When teachers and leaders take part in this process, their innovation has an impact beyond a single classroom.

Final Thoughts

Experts agree that schools and cross-curricular teaching teams working together on shared goals can make a significant difference. Both the schools and the teams should establish these shared goals using data from formative assessments that:

- focus on developing students as active, independent learners
- can be embedded in content teaching
- are shared by teachers across classes and subjects
- are shared with and reflected on by the students themselves
- are maintained and sustained across one or more years

The data from the end-of-year summative assessment can then be used to reflect on and refine team efforts and to set new goals for the next year.

Some of the richest examples of successful implementation of shared goals involve collaborative teaching among classroom teachers and among classroom and support teachers (e.g., resource teachers, librarians, literacy and numeracy coaches). These co-teaching arrangements are based on a shared ownership of the goal to improve student learning and lead to richer professional learning for the teachers involved. There are so many ways to collaborate! Samples of collaborative scenarios, of teachers working together to support student learning in the best ways possible, are found in chapters 5 through 12.

Chapter 3

Assessment that Supports Learning

By adopting the "assessment for learning" techniques that focus on the learners, teachers will find that their students' performance will improve because they are more likely to see themselves as learners. More students will be successful in achieving the curricular outcomes as the teachers learn how to target their lessons and help the students identify problem areas in their own work. (Clarke, Owens, and Sutton 2006)

Mention the word *assessment* and most teachers and students think of marks. Students check out their marks, compute their averages, compare their marks with each other. Unfortunately, receiving and examining marks is not what most affects student learning. We are in the business of learning. Our assessment practices should reflect this. The driving purpose of formative assessment is to inform teachers' instruction and students' learning. As Black, Harrison, Lee, Marshall, and Wiliam (2003) state, "formative assessment is a process, one in which information about learning is *evoked* and then *used* to modify the teaching and learning activities in which teachers and students are engaged."

To describe the two major types of assessment practices, we have adapted the succinct summation chart (Figure 3.1) prepared by Caren Cameron (BCELC, September 2007).[1]

---

1 Some researchers (Earl 2001) differentiate a third category of assessment—assessment *as* learning. We combine *for* and *as* in recognition that our ultimate goal is *for* the student to understand his role *as* a learner. We aim to involve students as much as possible in the learning process that, in our opinion, includes assessment of progress.

Figure 3.1 Assessment Practices

	Assessment OF Learning (summative assessment)	Assessment FOR Learning (formative assessment)
Purpose	Report out, summative assessment, measure learning	Guide instruction, improve learning
Audience	Parents and public	Teachers and students
Timing	At the end	Minute by minute, day by day, at the beginning
Form	Letter grades, rank order, percentages, scores	Descriptive feedback

As mentioned in chapters 1 and 2, the authors of the *Reading Next* (2004, 2006) study synthesized their findings by presenting 15 areas for educators to focus on in order to improve adolescent literacy. As math and science teachers, our favourite quote from this study is the mathematical equation $15 - 3 = 0$ which, according to the authors, means that, without 3 of the 15 key focus areas, significant change in student achievement is unlikely. The three key areas are:

1. **Ongoing professional development.** We must work together, over time, engaged in goal-directed, professional conversations about student work.
2. **Summative assessment.** Assessment *of* learning that helps us see whether the changes we make in our instructional practices indeed have an impact on our students' learning.
3. **Formative assessment.** Assessment *for* learning that is embedded in regular teaching practices and encourages students to develop independence as learners.

Both assessment *of* learning and assessment *for* learning are important. They serve different purposes. We have to include both in our teaching.

The National Council of Teachers of Mathematics (NCTM) and the National Science Teachers Association (NSTA) agree. Assessments must be authentic, integrated into instruction, and use a variety of sources of evidence (NCTM Principles and Standards <www.nctm.org/fullstandards/document/chapter2/assess.asp>). Assessment results should inform the teaching we do, particularly the important concepts that students must master, not only their knowledge of procedures. The NSTA agrees that meaningful science assessment requires teachers and students to share the responsibility for science learning and associated formative and summative assessments.

Assessment OF Learning

Assessment of learning (AOL) is that which takes place at the end of a unit of study when students either take a test or complete a project or performance in order to demonstrate what they have learned. This is not the assessment that most improves student learning. Teachers use the marks collected from these tests or projects to calculate a student's final grade for a report card. Like snapshots, the marks say, "At this particular point in time, based on the evidence we have collected, and against these criteria or this standard, we can say how much you have learned." Marks represent a way of telling others the measurement of a student's learning.

Different Kinds of Feedback

If assessment of learning is the main form of assessment used, then student learning is not maximized. Marks come too late to impact student learning. Marks describe how much has been learned. To improve their learning, students need feedback while they are still engaged in the learning activity so that they may use it to improve. They need to know what has been learned and what still needs to be learned. Teachers also need feedback on how their students are doing so that they may adjust their teaching to address the gaps in their students' learning. Every experienced teacher knows that just making a lesson plan does not guarantee that the lesson will work—or that it will work in the same way with each class. The learning process varies from student to student and from class to class. To increase student achievement, both leaders and learners need personal feedback along the way as part of the teaching/learning process, not the feedback that comes after the fact that was provided by marks and scores.

Assessment FOR Learning

When teachers shift to spending more time on assessment *for* learning (AFL, or formative assessment) and less time on assessment *of* learning (summative), they still collect marks, but usually fewer marks. Using the time they would normally use for marking, teachers give descriptive feedback *during* the learning when students can put the information to use. They do not give marks when assessing for learning; they give descriptive feedback. The more immediate and appropriate the feedback, the more likely the student will use it.

Michael Smith and Jeff Wilhelm (2002, 2006) suggest that we think of the feedback students receive when they play a video game. The players receive exactly what they need to know in order to progress. Teachers want to give their students feedback that is immediate (while students are still engaged in the work of learning), timely (when they need it and can use it), and personal (what they need, not what someone else might need). When the feedback is immediate, timely, and personal, student progress is enhanced.

Assessment for Learning Strategies

We use six specific strategies when assessing for learning based on the work of Black et al. (2003).[2]

---

2 Webcasts focusing on these strategies are available at <bcelc.org>.

1. Learning intentions

Learning intentions tell students what they can expect to learn—during this class, during the next learning sequence, during the unit. They are posted for students' and teachers' reference. Teachers articulate the learning intentions and frame them as "I will…" or "I can…" statements, allowing students to more easily own the statements. For example, in a grade 8 science classroom where students are working to explain the properties of visible light, the learning intentions are:

- I can make connections between the angle of incidence and the angle of reflection for visible light.
- I can record these connections in a chart.
- I can make use of this information to make predictions about how light will behave in other situations.

Knowing these clearly stated learning intentions, all students can keep their eye on the ball and work in a goal-directed way.

Setting up a learning intention in a math class involves giving students a context in which to work, a rationale for the learning and a reminder of the interconnectedness of the new concept to be addressed. One way of looking at learning intentions in math class is to consider the following example. In Jim Lovelace's grade 11 math class, the content goal is for students to add and subtract rational expressions with binomial and trinomial expressions. To introduce the learning and to make connections to what students already know and can do with fractions, Jim and Faye Brownlie present three equations to the students:

$$\frac{3}{5}+\frac{4}{5}=$$

$$\frac{7}{12}+\frac{5}{6}=$$

$$\frac{3}{7}+\frac{2}{5}=$$

The students work in pairs to explain how they go about solving these equations. Their comparisons of different methods used to solve the examples are shared and recorded for all to see. As a class, students review the set of brainstormed strategies and edit any misconceptions or inaccuracies. The teachers see a need to quickly review the concepts of denominator and numerator before moving on, but then focus the summary of the mini-lesson on the important connection that will take students forward into more complex content; that is, that we can use different strategies to add fractions with like and unlike denominators. From here, Jim and Faye extrapolate to an example with polynomials, helping students to see the connections between the simpler fraction example and more complex ones.

Notice that the work of math is concentrated at this point on building understanding of necessary background knowledge to really understand the new concept. No binomial or trinomial denominators are introduced until the prior knowledge has been activated and put into place as a point of connection to the new concept. Too often when the strategy or procedure is presented without building sufficient background, the students jump to completing the task without understanding the concept. In this model for teaching, math teachers connect to the previous day or to a related concept, then pose the day's problem, which is conceptually grounded in the important math for the day. The end of the lesson identifies the "big math idea" or "enduring understanding" the learning intention that, up to this point, has guided the teacher's planning and lesson design is made explicit only in this last summative conversation. Jim concludes the lesson on the learning intention by saying, "We can use different strategies to add and subtract rational expressions with binomial and trinomial denominators." This final summary statement (the synthesis of the classroom conversations about the content) makes the key math idea clear to students.

Another way to share a learning intention is by posing a "question for the day." The question communicates the area to be explored and simultaneously opens up the topic for exploration and meaning-making. We often begin the class with a question like *"What happens when…?"* or *"In what ways can you…?"* The questions and open-ended prompts both focus and support students' thinking and learning. As with written or stated learning intentions, they clarify the intent of the lesson and, when used again at the end of the lesson, help students monitor their understanding of the work.

2. Criteria

Criteria describe to students what a powerful performance (one that works well) or a product of their learning will look like. Criteria are best developed with the students, using examples either of published work or of work produced by the students themselves. In a science classroom where students write lab reports to explain what they know and have learned from the experiments they have completed, the process for building criteria requires several steps:

- Choose three or four student lab reports that the class can examine. Choose diverse student samples, each exhibiting different strengths.
- Discuss these samples with the class, focusing only on the strengths, never on criticism.
- After the discussion, ask students to write down their individual criteria for what a written lab report should include. Then have them choose their top three criteria.
- Move the students into groups of three or four to discuss and decide on three common criteria.

- Then have each small group present their top criteria to the whole class.
- Have students work with the criteria to categorize them and make a summary list.
- Add another criterion if the students have not identified an aspect of the curriculum that should be addressed.
- Work with the class for several days to ensure that their list of criteria works.
- Then have students keep a copy of the criteria in their science lab books for reference.
- Have students use the criteria during their work with future lab reports to self-assess, peer-assess, and set goals.

When Tim McCracken and Leyton Schnellert generated criteria with Tim's grade 8 science students, the class was able to organize their ideas into four categories:

1. predictions/questions
2. methods and observations
3. inferences and claims
4. organization

The students had come up with the same criteria that Tim and Leyton had in mind (observations, inferences, conclusions), but were more detailed in their thinking. The student-generated criteria led Tim and Leyton to build in more opportunities for predictions and questions that help students use and access their background knowledge. Setting the criteria as a class helps teachers see the learning through the students' eyes. In Tim's grade 8 classes, the students felt a greater ownership of the lab write-up process. Some students even designed their own formats for recording and reporting information related to these criteria.

3. Descriptive feedback

The backbone of assessment for learning is finding out what you need to know, when you need to know it. For the learner, descriptive feedback answers these three questions:

1. *What's working?*
2. *What's not working?*
3. *What's next?*

These questions guide our interactions with our students as we meet with them —whether individually in a side-by-side conference, in a small group, or as a class.

Bryn Williams and Rae Figursky are co-teaching Rae's grade 11 Principles of Math class in a demonstration lesson. They are applying students' conceptual understanding of the year's topics through problem solving. The students are working in triads, choosing from a wide selection of problems which logic problems they will work on. Three girls are sitting together, challenged by this problem, their first:

There are 20 socks in a drawer, 10 blue, 10 brown. What is the least number of socks you need to pull out to get a matched pair?

Gaby, one of the students has begun by stating, "I hate math, and I especially hate these kinds of problems." They have been working diligently for some time, but the frustration level is rising. Saruja asks, "Can you help? We don't know what to do." Faye Brownlie, who has been observing the lesson, responds with, "You bet. Let's figure out what's working so far." The answer at first is "Nothing," but we move on to discover that the girls have determined three things—what's given, what they know to be true, and what's unknown. They have also tried more than one plan. So "What's not working?" is an effective plan to proceed from this information. They have attempted to draw the drawer of socks and they have written out possible scenarios. Neither plan has moved their thinking forward.

Faye suggests that we let their pencils be the brown socks and their erasers be the blue socks, then see what happens when we randomly pull out socks—a step that the girls had suggested as a "What next?" Using their pencils and erasers as manipulatives, they quickly find a solution to the problem, and they are left feeling enabled and ready to try another challenge. It has taken longer than if we had just shown them what to do, but this kind of interaction gives students ownership of the problem, motivates them, and leaves them more confident and capable. Indeed, as the class ends and the girls leave the room, Gaby (the "I hate math" girl) said, "That was fun. I think I figured out something I could do today!"

As we circulate around the room while the students work on complex problems, we may see patterns in their thinking or in the strategies they use. Likewise, we may see misconceptions cropping up about the mathematical or scientific content presented. This is where we pause for a mathematical or scientific "commercial break"—a 30-second sound bite aimed at providing timely feedback on the strategies used, or at clearing up a minor misconception about the math or the science. In this way, all students receive feedback as quickly as possible—when they can still use the advice—and it does not interrupt the flow in the room.

Some misconceptions need to be addressed in a more thorough way. If, after collecting student work, we see a pattern in their responses that suggests a misunderstood concept or missing skill, then we teach a mini-lesson the next day either to the whole class or to the small group of students who need this instruction. Notice that giving descriptive feedback does not mean stopping teaching. When feedback is combined with effective instruction, student learning is enhanced (Hattie and Timperley 2007).

Coquitlam science teachers Joni Tsui, Aliisa Sarte, and Michelle Ciolfitto all use coloured highlighters when giving feedback to students—for example, during practice quizzes. These teachers like to have the students, in pairs, practise taking quizzes during class in order to consolidate their understanding. As the students are working with their partners, the teachers circulate, stopping by the partnerships and highlighting their work. Michelle uses orange to celebrate "You've got it," pink to say "You're almost there," and blue to say "Look at this again; let me know if you need more help." In a very short period of class time, they can give specific feedback several times and to all the students, helping them see where they need to target their learning. From their grade 8 and 9 science students to their AP biology and physics students, all cheer when their page is filled with orange!

4. Questioning

In a classroom that focuses on assessment for learning, teachers' questions are open-ended and invite reasoning. Teachers listen in a respectful way, intent on understanding their students' thinking and in engaging in real discourse. Students are invited to question themselves, to use their questions to guide their learning and to kindle their curiosity.

Questions are not used for control or for quick "Guess-my-thinking" games. All students are included in the discourse, so strategies such as "no-hands" may be used — that is, students do not raise a hand to answer a question. Rather we pose a question, students discuss possible answers with a learning partner, and then we call randomly on different students to answer the question. This strategy increases student reasoning and participation in the lesson, because some students can become reliant on those students in the class who consistently raise their hands, answer the questions, and do the thinking for everyone.

Another strategy is to use "stoplight cards." Students have three cards (red, yellow, green) or a cube painted red, yellow, and green on their desk. As the teacher is explaining, students move the cards or the cube to reflect their current level of understanding. When teachers notice yellows and reds appearing, they can pause and respond to questions rather than moving on, always assuming that their teaching is making a difference to students' learning. This is a visible way for students to cue a teacher that the content is challenging and to stay engaged. Just being physically present in the classroom does not ensure that a student is learning. Engagement in the learning process does.

In *Classroom Discussions: Using Math Talk to Help Students Learn* (2003), Suzanne Chapin, Nancy Canavan Anderson, and Catherine O'Connor outline five explicit strategies to help include more students in mathematical discourse — to ensure that all students are engaged in thinking through a mathematical problem. We like the way they have organized their questions and think this structure for questioning works equally well in math and science for all ages of students. Their strategies include the following:

1. **Re-voicing** (teacher – student): repeating what a student has said in a slightly different way.

   So you're saying that's an odd number?

   Work, according to you, means moving something?

   Why use it?
   • helps to clarify for student sharing
   • helps to clarify for others

2. **Re-phrasing** (student – student): asking students to restate someone else's reasoning:

   Can you repeat what he just said in your own words?

   Why use it?
   • involves students in re-voicing for one another
   • honours student contributions
   • gives another purpose for listening to students

3. **Agree-disagree and extending** (student – student): asking students to apply their own reasoning to someone else's reasoning

   Do you agree or disagree? Why?

   Why use it?
   • elicits respectful discussion of ideas
   • makes reasoning explicit
   • links and extends student thinking

4. **Adding on** (student – student) – prompting for further participation

   Would someone else like to add on?

   Why use it?
   • encourages contributions to classroom talk
   • makes explicit the expectation that we all have a voice

5. **Using wait time** (teacher – student)

   Take your time ... we'll wait...

   Why use it?
   • de-emphasizes speed in responding
   • involves more students in conversation
   • allows ESL learners and others to formulate thoughts

Used in a classroom regularly, these simple strategies for facilitating mathematical discourse defuse the "Wait for Michael to answer it" phenomenon, and create thinking classrooms where everyone is expected to contribute.

As the language of the task and its enduring understanding are tested, shared, and applied aloud, students take ownership of these new ideas in a powerful way. In the best of these conversations, the teacher is largely silent, simply moving the dialogue forward while students do the thinking work.

The teacher can then summarize and make explicit the big math ideas from the lesson.

The ultimate goal of questioning is to develop students who are inquisitive, who can reflect on their learning, set goals, and enjoy the process of thinking about their learning, being metacognitive. With this in mind, we work to develop students as independent thinkers. In our middle school and secondary school math classes, we support students in developing a metacognitive script that echoes these feedback questions. We ask:

- *What are you doing?*
- *Why are you doing it?*
- *How does it help you?*

When the students, in turn, internalize our questions, they begin to monitor their thinking and track their own progress through a task (Van de Walle 2001).

In a grade 6/7 math classroom, students work on a challenging problem involving ratio. As they apply the strategies that they have learned, we move through the group, asking students to explain what they are doing, why they are doing it, and how their chosen strategy helps them progress through the problem. One student explains that he is drawing a picture to help him make sense of the problem, but that the complexity of the ratio is making it hard to draw—his diagram has become overrun with once meaningful markings and he is lost. He looks up from his work and says aloud, "I think I'll make a chart instead." When students can evaluate the efficacy of their strategies while working, they are behaving and thinking like mathematicians. In substituting another, better strategy, students demonstrate what the National Research Council (2001) terms adaptive reasoning—the ability to reflect on and adapt their thinking.

Notice how the openness of the questions invites reasoning and participation. This is so much more than "match my thinking" or "find the right answer." These questions honour student thinking. Using the questions demonstrates a teacher's belief in all students' can-do attitudes to learning.

5. Self-Assessment and Peer-Assessment

Students need to be involved as much as possible in the work of becoming the best learner they can be. This requires that they clearly understand the task, the learning intentions or goals of the class, and what achievement will look like—that is, the criteria. When these are explicit and when we model how to work with the criteria, using open-ended questioning and giving descriptive feedback, our students can successfully assess one another's work. They follow the same guidelines that we have been modelling:

- Work with the end in mind.
- Use the criteria as a reference point for what the response should look like.
- Frame your descriptive feedback around the same three questions: *What's working? What's not working? What's next?*
- Invite a conversation with your peers; do not take control and tell.

As students work with peer-assessment, we are there to guide the practice and coach as necessary. Student conversations are authentic and helpful, so performance improves as each student has many more opportunities for feedback. When all feedback comes from the teacher, the odds of getting enough and just when you need it are not great! Ultimately, the student is self-assessing while working—the learner is the real locus of learning. Learners carry with them the ability to tell whether what they are doing is getting them what they want.

In the grade 10 science class, the students are beginning a new unit on motion. The teacher asks them, first, to write down in 2 minutes all the words about motion that they can think of; then, to join two other students and add more words to their lists. The energy is apparent. Their goal is to share ideas. They are engaged, talking to one another, building on each other's thinking. This is peer-assessment in the initial stages of a new concept. Later in the lesson, the teacher asks the students to explain the relationship between *vector* and *scalar*, using examples and language developed during the lesson—they are to have at least four points of comparison. The students begin alone, then again move into partners and triads to try and achieve success as a team. This, too, is peer-assessment: *What do you know that I need to know? How can I contribute to your learning?*

6. Ownership

The agent of learning is the student. When students are clear about the expectations, when they know how to participate, and when they recognize that their voices are valued in the process and that they are the ultimate consumers, they work harder. All the strategies of assessment for learning are geared toward inviting students in, toward giving them informed control, toward working with them to help them be the best they can be.

Ownership of the meaning can happen in math and science classrooms. In math classrooms where teachers model thinking strategies to allow students access to the mathematics, students know how to participate like mathematicians. When teachers support their learners in developing metacognition through simple questions (like *What are you doing? Why are you doing it? How does it help you?*), students learn to be self-regulating thinkers. When math and science teachers set clear criteria for student engagement and then provide feedback to students as they problem-solve, students learn to recognize success and the steps needed to achieve it. As teachers facilitate conversations about important concepts, students recognize the value of their own voice in that conversation, and their critical role in meaning-making in the discipline.

Assessment for Learning as a Grand Event

Most assessment for learning occurs day by day, minute by minute in the classroom. However, we also advocate a "grand event" formative assessment that is not a daily occurrence. As described in *Student Diversity* (Brownlie and Feniak 1998; Brownlie, Feniak, and Schnellert 2006), the Standard Reading Assessment is a performance-based assessment that helps teachers collect information about their students' reading that they can use to inform their teaching. Many schools choose to administer this performance-based reading assessment early in the year or early in the term. They examine the results of the assessment to find areas of strength and challenge for a particular group of students.

This is not an assessment for marks. The trends established from the assessment are used to help target specific areas of instruction. Repeating the assessment at a later date—another grand event—helps teachers monitor the effectiveness of their instruction, get feedback, and make new teaching plans. With the advent of the new science and math curricula, many schools are choosing to use their new science or math texts as the text for the assessment. This helps teachers see how able their students are at independently reading this text and its accompanying text features, and what areas they need to focus on in their teaching. When conducting the assessment, teachers:

- choose a passage (usually from a text they plan to use)
- build some background knowledge with their students
- set a purpose for reading
- pose several open-ended questions
- listen to students read orally and have a short interview with them

When coding the assessment, teachers:

- code individual responses by highlighting descriptors
- examine individual quick scales to find a pattern common to the class
- set class goals, based on the patterns of strengths and needs of the class

When planning with the assessment information, teachers

- share the strengths and goals with the class
- choose strategies to teach that help students achieve the goals

Notice that this process provides another form of descriptive feedback. The assessment takes a picture of a class or in-coming grade group that answers the questions for this particular snapshot.

Using the information gathered from the third descriptive feedback question (*What's next?*) informs subsequent planning. This is a curriculum-based assessment, created around the grade level expectations for proficient reading—that is, reading for information. It is a snapshot of independent, thoughtful reading. The passage is not tied directly to the content currently being taught. The intent is to see if students are independently and thoughtfully applying the skills and strategies for reading that are required—at this particular grade level, in this particular subject.

Performance-based assessment

There are several different ways to use this performance-based assessment. In Tait Elementary School, the assessment is scheduled five times a year. The year-long school calendar highlights the five assessment weeks. During these weeks, the teachers choose a 75-minute period in which to conduct their assessment. Resource teachers, librarians, administrators, or any other non-enrolling teachers sign up to conduct the assessment in the classroom, co-assessing with the classroom teacher. No teacher is alone in the classroom while conducting the assessment. Within the next two weeks, time is arranged for the staff members to code the assessments together. In September, enough copies of the grade level Quick Scale of the provincial performance standard are copied for each student. These same pages of the Quick Scale are used to record student progress throughout the year, with a different colour chosen to highlight each time. Teachers meet in teams to highlight on the performance standard what they have noticed about each student's work. Once each student's work has been recorded, a class summary is also created with notes on the strengths of the class and the areas of need. While the staff is together, the classroom teachers report on what they notice about their class as a whole, what their area of focus is, and what strategies they plan to use in addressing this area. The collaboration creates a climate in which shared learning is valued.

The assessments occur early in September, in November before report cards, in January, in March before report cards, and in May. Each assessment follows the same pattern: co-assessing, co-coding, and sharing the results and plans. The cycles of assessment allow teachers to see whether their teaching has made a difference in the students' learning. They can comment in the students' report cards on the growth they have perceived, but they do not record the assessment results as letter or number grades; rather, they prepare descriptive comments.

During the end-of-the-year assessment, some schools choose to change the descriptive comments to a numerical rating (depending on the rubric being used) as summative information. The staff can then examine this information to determine whether they have reduced, over time, the number of students who achieved below expectations and whether more students are achieving higher levels of proficiency. It is important to pause in our teaching to see whether we are, indeed, making a difference in our efforts to achieve our own goals.

In middle school or secondary school, the incoming group of students is typically assessed on their content-area reading. Again, a schedule is established among the teams of teachers who conduct the assessment. Together, the staff meet on a professional development morning to code the papers and to establish a profile of their incoming students—their areas of strength and their areas of need. The staff then moves into department groups to choose content-specific strategies to address the chosen area of student need. Although the text might have been in science, teachers of social studies, math, English, and the trades need access to this information as well. If the evidence indicates that students are struggling with effectively using text features such as charts and diagrams, their achievement will improve more rapidly if this need is addressed in all content subjects. Some schools repeat their assessments in January and May, others repeat them as a whole school only at the end of the year; individual teachers conduct similar assessments more frequently with their own classes. Several questions are always asked:

- *What is working?*
- *What can these students do?*
- *What is not yet working?*
- *What do these students need?*
- *What is my plan to address this need?*

Then, after the second assessment,

- *Is my teaching making a difference?*

Some schools code all the student assessments. This is very important in the case of the teacher (in whose class the assessment occurred) who is going to use the information to work with both class goals and individual goals. In a case where the information is being used to establish a goal for a grade group, all students will take the assessment, but only every third response will be coded. This is the pattern of the responses that teachers use to set the goal for a grade group and is, of course, much quicker to code but does not give information on individual students.

At Steveston-London Secondary School, the teachers chose to assess their in-coming grade 8 students using a section of their *BC Science Probe 8* text (Carmichael et al. 2006). Section 3.6, "Protecting the Body," had not yet been dealt with in class. It included many text features—sidebar notes, labelled diagrams, subheadings, figures and captions highlighting aspects of the text, and bolded key vocabulary. The students were asked to respond to the following questions:

1. **Predicting: Looking ahead** (answered after the teacher's instructions, but without reading the text)

   What do you think this reading passage will be about? Why do you think that?

2. **Summarizing: Making notes** (These questions are read aloud with the students before they read the text and before they complete the questions.)

   Read the sections "The First Line of Defence," and "The Second Line of Defence" on pp. 81–82. Make notes on these sections in an outline format or in a well-organized web. In your notes, make sure you show clearly which points are main ideas and which points are supporting details.

3. **Vocabulary: Defining words**

Define each of the following words. Explain how you figured out the meaning of each word.

Figure 3.2 Vocabulary: Defining words

Word	My definition	How I figured out the meaning
engulf (p.82)		
foolproof (p.82)		
transmitted (p.83)		

4. **Connections: Connecting to what you already know**

How are the body's defence systems (described in the reading) similar to the way that animals, individual people, or groups defend themselves from attack? You can write about what you've learned from school, other things you've read or viewed, or any personal experiences.

5. **Making inferences: Reading between the lines**

Consider a person whose blood test shows fewer white blood cells and antibodies than are within the normal range. How might this affect them? Why? Use evidence from the reading to support your answer.

6. **Evaluating: Supporting an opinion**

Imagine you have a scratch that is producing a large amount of pus. Would you go to see a doctor? Why or why not? Support your answer with evidence from the reading passage.

Notice that the students are cued to the type of thinking expected in each question. There is no time limit and most students easily complete the task within an hour. As well, each student reads a portion of the text to a teacher and responds to these interview questions:

- *When you come to a challenging word, how do you figure it out?*
- *If a reading passage does not make sense, what do you do?*
- *What was the main idea of the whole passage?*
- *Do you have any specific reading or learning strategy goals for this year?*

At Steveston-London, an interdisciplinary team coded the assessments. They found that the students were more capable of making connections and forming opinions, but they needed support with making inferences and using text features. This information was shared with all departments who taught grade 8 students. Within each department, plans were made to address these areas of need.

In a middle school or a secondary school, a department or an individual teacher along with the resource teacher may create a performance-based assessment to guide their practice. The cycle of the assessment is determined by the teacher or the department, depending on how frequently they want to examine snapshots of their students' independent work. During the repeat assessments and in regular classroom practice, teachers may want to focus only on one or two questions in order to target particular areas on which they and the students are working.

In mathematics, performance-based assessments play an important role in the cycle of assessment for learning, and are gaining more prevalence in classroom practice. Newly published textbooks include opportunities for performance-based assessment at regular intervals—at the end of each unit of study (a unit problem is used as assessment of learning) and also three times a year in the form of a cross-curricular investigation. These multi-day explorations include learning outcomes from a range of different topics; they consolidate the big ideas in pattern, data, number, and geometry into engaging real-world tasks.

Assessment of these rich learning tasks takes place through the use of a rubric, which focuses on students' competence in demonstrating their understanding of concepts, procedures, and strategies. When we embed these cross-curricular investigations (or math projects) every few units, we highlight the importance of focusing not only on paper-pencil tests of mastery but also on the application of these concepts. For adolescent learners who seek meaning in what they do at school ("When are we ever going to use this, Miss?"), the performance task as assessment tool validates and affirms that the math we study is important and has a useful place in our lives.

Performance tasks across the grades bring together important mathematics concepts and a context in which to apply those concepts. Consider the following example of a mathematical performance task:

> *Use what you know about the surface area of 3-D objects and tessellations to design an ideal box that will hold 24 chocolates. Justify your choice, referring to the cost of materials.*
>
> *What mark-up would you have to apply to the sale of this box of chocolates if you wanted to make a 20% profit?*
>
> *Create a design for the cover of your box that is eye-catching and includes at least 3 transformations.*
>
> *Write a set of instructions that manufacturing staff can follow in order to create the design and enact the flips, slides, and rotations required.*

This task can be used in grade 9 or 10 as a cross-strand investigation. It pulls together concepts from the measurement and geometry strands as well as learning outcomes from the number strand of the curriculum. This task can also be used midway through the first term to assess students' mastery of the concepts addressed, to determine what is missing, and to assess students' capacity to apply the concepts in a new context. Information from the analysis of the task sets the teacher up for what to teach next.

The research is very clear that assessment-for-learning strategies can have a profound effect on improving student learning (Black and Wiliam 1998; Black et al. 2003; Hattie and Timperley 2007) and for increasing engagement and motivation. We want to focus our energies on this area.

End-of-Unit Assessment of Learning

It is possible to design and implement highly effective assessment-of-learning practices that support all learners who are working in a differentiated environment. It is critical to this design to have clear targets and support along the way if the students and teacher are to achieve these targets. And, of course, what is being assessed to record as marks is only what has been taught and practised.

Consider the following summative project for grade 8, 9, or 10 (depending on the inclusion of the systems of equations and/or slope work). In asking students to demonstrate their understanding concretely, pictorially, and abstractly, it matches the algebra curriculum explicitly and provides an engaging task for students.

Use pattern blocks or other manipulatives. Create at least 4 stages of an increasing pattern, keeping track of the number of blocks used for each stage. Record a sketch of your pattern. Use words and numbers to describe the way in which your pattern changes, and which parts remain constant.

Translate this description into an algebraic expression that makes a generalization for the change for any stage. Use graph paper to express your increasing pattern in terms of a linear function. How does the slope of the line connect to the rate of growth of your pattern? What can you find out about the constant in your expression?

Lastly, compare your growing pattern to that of a classmate. Graph both expressions on the same set of axes. What do you notice? Do your lines intersect? What does it mean?

The end-of-unit math performance tasks are scored with rubrics. What is being assessed brings together important mathematical concepts and a context in which to apply these concepts. This is so much more than a paper-and-pencil test of mastery. Examples of such effective and fair assessments of learning are found in chapters 5 to 12.

Chapter 4

Frameworks and Approaches to Support Diverse Learners

> If we don't insist on the value of what we teach, have faith in our students, and persist in our attempt to make the education connections, then our invitation tends to have a shallow and possibly false ring. (Liston 2004)

Teachers need to have a working model in mind when designing lesson sequences for a class of diverse learners, and there are a number of well-researched frameworks and approaches to draw on. The two frameworks we use to design lessons and units that engage and support all learners are Universal Design for Learning and Backward Design. In this chapter, we explain these two planning frameworks and six well-known and inclusive teaching approaches:

1. assessment for learning
2. open-ended strategies
3. gradual release of responsibility
4. cooperative learning
5. information circles
6. inquiry

These approaches also address several of our key beliefs about teaching and learning:

- Learning is both individual and social.
- Learning should be personally meaningful and authentic.
- Learning builds from prior experience and background knowledge.
- Students from grade 5 through grade 12 must learn to work with teachers who may use different instructional styles and may convey different messages.
- Students from grade 5 through grade 12 must learn subject content and the subject-related thinking strategies to engage with, remember, connect to, process, and synthesize the content.

Universal Design for Learning

Universal Design for Learning, or UDL (Rose and Meyer 2002), is one framework we keep in mind when designing lessons and units. It can also be expressed as "designing learning to support all learners." This means that we design classroom activities that take into account the diverse strengths, challenges, and interests of all class members. We find that the accommodations we put into place for students with specific needs can benefit many other students' learning. Using the principles of UDL has moved us away from making a number of individual plans and toward using approaches that offer multiple ways for all students to engage in learning, to access ideas, and to show their learning.

UDL originated in the field of architecture known as "universal design," when architects responded to the increasing demand to make the built world more accessible to all. Yes, most buildings were accessible to the majority of people, but not to all people. Although most people enter buildings by stairs, some people—people in wheelchairs, people on rollerblades, mothers pushing baby strollers—find stairs a barrier to access. The big idea of universal design is that structures should be planned and then built with the diverse population in mind, not just a "typical" person. By also taking into account the needs of those who are not "most people," architects can design structures that meet the needs of all people. Ramps help not only those in wheelchairs or pushing strollers or on rollerblades but also anyone who has trouble going up a set of stairs, or carrying a box, or facing other unexpected and perhaps temporary challenges. When architects apply the principles of universal design, they plan multiple ways for people to access shelter, food, and water; meet with other people; or access resource people and services. Thus, most individuals can benefit from these design features at any time in their lives.

These concepts of universal design can be applied to education as a response to the varied individual ways that students learn and the means by which they access learning. At its core, UDL is an acceptance of and respect for diversity. It goes beyond physical barriers, taking into account students' sensory and cognitive needs. Rather than taking the perspective that we should "fix" children because they do not learn in a particular way, UDL takes a student-centred approach, which means designing many ways to engage students, many ways for them to access and process information, and many ways for them to express what they know and learn. We achieve this by using curricular materials and activities that provide multiple paths for students with differing strengths, interests, and abilities. These alternatives are *built into* the instructional design of educational materials; they are not added on after the fact. Universal design principles can apply to assignments, classroom discussions, group work, handouts, web-based instruction, and even lectures or demonstrations.

Three Guiding Principles

The three guiding principles of universal design are outlined in the paragraphs that follow. Within a particular unit of instruction and depending on the needs of our students, we might focus on one principle more than another.

1. Multiple means to tap into learners' interests and background knowledge to activate prior knowledge and increase engagement and motivation

Chapters 5 to 12 in this book offer lessons that use a range of ways to tap into learners' interests and background knowledge. In chapter 7, Nicole and Leyton use a connecting sequence to help students access their prior knowledge and experiences and link to the key concepts and approaches of the upcoming unit. They have students begin to think about the reading skills that scientists use. To move beyond the limits of the students' experiences, Nicole and Leyton place a bin of nonfiction reading materials on each table, and ask the students to continue their exploration of reading skills that scientists use, but now connected to text. Students have begun with individual work, then moved to a small group exploration with something concrete to examine. Finally, each group reports out to the class and they create a master list of reading skills which is then used to guide students in their non-fiction reading. Nicole and Leyton have the students as a class brainstorm what living things are, then move to record individually how living things are related to one another or what all living things have in common. The goals are common, but students have more than one way to engage with ideas and access what they already know.

In chapter 11, Catherine's classroom survey with the book *If the World Were a Village* (Smith, David 2002) is an excellent example of how to attract students' interests—in themselves—and make connections to a broader context. Students connected their nationalities, languages, and faiths to those prevalent in the world, and then made predictions about these aspects within another population. By examining each group, students were able to make predictions and inferences about them—thinking skills that are necessary for students to be truly numerate.

2. Multiple means for students to acquire information and knowledge that can help them process new ideas and information

The lesson chapters illustrate how teachers use multiple approaches to help students explore a key concept while at the same time developing thinking strategies. In chapter 10, students explore key mathematical concepts of area and volume by visualizing, building, and testing their conjectures about 3-D objects. Having the opportunity to touch and explore these real-world materials was critical in making the task meaningful for grade 8 students. One student was overheard to say in conversation with his peer, "This is great. You really have to know this stuff if you're going to build anything." He had made an important math-to-world connection, and by seeing the math applied, he could connect and process the information in a much more "meaning-full" way.

In chapter 8, Kristi Johnston and Jeremy Ellis provide multiple ways for their students to research their biome. Some students work online while others work with print text. In both cases, Kristi and Jeremy instruct the students in the ways to access information within their given format, and guide them as they explore their questions — questions that the students have chosen within the framework of the class's overarching question. Such a wide range of reading materials help keep the students from getting stuck in a text that they are unable to read, or stuck working in lockstep with everyone else, or stuck reading something they already know. They generate their own research questions, set their own pace (with goals along the way), and choose their own selections to read.

3. Multiple means for students to express what they know

We offer students a range of ways to show what they know, but recognize that we must first introduce the different ways and help them develop their ability to show their learning in a range of ways.

By the midpoint of a school year, Katie (chapter 9) has introduced and developed different ways for her students to show what they know — peer interviews, math journals, "build and share" — and students have practised these techniques. The students can choose to demonstrate their learning in the way that works best for them. Together, they establish criteria for a good math journal, and then they apply the criteria to their written work. As for expectations related to using manipulatives, they have also co-created criteria for their use. This is an essential step in middle schools and secondary schools because the use of models is often associated only with elementary school. These materials are not a crutch for those who struggle with mathematical concepts; rather, as mathematicians know, manipulatives are an essential tool in learning and making connections between abstract concepts. Students are, therefore, expected to demonstrate their understanding of concepts using models in order to master the concepts.

In Catherine's class (chapter 11), students who struggle to communicate in one modality have the opportunity to share their understandings in more than one way (like Vincent, whose oral language capacity far outstripped his ability to record on paper). The data management software likewise allows students to process information more efficiently and express what they know using multiple formats. All students have access to the important math ideas in this way.

In science classrooms like Nicole's in chapter 6, students have represented their learning throughout the unit in different ways — artifact strings, vocabulary representations, Venn diagrams, mind maps, journals, diagrams. As a final presentation, they can choose a scrapbook, a slideshow, or a personal option. Whatever their choice, they must demonstrate how water systems are connected and what that means to them. Since this is one project for a collaborative English/Science unit, their final project will include six poems exploring places that are special to them. The learning in both content areas has been guided by the essential question "How are we connected to our environment?" based on shared goals, but offering individual paths.

We use UDL because it acknowledges and accepts diversity as a reality and strength, and it helps us to plan and organize for teaching and learning with diversity in mind.

Backward Design

Planning and Teaching with Both Students and Content in Mind

Teaching in math and science is complex. It is easy to become overwhelmed by the content, the number of curricular outcomes to be "covered," and the sheer volume of material to be mastered. Teaching for understanding, though, means taking a step back from this long list of outcomes and examining instead the big ideas—the important things to know in the discipline. Teaching well requires us to determine the enduring understandings in mathematics and science, and the thinking strategies that students will need in order to demonstrate these understandings. There is much that we *can* focus on—for example, layers of facts, procedures and formulae, interesting data or experimental results—but deep learning needs to be rooted in a few core concepts. By *core concepts* we mean the big ideas that can be used to link all the information in a unit of study in a scientific or a mathematical strand. When we focus teaching and learning on core concepts, students can build connections between ideas and see them as interrelated components of a bigger concept. They see the "So what?" of learning math and science, and are able to find the conceptual forest among the trees.

For example, in science classrooms where meaningful, authentic, and concept-oriented learning occurs, students develop enduring understandings by relating ideas across explorations, texts they read and create, their prior knowledge and real world situations. To do this, we need to determine what is most important for students to learn and then design learning sequences that simultaneously develop conceptual understanding and the thinking skills they need.

In math classrooms where conceptual understanding is the end goal, the job of the teacher is to design learning tasks that allow students to draw upon their prior knowledge and apply it to new, problematic situations. The tasks themselves must be structured around an important math idea, an enduring understanding at which students arrive *in the act of solving the problem*. As students problem-solve alone and together using their background knowledge and the tools provided, they uncover the big math ideas for themselves; it is the teacher's role to home in on the enduring understanding in student discussions, to rephrase and elaborate on it, making the "So what?" of the lesson explicit as the final word.

We find that the Backward Design approach of Wiggins and McTighe in their book *Understanding by Design* (2001) is a helpful framework for our planning, assessment, and instruction so that we can build both the thinking strategies and the content knowledge of all students.

Backward design involves four key elements:

1. Identify key concepts from learning outcomes and organize lessons and learning sequences around the enduring understandings that we want students to develop by the end of a unit of study.
2. Identify what thinking strategies students need to develop and use to complete learning tasks, in particular, for summative assessments.
3. Align formative and summative assessments so that students know what is expected of them.
4. Explicitly teach and assess thinking strategies as part of a unit of study so that students become increasingly successful learners.

Chapters 5 through 12 present examples of teachers collaborating. Together, they decide what is most important for students to learn and do, and then support students in developing the understandings that are at the heart of the curriculum in math and science. They require critical thinking. In science, students must use thinking strategies to make sense of how real events, factors, and scientific principles relate to each other. In math, students must connect mathematical strands, topics, and principles in order to reason through problems, applications, and investigations.

To develop the thinking strategies required of mathematicians and scientists, students need to be engaged in a process of meaning-making. Learning in math and science requires these thinking strategies; teaching in math and science requires teachers to determine what the important ideas and enduring understandings are, what thinking strategies the students need in order to demonstrate these understandings, and then to explicitly teach their students how to develop these strategies. To begin:

- Look at the curriculum for related learning outcomes.
- Discuss what is most important for students to know and do in the unit.
- Brainstorm the big ideas to explore during the unit by linking the various things that are important for students to know and do.

We use just a few simple questions to guide our planning:

- *Planning:* What do I want my students to know and do by the end of the unit?
- *Assessment:* How will I know that they have developed these understandings and thinking strategies?

- *Instruction:* How will I engage students in constructing understandings and developing key strategies?

For example, in chapter 11, Catherine exposes students to a set of tasks that highlight the big math ideas, or enduring understandings, of the unit:

- We can draw inferences about data. When we make an inference from data, we must support our thinking with relevant data and explain why we think so.
- The predictions and inferences we make about a population come from making connections to what we already know. These connections are considered math-to-math, math-to-self, or math-to-world.

Catherine and Carole structure each lesson around these big ideas, and practise applying their strategies in different contexts — by reading charts, tables, circle graphs, and scatter plots. All students have a chance to develop deep understandings when inferring through data as they engage in whole-group discussions, partner check-ins, and online chats. Feedback on students' work, via email, keeps students on track with their learning, and mini-lessons provide targeted support for those requiring it.

Formative assessment is at the heart of our approach to Backward Design. In chapter 8, an overarching question guides the research process. Under the umbrella of this question, students create their own questions to guide their individual biome research. Kristi and Jeremy create content learning intentions and research learning intentions. Each student has a copy of these on the inside front cover of his research folder. The learning intentions that guide each day's lesson are initially chosen by the teachers, but on subsequent days, they are chosen by the students. Daily feedback from the teachers is based on how well each student accomplishes their chosen learning intentions. Because Jeremy and Kristi give daily feedback to their students, they are able to notice when more specific teaching is needed and adjust their lessons accordingly. The combination of all factors — clarity of task, daily descriptive feedback, feedback from self and peers, and controlled choice in questions and the order of fulfilling learning intentions — leads to greater ownership of their learning by the students. All students see clearly what is required of them because of the formative assessment given along their learning path in the form of feedback — rather than through a summative assessment at the end of a lesson.

Using frameworks like Backward Design helps us to develop learning-centred classrooms where all students engage in deep content learning that builds enduring understandings and thinking strategies. Using Universal Design for Learning also helps us plan for diversity. Next, we outline six approaches that help us to apply the principles of UDL while supporting students in their efforts to develop enduring understandings and to become strategic learners.

Applying the Principles of Universal Design for Learning

1. Assessment for Learning: Formative Assessment

When we use assessment for learning strategies, we make sure that every student gets personalized feedback in response to a class-wide focus. In chapter 3, we introduced the AFL strategies that make a difference:

- *Learning intentions:* By identifying learning intentions, students know where they are going and what they will be able to do. This can also be achieved through an inquiry question. In chapter 7, Nicole, Lori, and Leyton focus their students' learning by beginning the lesson with a question. Note that in mathematics, learning intentions are expressed as "big math ideas"—or the "enduring understandings"—of the lesson. These ideas or understandings are named explicitly to the students at the end of the lesson rather than described at the beginning of the lesson.
- *Creating criteria:* By including students in the development of criteria that will be applied to their work, students internalize criteria related to learning intentions.
- *Descriptive feedback:* Descriptive feedback helps students determine where they are in the process and make adjustments for further success.
- *Questioning:* Teachers use questions that are open-ended and invite and encourage students to develop their own questions.
- *Self-assessment and peer-assessment:* Opportunities to self-assess and give feedback to peers move students toward owning and personalizing criteria and self-regulating their actions.
- *Ownership:* Students come to "own" their learning, feel a shared ownership of the learning community and its activities, and work toward making a difference in their own and others' learning.

AFL focuses on getting information about students' use of thinking strategies and understanding of essential information. The AFL information is then used to make a plan. We often say "No plan, no point." Unless the AFL information is going to be used to set goals, to create plans to achieve those goals, and then to assess whether the goals have been achieved, it is not worthwhile collecting it. When looking at AFL information, we always focus on strengths first— *What can my students do? What's working?* Then we identify focus areas. We set class-wide goals that apply to *all* students, and we have students set their personal goals. Most importantly, we make sure that there are not too many goals, because we want to stay focused and see growth. The chosen goals should be goals that we practise throughout a unit and evaluate in our summative assessments. To have the greatest impact, we want students to get ongoing feedback from us (*What's working? What's not working? What's next?*), from each other, and ultimately from themselves by reflecting and continuing to set personal goals and working on them from activity to activity.

In each of the next eight chapters, we identify the AFL strategies used by teachers and how these relate to their summative assessments—assessment of learning (AOL). Backward Design helps remind us that our formative and summative assessments must line up. This helps us keep our summative assessment authentic. There may be many criteria on a rubric, but we only summatively assess the thinking strategies that we have taught in class and that students have practised. If we didn't teach it, we won't evaluate it. Our assessment of learning aligns with what we have actually taught, and we assess thinking strategies that students have had a chance to work on over time.

2. Open-Ended Strategies

We find that instruction using open-ended strategies is a key ingredient in classrooms that are learning communities. Open-ended instructional strategies do not set a ceiling on what students can learn and do. Rather, they allow students to stretch as far as they can go in using language and pushing the edges of their current knowledge. At the same time, they support all learners in thinking about their learning and contributing to the learning of others. By using open-ended strategies, all students have opportunities to learn, identify, and share relevant background knowledge. The first principle of Universal Design for Learning is to give students opportunities to use their own interests and experiences. Open-ended strategies also set students up to construct their own understandings.

When using Backward Design principles, we plan instruction around curriculum expectations, and we design opportunities for students to move from their current learning place to the learning place described in the curriculum. We believe that all students can and should build on and from their prior knowledge; thus we use instructional strategies that ask students to find information, relate it to other information, and develop possible interpretations. Using open-ended strategies engages students in meaning-making and knowledge construction.

As discussed in chapter 1, we divide open-ended strategies into three categories—these are the strategies that help students in *connecting*, *processing*, and *transforming and personalizing* information. You will find an example of *connecting strategies* in chapter 9. There you will notice that Carole and Katie begin a lesson by asking students to connect what they already know to the ideas and concepts that they are studying. We often start a learning sequence by asking students to predict, link, or compare key words, ideas, images, or relationships before engaging with new content. Activating prior knowledge helps students connect what they are learning to what they already know. In chapter 6, Nicole and Sue help students in their science class connect and activate prior knowledge with a graffiti strategy on the topic of water combined with examining images of scenic locations in English class. They use this activated, shared knowledge to build community in the class, to assess what the students know already, and to lay a foundation for the new curriculum content.

For the second category of *processing strategies*, our teaching helps students draw out, link, and compare key information from tasks or texts. In math and science classrooms, we help them master the content and the discipline by problem solving, reasoning, and making connections, which can be practised and applied while engaging in a task or with a range of texts—print, media, visual, and oral. In mathematics classrooms, the content itself becomes a text to be connected, and the focus of the lessons, then, is on the math-to-math connections that can be made within and between lessons. In chapter 11, Catherine has students develop and compare their inferences and reasoning about data with other students online. In chapter 7, Leyton and Nicole ask students to make notes from text using the magnet strategy and two-column note strategy. In both these examples, the teachers are focused on students using strategies to make meaning and think critically in relation to key questions, not engaging in a rote activity like finding the "right" answer. Open-ended instructional strategies require students to do their own thinking to find information, to relate it to the topic, and to devise and support their unique interpretations. The students have to engage in the process but they can do so in ways that draw upon their own background knowledge and their strengths as learners.

The third type of open-ended teaching strategy—*personalizing and transforming*—requires students to personalize and transform the information and ideas they have engaged with. They focus on figuring out what the elements of information are and how they go together. When possible, we ask students to take information from multiple sources, combine it, and communicate how the information can be pieced together to show a principle, a theme, or a big idea. If the information comes from a single source, it is doubly important that students go through the process of transforming the information into another form (e.g., the ideas from an activity or textbook are shown as an icon or diagram). This activity helps them determine the importance or relevance of certain information. Personalizing and/or transforming strategies involve synthesizing information. Synthesizing involves more than summarizing; it requires students to show that they have made sense of how the information goes together, have made decisions about what is important and how they can best communicate their understanding. In chapter 10, Carole asks the students to develop and show their understanding of the relationships between the area and volume of cylinders as they work through "The Paper Problem." Starleigh and Mindy in chapter 5, have their students create a demonstration, present a scenario, or create a model to demonstrate their understanding of how materials hold and transfer electricity.

Open-ended instructional strategies are a powerful way to teach while keeping all learners in mind. These strategies require students to make connections, process information, and transform it in a variety of ways. By using these strategies, we build in a range of seamless supports and prompts as we encourage students to personalize and share their responses. Students with learning challenges are included as members of the learning community and as part of the classroom conversation, while they are engaged in quality teaching and learning through such open-ended strategy sequences. They construct meaning with the support of peers rather than by working on separate lessons that remove them from the learning context. For us, a supportive classroom is one that welcomes and celebrates all learners, one in which teachers use instructional strategies to help students develop their thinking and their knowledge.

Open-ended strategies in mathematics involve working on a problem that has more than one right answer or more than one solution method. Diversity in the classroom is supported by posing problems that are complex enough to be compelling and open-ended enough to engage all students whether they are struggling or excelling. Central to these open-ended tasks is the enduring understanding, or the big math idea. By drawing on a common "So what?" for the lesson, teachers can pull together all their students—regardless of their level of skill—to highlight the enduring understandings. In this way, all learners have a chance to touch the important mathematical concept of the lesson and also see other ways of engaging with it. This is a powerful learning structure, and one that allows teachers to keep their classroom communities intact for learning. We are, after all, smarter together.

3. Gradual Release of Responsibility

Another approach that supports diverse learners is the *gradual release of responsibility* (Pearson and Gallagher 1983). When key thinking strategies are identified for a unit of study, teachers can gradually release the development of their students' capacity as thinkers and doers, moving from modelling to guided practice to students practising in small groups, to independent practice. We watch for students' independent application of these key thinking strategies, applying them in new contexts without teacher prompting. As with open-ended strategy instruction, we focus on having students personalize and apply approaches with increasing independence.

In chapter 7, Nicole, Lori, and Leyton gradually release students' development of note-making strategies into their students' control. Students then choose and use their various note-making strategies to work on a team and create or design a team poster, game, skit, comic strip, rap song, or other demonstration of their choice to explain the Five Kingdoms—information gained from independent and peer research. Later they use these strategies to collect information and write to persuade others about the need for laws to protect the environment. Successful completion of these summative assessments requires that they use the strategies introduced and modelled by the teachers.

4. Cooperative Learning

Cooperation plays a key role in learning and in one's ability to contribute to and participate in society. Cooperative learning is also an instructional approach that honours and builds on student diversity. Cooperative learning involves having students work together in peer-mediated groups. Cooperative learning helps students develop thinking strategies and make meaning together. We say to students: "You should leave this group smarter than when you entered it." Cooperative learning will serve students well both during and beyond school. A key aspect of an effective workplace is the ability of co-workers to confront and resolve conflict. The most common aptitudes found in job descriptions relate to communication skills and to interpersonal skills. Working together provides students with opportunities not only to learn content but also to build their understanding through interaction. Many researchers have shown how learning is socially constructed. Similarly, neurologists argue that talk is essential for intellectual growth. Our math curriculum highlights the importance of talk and has built communication and representation of mathematical ideas into almost every prescribed learning outcome from kindergarten to grade 12.

Cooperative learning in mathematics and science requires social skills, communication skills, and critical thinking skills. Within a unit of study, a teacher may choose to help students develop skills in one or two of these areas. Social skills include taking turns, showing mutual respect, and encouraging others. Communication skills include paraphrasing, seeking clarification, and accepting and extending the ideas of others. Critical thinking skills include suspending judgment, considering multiple perspectives related to an issue, taking into account multiple factors, and recognizing bias.

We have experienced the power of cooperative learning in K to 12 classrooms. One of the most powerful ways to engage students in active learning is to have them talk to one another about what they have just done, observed, or read. Another is to have them share and give one another feedback regarding a project or composition that they have worked on over several classes. The cooperative learning approaches used by teachers in this book are collaborative, in that they require students to share their thinking at several points along the way. In some cases, cooperative learning is a means of helping students explore ideas, develop possible understandings, share works in progress, and get feedback. In other examples, teachers teach and assess the communication and collaboration skills as part of their unit, for example, Katie's "peer interviews" in chapter 9 on understanding polynomials or Nicole, Lori, and Leyton's "Five Kingdoms Team Project" in chapter 7. Whether the focus is on having students scaffold one another's thinking over time, or building students' social and communications skills, or developing critical thinking skills, cooperation plays a key role in the learning community.

5. Information Circles

One of the most effective ways to engage and support all learners is to use diverse texts. Within a unit of study, we collect a range of texts on the same theme but with as wide a range of reading levels and genres as possible. Texts may include picture books, short articles, and visual texts such as art, advertisements, and online texts. We often start a new unit by building students' background knowledge using a common text or several short pieces of text, then we ask students to dig deeper into a topic by choosing from and reading several more related texts.

For example, in chapter 8, Kristi and Jeremy have their students choose their own materials for research, both print and online. In chapter 6, Sue and Nicole have their students work with different newspaper articles to examine the human impact on water systems and read different poems in English as they build toward their essential question "How are we connected to the environment?"

Information circles involve taking the literature circle structure (see Brownlie 2005; Brownlie, Feniak, and Schnellert 2006, Brownlie and Schnellert 2009) and applying it to information texts, including textbooks. Students have discussions in small, peer-led groups about the text they have chosen to read. Information circles offer students a choice of text in the science classroom. They help teachers gradually release the use of particular thinking strategies and allow a deeper investigation of key concepts first explored as a whole class. Of course, the power of talking together helps to enhance the students' understanding. All students get a chance to share ideas and develop meaning together without deferring to the teacher. Like literature circles, information circles have several key components:

- Students choose the reading materials from texts that the teacher has introduced.
- Students who have chosen to read the same article, chapter, or book form an information circle.
- Students keep notes to guide both their reading and discussion (e.g., a journal entry, a graphic organizer, sticky notes, annotations in the text).
- Groups meet regularly to discuss their reading.
- Discussion points and questions come from the students, not from the teachers or the textbooks.
- Personal responses, observations, and questions are the starting point of discussion.
- The teacher acts as a facilitator and observer.
- When information circles finish a cycle, groups may share highlights of the reading with classmates through presentations, discussions, dramatizations, or other media.
- New groups form around their new reading choices, and a new cycle begins.

For certain strands of mathematics, (particularly the data management and geometry strands), students find discussions in information circles meaningful. Using samples of real-world texts, students access data drawn from a variety of sources — newspapers, magazines, online websites, and advertisements — in order to interpret the graphs and tables, to make inferences about the results and to apply their developing understandings of bias. Students engage in discussion of these key aspects of the mathematics while comparing and contrasting their chosen mathematical text — the data set or graph they selected. In a similar way, art and architecture as well as other graphics become the "texts" to be compared in an analysis of the attributes of geometric shapes, or an investigation of transformations, or an exploration of the area of circles, triangles, and parallelograms.

6. Inquiry

Inquiry is another approach that engages and supports all learners. Inquiry provides a planning structure to help students develop thinking strategies that lead to deeper understandings about concepts. Inquiry can also help us match our teaching to our students' learning. When working with an open-ended question over the course of either several lessons or a full unit of study, students collect, compare, and synthesize information over time. Embedded within an inquiry are several thinking skills. In chapters 5 through 12, you can see how thinking skills can be introduced and used to explore big ideas in relation to an overarching question or to encourage student questioning within the unit of study. The teachers you will meet in the following chapters use open-ended inquiry questions that set a purpose for learning. Students read, write, explore, make meaningful connections, and apply what they are learning to new texts and situations.

Nicole and Leyton have their students keep Wonder books. Catherine and Carole focus on inferring in chapter 11; Mindy and Starleigh in chapter 5 focus on connecting vocabulary and concepts to everyday life through accessing prior knowledge, predicting, inferring, and visualizing. Catherine's students (chapter 11) engage in inquiry when they compare first-hand data from peer groups of students across the country, and make inferences about the lifestyles of those groups. Katie's students (chapter 9) use inquiry in their polynomial explorations to establish math-to-math connections, modelling and simplifying expressions using algebra tiles. Students engage with inquiry when they investigate relationships between the area and volume of cylinders, and then connect those understandings to materials they use in everyday life (chapter 10). In chapter 5, Mindy and Starleigh's students wonder what happens when you rub a balloon on your hair. Nicole's science students and Sue's English students create a common project to address the questions: *What are the different ways we can be connected to our environment?* and *How does what we know as scientists matter to what we love as poets?* (chapter 6). In chapter 7, Nicole and Lori's students use inquiry as they work with "reciprocal teaching." And finally, Kristi and Jeremy's students follow their research questions into the library as they learn about biomes (chapter 8).

Conclusion

Together with our colleagues, the teachers you will meet in the next eight chapters, we are committed to working and learning together. Teaching in ways that support thinking and learning in all of our students continues to fuel our own process of inquiry. Along the way, we have discovered and tailored frameworks and approaches that support the diverse learners of our classrooms. We embrace the diversity in our classrooms. We want to help all students develop and use their strengths and interests while also developing thinking strategies and conceptual understandings. We invite you to adapt these ideas for the grades and units that you teach. Make them your own. Although the content of each chapter is specific to a grade or grades and matched to the most current math and science curricula in Canada, the frameworks and approaches introduced are not grade-specific or topic-specific. The planning structures themselves can easily be applied at any grade level and with a range of topics. Turn to the chapter that interests you most and think about how you might adapt the approaches described—assessment for learning, open-ended strategies, gradual release of responsibility, cooperative learning, information circles, inquiry—for your students.

Chapter 5

Introduction to Electricity

Grade 9—Science

Assessment FOR Learning	• Connecting • Exit slip • Providing feedback
Gradual Release of Responsibility	• Scientific skills and strategies modelled • Guided application for students • Creating scenarios and demonstrations • Stategic learning in lesson sequences
Thinking Skills	• Connecting vocabulary • Predicting • Inferring • Visualizing • Accessing prior knowledge
Inquiry	• Essential question
Differentiation	• Partners • Predict-Observe-Explain (P-O-E) format • Open-ended performance tasks • Varied levels of support • Student choice of representation
Assessment OF Learning	• Performance task • Peer-assessment

The Collaboration

Mindy Casselman and Starleigh Grass worked together for a few years at Kumsheen Secondary School (KSS) in British Columbia and now teach at Lillooet Secondary School (LSS). Both schools are small and rural: Lillooet Secondary School encompasses grade 8 to grade 12, but has 260 students in total enrolled over the five grades. Seventy per cent of the students at LSS are from the St'át'imc First Nation. The school is served by seven buses because some students travel up to 50 km to school; students who live more than 100 km from the school stay and board in town during the school week, and go home on the weekends. The Ministry of Education has identified 9 per cent of the students as having special needs. Mindy teaches science to both junior and senior classes as well as physical education; Starleigh teaches junior social studies, English, and science.

For the past three years, both teachers have participated in a district-wide learning community on Universal Design for Learning facilitated by Leyton Schnellert. With what they learned during these sessions, they began to collaborate with other teachers from their school and across the district on strategies that work well within their school contexts. During learning community meetings, both groups of teachers had opportunities to co-plan and reflect.

Mindy and Starleigh collaborate at the school level through meetings at which staff members are divided into groups to share their progress in implementing formative assessment strategies, a goal of the whole school. They are also part of a school-based team with whom they discuss their initiatives for improving academic performance; the team sets goals for creating common structures in their classroom and facilitating skill transfer across grades and across disciplines. Because Starleigh and Mindy share students, they have found that they have exciting opportunities for co-planning and reflection in their rural school.

The Context

In this introduction to the electricity unit for Science 9, Starleigh and Mindy applied planning principles such as organizing instruction around ideas and developing content-specific thinking skills. This chapter is the first part of the larger unit, the Characteristics of Electricity, one quarter of the Grade 9 Science curriculum. The concepts dealt with in this section, such as understanding electron transfer, are essential to understanding ideas that come later in the course. At LSS, Starleigh and Mindy work within an inclusive classroom model, where teaching assistants and a learner support teacher provide support to students who are struggling in class. In this model, a teaching assistant sometimes moves around the classroom to support a different small group each day. During a unit such as this one, the role of the teaching assistant includes modelling inquiry and inference, asking thought-provoking questions during hands-on activities, clarifying instructions when needed, and generally supporting students as they complete their task.

Because of their shared classroom experiences (Starleigh taught social studies and Mindy taught science to this group of grade 9 students), it was clear to them that their students needed highly engaging, interactive activities and that they thrived in an environment offering a high degree of autonomy in social learning situations. Teacher-centred, direct instruction did not work for this cohort; but when given structured activities that allowed them some freedom and creativity—with teacher support, the students helped each other and explored issues with fervour. After co-planning the lessons with Starleigh, Mindy taught the lessons herself.

Mindy and Starleigh are both strong believers in interactive and energetic activities in science. They know that creating enthusiasm for science is critical in grade 9 because these students will soon be deciding whether or not they will include senior level science courses. By showing students that science is full of exploration, inquiry, and discovery, they hope that all students will develop a lasting love for the discipline, and that some students will perhaps consider a career in science.

Key Structures

Assessment for Learning

- Connecting strategies and Exit slips help both teacher and students monitor the learning.
- Using an essential question helps students keep their learning on track.

Gradual Release of Responsibility

- Teachers model the skill or strategy, then do it with the students as a guided practice, then provide individual feedback while the students are working at applying the skill or strategy in independent practice.
- Students are supported as they increase their content knowledge and thinking skills in a series of lesson sequences so that they are prepared to apply their knowledge for assessment of learning tasks.

Differentiation

- The strategy of Predict-Observe-Explain (p-o-e) is a common structure within which students can choose different ways to show their understanding; for example, they can choose to draw and label, write in sentences, or take jot notes.
- The open-ended performance task sets expectations so that all students can be successful while none are restricted in their achievement.
- Activities are structured so that students can receive varied levels of support, depending on their need.

Thinking Skills
- Students routinely connect vocabulary and concepts to their everyday life, which not only meets the learning outcomes of the course but also nurtures lifelong scientific thinkers.
- Skills such as predicting, inferring, visualizing, accessing background knowledge, and connecting are practised within the context of experiential learning situations.

Assessment of Learning
- Students peer-assess the performance task.

Essential Question

Students are invited into the study of electricity through the essential question: How do materials hold and transfer electric charge?
- Students have multiple opportunities to expand upon this key question throughout the unit.
- This question helps students organize their learning around the major concepts of the unit.

Enduring Understanding

- At the end of the unit, students should be able to understand that electricity is created by the movement of electrons.

Lesson 1—Rationale

Making connections is at the heart of science education. This activity allows for the connection of two major portions of the Science 9 curriculum, chemistry and electricity. Students have already learned about the structure of atoms in the chemistry unit. This activity helps students carry information from the previously learned chemistry unit into the electricity unit. It will remind them of what they know about the structure of an atom or rebuild this knowledge for those who might have forgotten. Recalling atomic structure will provide the content base necessary to understand that electrons have the ability to move from object to object. A can-do attitude can enhance student engagement and confidence as they begin a challenging unit. Students will also need to continue developing collaborative relationships in a community of learners who share their thinking.

Accessing Background Knowledge

- Give students 2 minutes to work independently to list what they can recall about the structure of an atom. Giving students this opportunity to activate their background knowledge will help them lock in new information when it is presented.

- Have students leave their seats and form groups of 3 to review and revise the lists they have made. This collaborative work gives the students an opportunity to self-assess and have their peers assess their existing knowledge. Also, because this unit is highly interactive and relies a great deal on students' sharing their thinking with others, this activity acts like a warm-up. Later, when students have to work together on more challenging tasks, they are already in the habit of sharing their ideas with others and building upon each other's thoughts.
- While students are discussing atoms with each other, circulate and listen to their discussion to determine what the class understands about the structure of the atom, and what misconceptions exist.
- Listening in on student conversations is one way to tell where their strengths lie and whether or not there is any information missing. Offer supportive comments to students as they sort out their thinking with others, and ask probing questions when students are stuck:
  - *What else can you think of?*
  - *How do you think you know this?*
  - *How are parts of an atom different?*
- One additional step is to give each group of 3 students a computer with Internet access and ask them to see what else they can find out. This would be particularly helpful if students have not done any work related to the atom yet.
- Finally, call on students as a class to create a summary list from their recollections about the structure of an atom. This step is important in order to clarify any confusion and celebrate what the students recalled from previous classes.
- Edit this list to include the following key concepts about the structure of an atom:
  - All matter is made of atoms.
  - Atoms have electrons, neutrons, and protons.
  - Electrons move; protons and neutrons do not move.
  - Electrons have a negative charge; protons have a positive charge.
  - Protons and neutrons are located at the centre of the atom, in the nucleus.
  - Electrons orbit around the outside of the nucleus, in energy "shells."
  - An atom can become a charged ion when it loses or gains electrons.
  - When an atom loses electrons, it becomes positively charged.
  - When an atoms gains electrons, it becomes negatively charged.
- Ensure that students edit their own lists to include these ideas.

Atomic Vocabulary … it's all Greek to me!

Using the model chart (Figure 5.1), which provides the root origin of key words in the field of electricity, have the students work alone or in partners to brainstorm ideas and record their thinking in the 2 blank columns in the chart—Our Definition and Our Thinking. Use the 2 questions below the chart to discuss their responses and help them consolidate their learning.

- Have students meet in groups of 2 or 3 to compare their answers. Did they omit anything important?
- Review the answers in the chart with the whole class.
- Ask each student to report on their partner's thinking about the consolidating questions. This reporting out on their partner's work rather than on their own provides another reason for students to listen carefully to each other, forming a more cohesive learning partnership.

Visualizing the Atom

Using terms from the Atomic Tea Party Chart, ask students to work in pairs to complete Figure 5.2, labelling a diagram of an atom. After they have a draft, join two pairs of students together to explain their thinking. Have groups report out. Then show students a completed diagram on the board or in a textbook and ask them what they need to change in their own work and why (Figure 5.3).

Figure 5.3 Labelled atom diagram

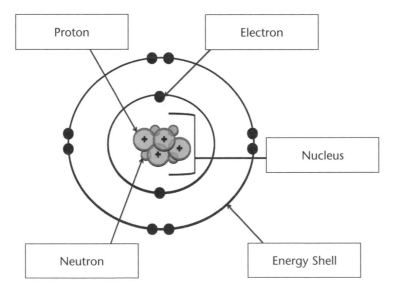

Figure 5.1 Key words in field of electricity

Name: _____

Key words in field of electricity

Word	Origins	Our Definition	Our Thinking
Atom	From ancient Greek word *atomos*, meaning *indivisible* (something that cannot be broken down into smaller parts		
Proton	From ancient Greek word *protos*, meaning *first*		
Neutron	From ancient Greek prefix *ne* meaning *not* (neither positive nor negative)		
Electron	From ancient Greek work *electron*, meaning *like amber* (which, when rubbed, produces static electricity)		

Which of these words will be the key item in learning about electricity?

Does the definition for the word atom match its word origin? Why do you think so?

Figure 5.2 Labelling an atom

Labelling an Atom

Label the atom diagram with the folowing terms:

- Proton
- Nucleus
- Energy Shell
- Electron
- Neutron

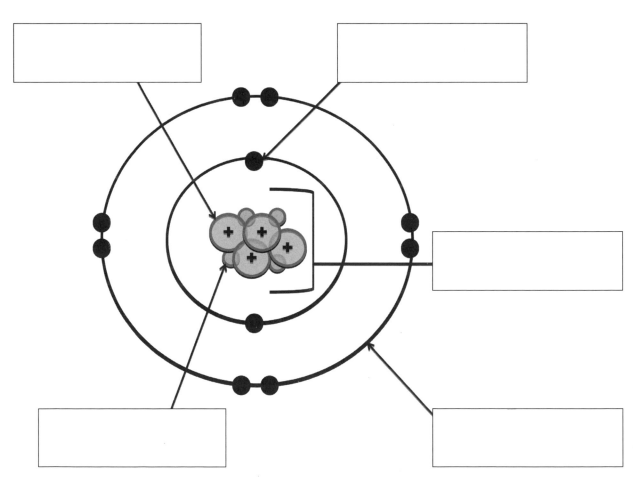

Lesson 2—Rationale

In this lesson, students draw on their prior knowledge of magnetism to produce their first Predict-Observe-Explain (p-o-e) chart, which is a key strategy in this unit. It provides an open-ended structure of representation so that learners can grasp and demonstrate their understanding in a variety of ways. For example, some students might not be able to show their learning on a pen-and-paper test, but they can explain their learning orally, or by illustrating their understanding of concepts. Some may prefer writing down what they've observed and then use inductive reasoning to come to a conclusion. Starleigh and Mindy have found that allowing students to demonstrate their learning in multiple ways assists them in achieving the content outcomes for the course. Moreover, they found that when they used Predict-Observe-Explain to introduce these concepts, students became more enthusiastic about—and engaged in—their learning. Students were speculating about possible applications and creating analogies to other situations in their lives where this rule could apply.

Constructing the rules of electricity

- Positively charged objects are attracted to negatively charged objects.
- Negatively charged objects repulse negatively charged objects; positively charged objects repulse positively charged objects.
- Neutral objects neither attract nor repulse each other.

Materials:

- 2 bar magnets with the poles clearly labelled
- handful of paper clips
- blank handouts of Predict-Observe-Explain (Figure 5.4) for distribution

- Review previous vocabulary (positive, negative, neutral).
- Explain that the rules that govern electricity are similar to the rules that govern magnetism, and that some vocabulary learned previously for magnetism (positive, negative, neutral) also applies to electricity.
- Ask students to *predict* what will happen when you put one paper clip next to the other paper clip. Then, ask them to *observe* and illustrate.
- Ask students to observe and illustrate what they observe when they put a paper clip next to the negative pole.
- Circulate throughout the room, asking students to notice if there are any patterns developing. Once students have tried out all of the paper clip/magnet combinations, ask them to put two positive poles together, two negative poles together, and finally a negative/positive combination.

Figure 5.4 Template for Predict-Observe-Explain

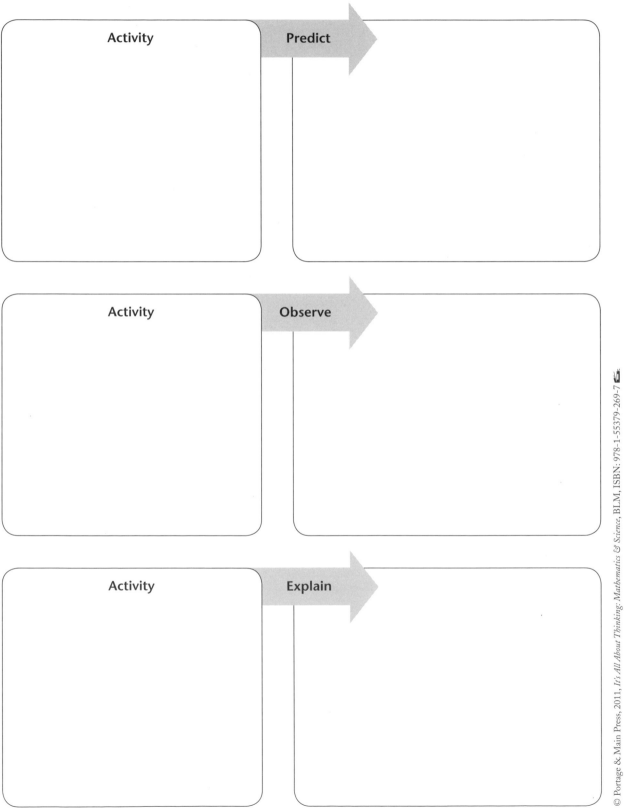

- Invite students to try different versions of how to record their thoughts on the handout for the p-o-e activity (notes in point form, full sentences, labelled illustrations). Figure 5.5 is an example of one student's completed p-o-e graphic form.

- Because this activity introduces a new strategy, the students will require more feedback about how to fill in the p-o-e form. Build time into the lesson to circulate among the students and give feedback on their choices for representing their ideas. Encourage students to take ownership of their learning and use the form of representation that makes their communication most effective.

- Have students sit with a partner at the end of the activity and compare their p-o-e forms, commenting on one thing that makes the other partner's responses effective. Encourage students to ask a question about something in their partner's thinking that they would like to know more about.

Figure 5.5 Student's response on the P-O-E template

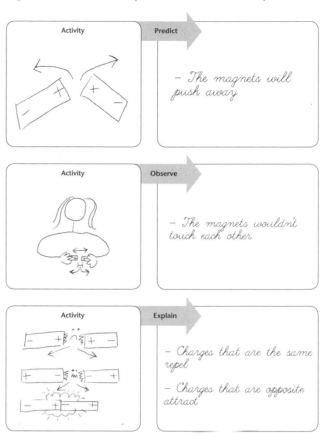

Assessment for Learning

Exit Slip

- At the end of the class, have students explain the rules for the phrase "opposites attract" on a small piece of paper.
- When doing so, students should use the words: *attract, repulse, negatively charged, positively charged, neutral.*
- Collect their Exit slips. Use them as feedback for yourself on the students' understanding of the content. Ask yourself: Do the students understand the key concept? What is missing? What do I need to do next, at the beginning of the next lesson, to ensure understanding?
- An Exit slip is a quick way for students to synthesize their understanding and for teachers to see if the lesson has worked.

Lesson 3 — Rationale

In order for students to demonstrate their understanding later in the unit, they have to be able to illustrate positive and negative charge. Graphic representation of objects that possess electric charge will be used throughout the electricity unit. It is essential for students to understand how to differentiate between illustrations of neutral objects and illustrations of positively and negatively charged objects. As the unit progresses, these illustrations will be used to show the transfer of charge. Students' familiarity with the illustrations will allow them to communicate their knowledge of charged objects and a transfer of charge. This activity introduces the concept that everyday objects can possess electric charge, and it gives students a simple tool to represent a charge within those objects.

Illustrating Charge Using plus (+) and minus (-)

- Show students how to illustrate positively charged and negatively charged objects. Be creative with your illustrations! The top of Figure 5.6 is an example of how to model drawing objects that are positively charged (+), negatively charged (-), and neutral (same number of + and − signs).
- Ask students to illustrate the rules for "opposites attract" by including the standard form for illustrating positively and negatively charged materials. These rules include:
    - When illustrating a positively charged object, there should be fewer minus signs (representing electrons) than plus signs (representing protons).
    - When illustrating a negatively charged object, there should be more minus signs than plus signs.
    - When illustrating a neutral object, the number of minus and plus signs should be equal.
- Circulate while students are creating their illustrations to give descriptive feedback about their negatively and positively charged diagrams (Figure 5.7).
- Have students compare their drawings. Ask:
    - *Do they communicate the same message?*
- Arrange student drawings in a "gallery" and have them view each other's work. This opportunity for students to re-assess their own work along with the work of their peers increases their engagement. Talking also helps to solidify meaning, as students learn through networking and sharing.

Figure 5.6 Model for drawing charged objects

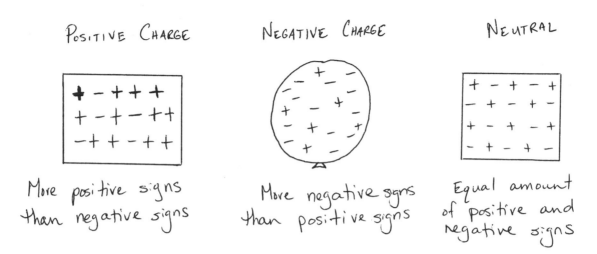

Figure 5.7 Student drawing of charged objects

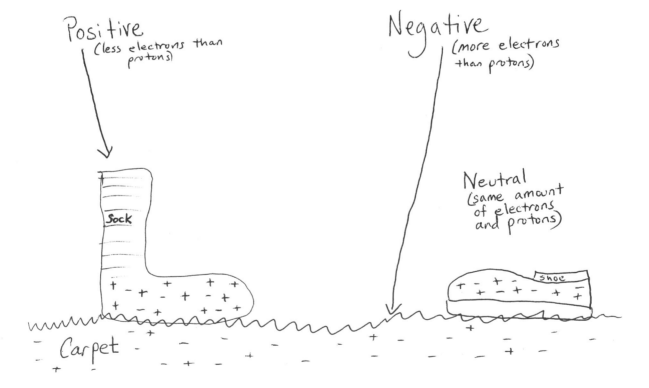

Figure 5.8 Suggested instruction for activity using P-O-E template

Activity	Predict
Make 3 predictions about what might happen if I rub a balloon on my hair.	

Figure 5.8A gives an example of student responses. Figure 5.8B provides explanations to help the students understand that electrons move from object to object, and friction causes electrons to move. When electrons are transferred between objects, one object becomes positively charged, and another becomes negatively charged.

Figure 5.8A Sample student predictions and observation

Activity	Predict
Make 3 predictions about what might happen if I rub a balloon on my hair.	Sample responses: · Hair will stick to balloon · Balloon will pop. · Balloon will be repelled by hair.

Figure 5.8B Sample teacher explanation

Activity	Predict
Make 3 predictions about what might happen if I rub a balloon on my hair.	

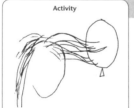

Activity	Observe
	· The balloon was rubbed onto hair. · The hair lifted and stuck to the balloon.

Activity	Observe
	· The balloon was rubbed onto hair. · The hair lifted and stuck to the balloon.

Activity	Explain

Activity	Explain
· The friction between the hair and the balloon causes the transfer of electrons. · The balloon wll pick up electrons from hair and become negatively charged.	· The hair wll lose electrons to the balloon and become positively charged. · The hair and ballon are now oppositely charged and become attracted to one another

Lesson 4—Rationale

By this point in the unit, students should know that oppositely charged objects are attracted to one another. In this P-O-E activity, students apply and construct their knowledge of charged objects and the laws of force to what they see when a person's hair is rubbed with an inflated balloon. This friction results in the transfer of electrons from one object to another. Students use their understanding of atoms and electrons to connect the idea that gaining and losing electrons results in objects becoming negatively and positively charged. This will once again allow for information taught previously in the chemistry portion of the course to be connected to the current concepts of the electricity unit.

Key Concepts for Creating Electric Charge

- Electrons move.
- Friction causes a movement of electrons.
- When electrons move, atoms become negatively or positively charged.
- If an object loses electrons, it becomes positively charged.
- If an object gains electrons, it becomes negatively charged.

A Hair-Raising Exploration of Electric Charge

- Have students record in the Predict section of a P-O-E template (Figure 5.8) what they think will happen when a balloon is rubbed on hair.
- Rub a balloon on your hair, and have students illustrate or write their observations.
- Together, with student assistance, fill out the Explain box in the template on an overhead. This is the second Predict-Observe-Explain that students have done, so it is critical to begin by modelling your thinking while filling out a section of the table. Use student input to fill in the remainder of the table together.
- Ask for a student volunteer. Have the volunteer rub a different balloon on his or her hair. Ask the students to predict whether the two balloons will attract, repulse, or remain neutral, based on their understanding of positive and negative forces from the previous lesson. Have students fill in the Predict box.
- Place the balloons near each other, and see what happens. Have students fill in the Observe box.
- Ask students to fill out their Explain box, using the standard form for illustrating positively charged and negatively charged objects. Figure 5.9 provides an example of student work.
- Provide immediate descriptive feedback to students as they fill out their tables.

Figure 5.9 Student response on P-O-E template

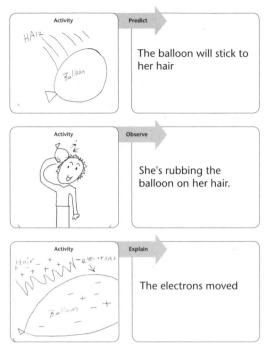

Assessment for Learning

Exit Slip

- Present two scenarios:
    1. Your white cat rubs against your black shirt.
    2. A dryer sheet sticks to your clothing in the dryer.

- Ask students, with a partner, to choose one scenario and either write to explain what happened, using the words friction, static charge, positively charged, negatively charged, electric force, and electrons, or illustrate their explanation of what is happening.

- While the students are working, circulate in the room to collect information on how well they understand the concepts. As students move toward independence, they may still need you to offer prompts and clues to help guide their thinking. Initially, some students may struggle to transfer the concepts from one situation to another. Working with a partner can help them process the new information they have taken in, and work through the concept when applying it to a new situation.

- Mindy and Starleigh use cooperative learning a lot in their classrooms. As a PhysEd teacher, Mindy knows that students would rather play soccer with a group of friends than kick the ball around alone. Academically, this means that students will share what they know with each other, and they are quite willing to both help and accept help from others when presented with the opportunity. As an English teacher, Starleigh knows that working together helps us form new ideas that we may not have thought of otherwise—recognizing that other people stimulate our creative thinking.

- Try to ensure that the tone of your classroom matches the tone of the scientific community. Scientists do not work in isolation — they talk things over, share results, and compare notes. They ask each other questions and challenge each other's conclusions. Rich learning happens on a peer-to-peer level as students speculate about the possible applications of what they are learning. If we are to raise an exciting new generation of scientists to take on the many scientific challenges that society has waiting for them, then we must nurture them as scientists in a social sense early and often.

Lesson 5 — Rationale

The three big ideas of induction/conduction, the electrostatic series, and electric force are interrelated. This lesson involves speculating on how to prove these concepts, which helps students access their prior knowledge and pose real questions. The purpose of this connecting activity is to get students ready to begin their journey toward an expanded understanding of the limits on the transfer of electrons, the varying ways in which electrons move, and the measure of how electrons move. Students are given the opportunity to connect prior knowledge and real-life situations to classroom concepts and to share their ideas with the rest of the class.

Key Concepts

- Transfer of electric charge can happen in two ways (see Figure 5.10).
  - Conduction — contact between neutral and charged objects results in the transfer of electrons; neutral objects gain charge.
  - Induction — close proximity between neutral and charged objects creates the movement of electrons within objects, which results in temporary charge in neutral objects.
- Materials that store and transfer electric charges can be sorted along a series. The further apart they are on the electrostatic series, the greater their charge, and the greater their force.

Method

- To form groups of 3 or 4 students, cut several pages of coloured paper into four pieces — enough to provide a one-quarter page of coloured paper for each student in your class. Place the papers in a container.
- As students come in the classroom door, have each draw one piece of paper out of the container. Ask students to hold their paper aloft, then form a group with other students who have the same colour.
- Introduce handouts of Figures 5.10 and 5.11. Display Figure 5.10 on an overhead.
- Then ask these randomly formed groups to review a statement on the board: "Some materials store electricity (insulators) and some materials let electricity pass right through them (conductors)."

Figure 5.10 Demonstration of induction and conduction

Inductive Charging

When you move a charged object near a neutral object, the action causes a movement of electrons within the neutral object.

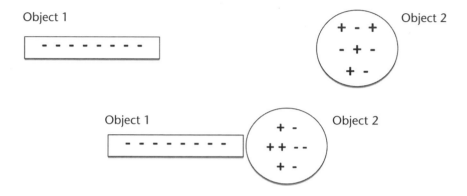

When you move a negatively charged object close to the neutral object, the electrons within the neutral object move away from the negatively charged object. The action causes the end closest to the negatively charged object to become positively charged.

Conductive Charging

When you move a charged object into contact with a neutral object, electrons transfer from one object to another, creating a charge within the neutral object.

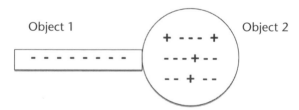

© Portage & Main Press, 2011, *It's All About Thinking: Mathematics & Science*, BLM, ISBN: 978-1-55379-269-7

Figure 5.11 Electrostatic series

Electrostatic Series

More likely to lose electrons
or become positively charged

Glass
Human Hair
Cat Fur
Cotton
Human Hair
Plastic
Rubber

More likely to gain electrons or
become negatively charged

- Ask students in their groups to prove that this statement is true by finding examples in real life to back up the statement. If students are struggling as you circulate around the room, ask questions to prompt their thinking. For example, ask:
  - *Why don't we get electrocuted when we touch power cords?*
  - *Why can't you use electronics in the bathtub?*
  - *Why is it that, if you lick a battery, you'll get shocked, but if you touch it with your finger nothing happens?"*
- Share group responses with the whole class.

Holding an Electric Charge—Rationale

This activity introduces students to the idea that the ability of objects to hold electric charge varies along a continuum. In this activity students roll a pop can from a starting line to a finish line using static charge, inductive charge, and the resulting electric force. It helps students understand that the capacity of materials to build up electric charge varies. Students are to predict which materials will move the can, then test their prediction and, after noting that result, go back and use the information from their trial to test another material. This hands-on inquiry-based activity will provide experiential learning that will serve to deepen their understanding of how friction can build electric charge and how the charge can be transferred. Students will be able to witness first-hand how some materials are able to build up and hold more electric charge than others and how this charge can be transferred to other objects. By allowing students to explore through trial and error, they are given the opportunity to construct their own knowledge of the key concepts, which deepens their engagement and can lead to enduring understanding.

Key Concepts

- Friction builds up static charge.
- Induction can be used to create a temporary charge by bringing a charged object close to a neutral object.
- Induction causes the movement of electrons within an object, but not the transfer of electrons.
- Materials vary in their ability to hold and transfer electric charge.

Materials

pop can, wool, balloon, glass rod, straw, paper towel, plastic strip, handout copies of Figures 5.12 and 5.13.

Method

- Ask students to predict which materials will move the can.
- Students charge different materials by rubbing them together and practise moving the pop can.
- Students use trial and error to decide the two best materials to build a static charge.

Figure 5.12 Electric force + distance

Electric Force

There are 3 laws of Electric Force:

Law #1: Like charges repel.

Law #2: Opposite charges attract.

Law #3: Neutral objects are attracted to charged objects.

The amount of electric force between two objects depends on—**the distance between two objects**

Scenario #1

Scenario #2

Scenario #1 has a greater electric force than **scenario #2** because there is less distance between the two objects.

© Portage & Main Press, 2011, *It's All About Thinking: Mathematics & Science*, BLM, ISBN: 978-1-55379-269-7

Figure 5.13 Electric force + size of charge

Electric Force

There are 3 laws of Electric Force:

Law #1: Like charges repel.

Law #2: Opposite charges attract.

Law #3: Neutral objects are attracted to charged objects.

The amount of electric force between two objects depends on—**the size of the charge the objects have.**

Scenario #1

  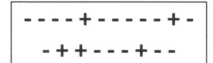

Scenario #2

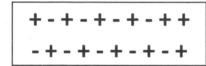  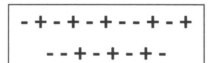

Scenario #1 has a greater electric force than **scenario #2** because the objects in **scenario #1** have a greater charge than **scenario #2**.

© Portage & Main Press, 2011, *It's All About Thinking: Mathematics & Science*, BLM, ISBN: 978-1-55379-269-7

- When students have chosen their two best materials, they line their pop can up at the start line.
- Give students 30 seconds to 1 minute to charge their insulating materials.
- On the word Go, have students bring the charged material close to the pop can and try to roll it over the finish line.

The Post-Game Analysis

- Using the Electrostatic Series information sheet (Figure 5.11) and the Electric Force handouts (Figures 5.12 and 5.13), explain to students the laws of electric force.
- Ask students, in pairs, to briefly discuss how the size of charge affects the amount of electric force and how this affects their ability to move their pop can.
- Circulate through the room and have mini-discussions with students to check their understanding, clarify the laws of electric force, and reinforce understanding of the relationship between size of charge and amount of electric force.
- After the partner talk-time, have students share out their explanations of how the size of the charge and the resulting electric force impacted the speed with which their pop can moved. In an activity such as this, talk time is especially useful because students are exposed to the thinking processes of others, and it helps them process their own experiences and understandings.

Assessment for Learning—Exit Slip

- As an Exit slip, have students either create a diagram of the objects that represent both the charge and the resulting electric force (between insulating materials) and conductive charging (between insulating material and pop can), or explain in words why some materials worked better than others (e.g., their position on the electrostatic series).

Lesson 6—Rationale

Classroom discussion of the types of force naturally leads into how force varies. In this lesson, students will be reaching a higher level of autonomy in terms of their ability to show their thinking during a Predict-Observe-Explain activity. They will also apply their knowledge of the electrostatic series to a hands-on activity. Activities such as these help demonstrate to students that science—and scientific thinking—can be a rich experience full of exploration and discovery. A scientific community explores new ideas and activities and works together on collective inquiry questions.

Key Concepts

- Insulators build up or hold static charge.
- Conductors do not allow for the build up of static charge because electrons pass through them.
- Induction creates a temporary charge in neutral objects.
- Neutral objects are attracted to charged objects.

Materials

rice crispies, fur, wool, plastic straw, balloon, vinyl swatch, overhead transparency, hair

- Distribute students' materials.
- Have students predict which combination of two materials will pick up the most rice crispies.
- Have students use the table in the pre-made P-O-E to keep a running record of which combinations pick up the most crispies.
- When students have tried at least two pairs, have them return to Figure 5.10, Electrostatic Series. Ask them to infer some logic in the relationship between where items lie on the series and their force, or ability, to pick up the rice crispies.
- Circulate, checking students' understanding. Ask leading questions such as:
  - *What do you think the charges of the two objects you used are?*
  - *What are the positions of your objects on the electrostatic series?*
  - *Is there a relationship between the location of objects on the series and their force, or ability, to pick up rice crispies?*
  - *Why would one material pick up more rice crispies than another?*
- As students finish their trials, ask them to come together and share their hypotheses.
- Review the theory, referring to Figure 5.12 and Figure 5.13, and ask students, in partners, to illustrate or explain in words which set of materials picked up the most rice crispies and why.

Lesson 7—Rationale

Wrapping Our Minds around Insulators

In order to answer this unit's essential question—How do materials hold and transfer electric charge?—students must be able to differentiate between insulators and conductors. Conductors allow charge to pass through them and insulators allow for the build up of static charge. In this activity, students can apply their observations from the activity Energetic Pick-Me-Up to insulating and conducting materials. After direct instruction on the characteristics of insulators and conductors, students can use their previous knowledge and observation to label the objects used in the activity as insulators or conductors. Students will begin to see that all the metal objects in the previous activity did not pick up rice crispies and therefore were not able to build up static charge. This will lead to the understanding that conductors allow electrons to pass through them; they will not be able to pick up rice crispies because they remain neutral. Insulators are able to build up a static charge, which means they can pick up the very light-weight and neutral rice crispies. This is an example of charging by *induction* when the insulator is brought close to the rice crispies and charging by *conduction* when the rice crispies actually touch the charged insulator. Connecting back to previous lessons on charging by conduction and induction helps strengthen their overall understanding of these difficult concepts. Students can then begin to label metals as *conductors* and non-metals as *insulators*, which again links back to the chemistry unit and the properties of elements.

Key Concepts

- Insulators build up static charge.
- Conductors allow charge to pass through them.

Wrapping Our Minds around Insulators

- Remind students of the previous lesson by demonstrating the rice crispies activity that they have already performed.
- During the demonstration, explain to students that some materials are insulators, which build up static charge and hold it in place, and some materials are conductors, which allow charge to pass through them but do not build up static charge.
- Explain that anything that can build up static charge is an insulator. Picking up rice crispies is a sign that something has built up a static charge. If something cannot pick up rice crispies, it probably doesn't have the ability to build up static charge because it is a conductor and the charge flows right through it, rather than storing it.
- Ask students to sort the following materials into insulators or conductors, based on whether or not they can pick up rice crispies.

Materials

glass rod, balloon, strip of plastic, wool, vinyl, cotton, fur, paper clip, copper wire, tin can, knife, keys

Explaining Our Thinking

- With the students in pairs, assign one partner to be the speaker and the other partner to be the illustrator.
- The speaker's job is to tell the illustrator what to draw. The illustrators in each pair may ask the speakers leading questions to help them expand upon their thinking; however, they must draw only what the speaker says. This activity helps develop precise language and assists the students in gaining control over their developing scientific vocabulary.

- Each partner must illustrate and label one material that is a conductor and one material that is an insulator.
- Using their knowledge of charge, have students illustrate their conductor/insulator examples.
- As a class, come together to share illustrations and articulate how each illustration explains how conductors *do not* build up charge while insulators *do* build up static charge.
- Ask students to identify any similarities between the materials that they labelled as conductors.

Assessment for Learning—Exit Slip

In ten words or in an illustration, explain the answer to the question: *How can we store and move electric charge using common materials?*

Assessment of Learning

This is an opportunity for students to bring together their increased ability to answer the essential question for the unit: How do materials hold and transfer electric charge?

For their summative assessment, students will create a demonstration, present a scenario, or create a model to demonstrate their learning of the key concepts and vocabulary. Students will be expected to use the vocabulary in their demonstration or elicit the vocabulary from participants and affirm or correct it during discussion, and to explain how their demonstration/scenario/model relates to the main ideas. Figure 5.14, the rubric for this activity, will help students understand how the activities they have been engaging in over the last seven lessons were preparing them to complete this task. The key concepts and thinking skills that have been targeted in the teaching and assessment for learning activities match up with what students do and show in this task.

A Media Scrum—Rationale

In order to support students while they plan their activity, have students explain their plans to a partner. Provide them with a structured format with which to plan their performance piece. We recommend using a media scrum format. First, students will interview each other in character as journalist/scientist. Then, students will rehearse and perform their interviews "on-air" in front of the class. In addition to giving students an opportunity to plan their presentation in a structured format, this gives students the benefit of seeing what others will be doing. Seeing how their peers plan projects helps students monitor their own planning and gain inspiration for their own projects. Like scientists, students feed off the creativity of one another.

- Assign one partner to be a journalist and another partner to be a world-renowned scientist who has just discovered some key principles of electricity. The scientist will perform a demonstration to the audience in an upcoming conference of key thinkers in the scientific community. The journalist's role is to interview the scientist using key questions such as:
    - Why should the public care about electricity?
    - How will you demonstrate these principles of electricity?
    - What do you hope people will learn from your presentation?
    - What materials will you be using?
- Emphasize that the journalist's role is to "get the story" while the scientist's role is to build excitement so that people will come to the conference. Some students will take on kooky personas such as the scientist who wants to take over the world or the scientist who has spent the last ten years in a laboratory perfecting his demonstration.
    - Give students time to rehearse each role.
    - Have students perform their interviews for the class.

Today a Flow Chart, Tomorrow the World!—Rationale
Successful presentations rest heavily on classroom time for students to plan, try out and adapt their work as they receive feedback throughout the planning process. Although we believe in structured planning, we also believe that self-regulated learning happens when students have autonomy in their planning process. Setting daily goals helps students learn to be accountable for the planning time provided. Checking in with a partner at the beginning and the end of the lesson provides them with a peer support network, people who can encourage them and cheer them on toward success. Providing class time to assess their progress also gives the teacher an opportunity to remind students of project goals by keeping their focus on the rubric.

- For each day that you allow students to plan, begin the class with a review of the rubric, Figure 5.14.
- Ask students to jot down three goals that they hope to accomplish during the course of the class and have them share their goals with a partner. Remind students that successful projects are the product of careful planning and strategic goal setting.
- Circulate during the planning time, and provide students with specific, descriptive feedback on areas of strength. If there are areas that seem to be vague or missing, gently ask students how they are planning to meet that specific aspect of the rubric.
- At the end of the class, have students check in with their partner so that their partners know which goals were met, which goals they plan to work on between classes, and which goals they are thinking of setting for the next class.

Figure 5.14 Assessment Rubric of student understanding of electric force

PLOs	Minimally Meeting Expectations	Fully Meeting Expectations	Exceeding Expectations
Explain or illustrate how static charge is created. Vocabulary: · static charge · protons · atoms · electrons · neutral	Student can comprehend discrete vocabulary, but has difficulty making connections between vocabulary words and the main idea.	Student can demonstrate that they know the vocabulary, can make connections between vocabulary words and the main idea.	Student can demonstrate that they know the vocabulary, can make connections between vocabulary words and the main idea, and can apply both vocabulary and the main idea to real world scenarios.
Explain or illustrate how static charge is transferred. Vocabulary: · insulators · conductors · coulomb · grounding · electric force · conduction · induction	Student can comprehend discrete vocabulary, but has difficulty making connections between vocabulary words and the main idea.	Student can demonstrate that they know the vocabulary, can make connections between vocabulary words and the main idea.	Student can demonstrate that they know the vocabulary, can make connections between vocabulary words and the main idea, and can apply both vocabulary and the main idea to real world scenarios.
Use the laws of electricity to predict the behaviour of electric force.	Student can comprehend discrete vocabulary, but has difficulty making connections between vocabulary words and the main idea.	Student can demonstrate that they know the vocabulary, can make connections between vocabulary words and the main idea.	Student can demonstrate that they know the vocabulary, can make connections between vocabulary words and the main idea, and can apply both vocabulary and the main idea to real world scenarios.

© Portage & Main Press, 2011, *It's All About Thinking: Mathematics & Science*, BLM, ISBN: 978-1-55379-269-7

Figure 5.15 Descriptive feedback on assessment from peer

PLOs	Minimally Meeting Expectations	Fully Meeting Expectations	Exceeding Expectations
Explain or illustrate how static charge is created.			
Explain or illustrate how static charge is transferred.			
Use the laws of electricity to predict the behaviour of electric force.			
I liked the way that you...			
Maybe next time you could...			

For My Next Act, I'm Going to Transfer Electrons!

Celebration! Students now demonstrate their learning to the class. They have learned key concepts, focused on an essential question, and had meaningful conversations and feedback.

- Provide each student with a peer-assessment handout (Figure 5.15).
- Ask for volunteers who would like to go first; post their names and project titles on the board.
- Determine the order for the rest of the students by using arbitrary criteria (e.g., by birthday, alphabetically by first name, by height), then post their names and project titles on the board. Letting students know what to expect and when to expect it provides them with a sense of security around the process.
- Ask for a volunteer for the role of emcee, who will announce each presenter's name and project titles with gusto and will thank each presenter for their presentation.
- Allow students time to complete their peer-assessments between presentations, and hand them to each student-presenter as soon as they have finished. Students relish timely, personal feedback from their peers.
- After the presentations are over, have students write a quick reflection on the prompt: "What did I do well? What would I do differently if I were to do this again?"
- Ensure that presenters hand in their peer feedback forms on their way out the door.

Reflections by Starleigh and Mindy

We discovered that working together helped us draw out the strengths from both of our practices and combine them to create something better. We both could ask questions about each other's practice and wonder aloud about what we might try in the future. We were learning in various settings about structures and strategies that we could then try out in our classrooms independently. Our ongoing planning sessions provided opportunities to explore and reflect on the effectiveness of our strategies. Although we teach the same students at the same school, each of us brought different styles and skills to the table, which resulted in something far more dynamic than either of us could have come up with alone.

We work with many students for whom the traditional form of schooling is not successful. We believe—and support each other in this belief—that all of our students can be successful when we make the effort to figure out how to best support them in their learning. In science and in life, people process information and interpret events in diverse ways. By allowing our students to experience this diversity, they see that others who might think or work differently have interesting and worthwhile contributions to make to collaborative explorations, activities, and discussions. In reality, we are preparing them for life and possibly for a future in science. We believe that science classrooms can provide a great service when they allow students to experience science rather than just listen to someone tell them about it. Our collaboration was a science of exploration and discovery for us as well. We were thrilled with our students' results and are encouraged to continue.

Chapter 6

A Cross-Curricular Collaboration

Grade 8—English and Science

Assessment FOR Learning

- Quick-writes
- Peer-mediated conversations
- Midway check-in
- Peer-assessment and self-assessment
- Criteria-setting
- Student exemplars
- Co-created rubrics

Gradual Release of Responsibility

- Metacognition
- Goal-setting
- Targeted skill and strategy instruction
- Model it

Differentiation

- Open-ended strategies
- Use of manipulatives
- Extensions/adaptation provided

Assessment OF Learning

- Portfolio assessment
- Cross-curricular final project

The Collaboration

Nicole Vander Wal teaches Science at Westview Secondary in Maple Ridge, and Sue Schleppe works as a district facilitator. Previously, the two had collaborated on a literacy-rich Science 8 unit on water systems. When Nicole enrolled in her master's program in Learning Environments and Ecological Education, she asked Sue to create a complementary English 8 unit to further involve students in the environmental theme. At Westview Secondary, the grade 8 students are enrolled in a transition program. This is a middle-school concept within the confines of a secondary structure. Because the students are "podded," the teachers within one pod share the same students, which facilitates teacher collaboration.

Typical combinations have been teachers of English collaborating with teachers of social studies, and mathematics teachers with science teachers. In contrast, this unit represents an atypical collaboration in that the Science portion runs concurrently with the English unit. The students attend both classes within the timetable—the two classes are not integrated. Because both subjects share the same essential question, "How are we connected to our environment?," they reinforce similar teaching strategies and skills. One goal of the collaboration is to help students view the world as interconnected. Although Science and English might not always seem like the most obvious pairing, Nicole and Sue enjoy working together and have learned, over time, that there are more connections than they had originally thought.

The Context

Nicole and Sue have created a unit that explores the essential question and leads to a final project that both units can share. The idea of turning in one project to satisfy the same inquiry question for English and Science is exciting. The teachers introduced both the essential question and the unit's final project during the first classes, so their students spent their time in both subject units working toward the goals. They were able to understand how what they were doing applied to their project, and they had the opportunity to continue improving upon their work. Both units explore the concept of place-based education, expanding the curriculum to the outside world and inviting the world into the classroom.

For English, the unit looked at the students' connections to their environment; elements of all the curriculum organizers were covered— reading and viewing, writing and representing, and oral language. More specifically, activities and rubrics were provided to engage the students' metacognition and promote goal-setting in discussions, reading of poetry, and writing of poetry. Strategies for before, during, and after (connecting, processing, and transforming/personalizing) the reading and writing served to prepare students for the tasks but, more importantly, these strategies played an important role in enabling the students to better extend their thinking while connecting them to the content. Finally, students worked on the skills associated with viewing and representing, and on how they could enhance poetry and their connection to their environment. In Science 8, this unit enabled students to complete the following prescribed learning outcomes:

- Explain the significance of salinity and temperature in the world's oceans.
- Describe how water and ice shape the landscape.
- Describe the factors that affect productivity and species distribution within aquatic environments.

The goal of this unit was to link the students' home surroundings, their environment, to their learning, with the aim of instilling a deeper connection to the environment in which they live.

Essential Question

- How are we connected to our environment?

Key Structures

Backward Design

- Students start the units with the end in mind: their final project. The work they do throughout the unit contributes to the project, and the students are offered some degree of choice as to how they will represent their learning.
- The project represents the largest piece of the unit's assessment of learning.

Assessment for Learning

- Students keep their work in portfolios; as the units proceed, they select the work they feel will best represent their learning in the final project.
- Students develop and work with rubrics, which they use to self-assess and peer-assess with specific goals of improvement in mind.
- Nicole and Sue provide the students with specific feedback as they progress.

Place-Based Education

- By placing students' learning in their environment, the teachers' lessons become more meaningful.
- Throughout the unit, what the students are learning guides them as they become more connected to their local environment through activities for both Science and English that are situated in the "place" or in the classroom.

Lesson 1—Rationale

Both units are based on the backward design model. Sue and Nicole created one final project that could be used for both English and Science—and each introduced the students at the beginning of the unit to the combined Science-English summative assessment (final project). This early focus on the ongoing project meant that the students could focus better on their goals throughout the unit.

English

Content Connections

The unit begins by exploring the topic as a "hook" to refresh prior knowledge. Then, students are introduced to the final project. (Note: Keep student samples to show to next year's classes.) The students have journals in which to write any "gem" or "treasure" (i.e., evocative) words or phrases that they collect as part of their pre-writing activities.

- Introduce a PowerPoint presentation of scenic locations from around the world. Have students jot down their thoughts as they view it, particularly any powerful descriptions or reactions, in their journals—their personal archive of readily accessible inspiration for their writing.
- Ensure that the final slides in the presentation are local images. These tend to evoke a different emotional response than the others.
- Have students share their observations, borrowing any terms, words, or ideas that resonate with them, and adding them to their journals.
- Introduce the final project for the unit. The essential question in Figure 6.1, How are we connected to our environment?, is the final project for both English and Science.

Science

Activating Prior Knowledge

Backward design in Science allows the students to visualize how all the concepts they learn are connected. The connections help focus the students' learning. The graffiti strategy builds on students' prior knowledge, provides assessment for learning, and creates a social learning experience.

Graffiti

- Write titles such as Humans and Water, Your Town and Water, Weather and Water, Pollution and Water, Sea Life and Water on pieces of chart paper, and place them around the classroom.
- Group the students and assign each group a coloured marker. Each group uses this coloured marker to identify their contributions to the activity during the summary session.
- Ask that each group move to one of the charts, discuss the title, and write their questions, comments, examples, or diagrams on the chart paper.

Figure 6.1 Instructions for Final Project

Essential Question: How are we connected to our environment?

The environment is very important to us for many reasons. In Science class, we will investigate how water systems are connected and how the connections matter to our community. In English class, we will examine the places that have special meaning for us, and how they become a part of us. We will also research similar topics, sometimes through the eyes of a scientist, sometimes through the eyes of a poet—sometimes through both sets of eyes.

Your end-of-unit project serves as the final assessment for both English and Science. As you progress through this unit of study, add these variations on the essential question:

- In what different ways are we connected to our environment?

- How does what we know and learn as scientists matter to what we love as poets?

Shape your ideas and gather evidence to show both scientific and poetic responses to these questions. Think as well about the format you'd like to use to present your response: a scrapbook? a slideshow? or a personal variation? Discuss your ideas about your project's format with your teachers early in your planning.

For your Science mark, you must show your understanding of the following concepts:

the water table	water distribution in the world
weather and climate	aquatic biodiversity
erosion	influences on currents, glaciers, and tides
human impacts	comparing salt water and fresh water

Try to demonstrate your learning in your own words, using original examples in an original format that moves your work a bit beyond the text or our class work.

In English class throughout this unit, we will explore poetry as a powerful expression of ideas; we will also explore places on the planet that are, or seem, special to you. For your English mark at the end, try to express what they mean to you in an interesting, powerful way and through different representations that enhance your message.

Final Checklist for Your Project

	Science	English
Required Elements	Present the concepts in a way that clearly shows your understanding.	Choose six (6) original poems that explore a connection to places important to you.
Presentation Goals	Decide how you want to present your learning. Choose a format and make it your own original.	Represent your poems in a thoughtful way that enhances their meaning.
Bringing It Together	As you bring the elements of your project together, think about how your work in Science and in English are related. In what ways are the two perspectives important to each other? Be prepared to answer this question in a short conference with your teachers.	

- Allow the groups to work for 5 to 7 minutes, then ask them to move to the next chart, where they again discuss the topic and add comments, questions, examples, or diagrams.
- After the groups have worked on each topic, have someone collect the papers and bring them to the front. Have students as a class discuss their collective work by reading aloud what was written. You might ask more questions, acknowledging each group's contributions as identified by their coloured marker, and tying the topics into their future learning outcomes.
- Write the students' insightful and relevant questions on a separate chart paper titled Wonder Wall. Then use this chart paper as the place to add questions as the unit progresses. It can also be used for inspiration during the students' final project.

Lesson 2—Rationale

This lesson emphasizes gradual release of responsibility. Its main objective is to take students through the process of reading, responding to, and writing poetry. It relies on modelling, rubrics, and self-assessment. It is a slow process initially, but worth the effort. Because it is quite an involved process, students are given the tools to practise the skills with a fair degree of confidence. The lesson is much more about the skills than it is about the poem itself.

English

Reading, Responding to, and Writing Poetry

- Model a think-aloud using a few lines of a poem like "Nature" by H. D. Carberry, a Jamaica-born lawyer and poet (*Crossroads 10*, p. 322, Figure 6.2A).
- As you continue, invite the students to share some of their thoughts.
- Have students highlight what they think are the three most important words or phrases.
- Then ask them to identify one image that strikes them the most—they may wish to sketch it.
- Have students write down two connections they have to the poem.
- Allow students a few minutes to write down 2 or 3 questions they may have either about the poem or stemming from the poem.
- Ask the students to jot down anything they may know about the speaker.
- Have students add words or phrases that they consider gems to their journal.

Figure 6.2A "Nature" by H. D. Carberry

Nature

We have neither Summer nor Winter
Neither Autumn nor Spring.

We have instead the days
When gold sun shines on the lush green canefields —
Magnificently.

The days when the rain beats like bullets on the roofs
And there is no sound but the swish of water in the
  gullies
And trees struggling in the high Jamaica winds.

Also there are the days when the leaves fade from off
  guango* trees
And the reaped canefields lie bare and fallow in the
  sun.

But best of all there are the days when the mango
  and the logwood blossom.

When the bushes are full of the sound of bees and
  the scent of honey,
When the tall grass sways and shivers to the slightest
  breath of air.

When buttercups have paved the earth with
  yellow stars
And beauty comes suddenly and the rains have gone.

H.D. Carberry

Guango: "This is the usual name in Jamaica; more commonly known in other parts of the Caribbean as saman [Native name]. A tropical American tree of the bean family *Pithecolobium saman*, the pods of which are used as cattle fodder." Source: *New English Dictionary*.

Source of Poem: *Caribbean Voices, An Anthology of West Indian Poetry, Selected by John Figueroa, Volume 1, Dreams and Visions*, Evans Brothers Limited, London, 1966, page 25.

- Students who are struggling may find the suggestions and questions on Figure 6.2B helpful in thinking through and describing their response to and feelings about the poem. Allow students time to share their observations with a partner.
- Bring the conversations back to the class level, while introducing the self-assessment tool in Figure 6.3. After students have used this rubric, you might discuss their self assessment using probing questions such as "What do you think you should keep on doing?" "What do you think you should try next time?"

Figure 6.2B Suggestions for reading and thinking about a poem

Reading and Thinking about a Poem

1. Write the title of the poem and your first thought about its title.

2. Read the poem slowly, then write the first ideas you found in it.

3. List some words or phrases from the poem that brought vivid images to mind.

4. Write one or two personal connections that the poem made you think about.

5. List the poet's words or phrases that seem powerful or unusual to you.

6. Do some of the poet's words or phrases seem ambiguous or confusing to you? Try to frame questions about them that you would pose to the poet if you could.

7. What do you know about the poet, just from reading this poem?

8. How and where might you learn something factual about the poet?

9. What new ideas does the poem give you?

10. If you found any "gems" or "treasure words" for your journal, write them here.

© Portage & Main Press, 2011, *It's All About Thinking: Mathematics & Science*, BLM, ISBN: 978-1-55379-269-7

Figure 6.3 Self-assessment tool for responding to a poem

How do I respond to a poem?

4 I'm a star!	3 I've got it!	2 I'm almost there.	1 I'll keep working on it.
· I can understand this on my own, and I can explain how some of the figurative language works. · This poem makes me see things in a new way, and I can relate that viewpoint to other things I already know about. · I can support these new ideas with many examples from the poem.	· A few parts are tricky to understand, but I can see how some of the figurative language works well. · I can relate this poem to things I already know about. · This poem has given me some new ideas. · I can use examples from the poem to back up what I think.	· I need some help with this poem. · I can find some figurative language. I can connect it to a little that I already know about. · I can find a little bit in the poem to back up what I'm saying. · I would have more to say about this if someone asked me some questions.	· This poem frustrates me. · I didn't connect it to much that I already knew about. · I do not understand the figurative language. · My response is pretty basic, and I can't find much in the poem to back up what I'm saying.

- Next, model a discussion of a poem with a few student volunteers. Using the criteria from Figure 6.4, have students reflect on the discussion with specific reference to the criteria. If it seems appropriate, work with the class to create more appropriate criteria. When your students consult this self-assessment rubric, follow up with them to explore their rationale for evaluating their own work.

Figure 6.4 Self-assessment for participating in a discussion

What makes a good discussion?

4 I'm a star!	3 I've got it!	2 I'm almost there.	1 I'll keep working on it.
· I had prepared thoughtfully. · I encouraged others, and I was able to come up with new ideas based on what others had said. · I asked interesting questions, and when I answered questions, I outlined new ideas that occurred to me.	· I was well prepared to take part. · I was clear, and I kept the conversation going by encouraging others and adding ideas. · I asked relevant questions, and I gave thoughtful answers to the questions posed to me.	· I was prepared to take part. · I shared what I had prepared with the group, and I may have asked some questions. · I answered any questions briefly.	· I was somewhat prepared. · I told some of my ideas to the group. Mostly, I just read a few things I had prepared. · I asked some questions, but they weren't actually important to me. · I didn't really answer any questions.

Science

Connecting and Sharing Background Knowledge

This activity asks students to reflect on their prior learning experiences with water and to share them with the class. To establish how the content has relevance to the students' daily lives, probe for their previous conceptions of water, listen to their interests, and ask them to share their knowledge. The students learn more about each other, which helps to build a stronger, more cohesive group. This hybrid activity was collaboratively designed by Nicole and her classmate, Tina Kaminiarz, based upon one designed by David Zandvliet and on a Family Tree assignment found in *From Ordinary to Extraordinary* (Vieth 1999).

Artifact String

- Discuss the artifact string assignment with students, using the outline (Figure 6.5) and the rubric (Figure 6.6).
- Model the activity by showing an artifact string of your own. Explain the significance of each object—be very specific when explaining how your objects and stories tie into the topic of water.
- Have students bring in from home any objects that represent their own water-related learning experiences, and have them create their artifact strings in class.
- Ask students to organize in groups of 3 or 4 to share their artifact string stories, then peer-assess the artifact strings using the rubric.
- Afterwards, hang the strings around the room where they may serve as a source of inspiration for the students' as they develop their final project (Figure 6.7).

Figure 6.5 Outline of Artifact String assignment

Artifact String Assignment

Select at least 4 and up to 6 artifacts (objects or pictures) that represent your learning experiences connected with water. Select a type of string—which could be a shoelace, or a piece of fishing line, or yarn, or something similar—that is strong enough to hold the artifacts you selected. As you attach them one by one to the string, think about the meaning each has for you. When you have finished your artifact string, volunteer to share your stories about them with your classmates and teachers.

Figure 6.6 Rubric for the Artifact String project

Assessment rubric for Artifact String activity

	3 I've aced it!	2 I've got it!	1 I'm still working on it
Water Story	My stories about my artifacts clearly demonstrate a time when I learned something relevant about water.	My stories about my artifacts demonstrate a time when I learned something about water.	Although my stories and artifacts clearly are about water, they are not linked to a learning experience.

Figure 6.7 Student's account for Artifact String

Artifact String

Water is all around us and is an important thing of enjoyment to life.

When I went to Mexico we would spend everyday that we were there sitting on the hot sunny beach and going into the nice refreshing ocean. I learned that there are many different species of salt water fish in the ocean. I'm going to represent this by using sea shells that we brought home from Mexico.

The rivers and lakes are an important fact of a food source because they hold fish. I love to go out fishing and bring home a nice fish to grill and eat. I learned from fishing that lakes are fun to swim in but are also very important for fishes habitat and pumping water to homes and cabins. I'm representing this by fishing tackle.

Lesson 3—Rationale

This lesson takes students slowly through the process of writing a poem. It begins by asking them to think about the poem "Nature" from last class, and allowing them to play with poetic terms, and to create only short snippets of examples that tie in with the environmental theme. It also serves as a pre-writing activity for the students and gives them something to build on when they apply this skill to the creation of a poem. This process provides support for those who may be unsure, but allows freedom for those who are more confident.

English

Poetic Terms and Writing Poetry
Give students the opportunity to play with writing, to experiment using poetic devices when describing their environment. Sue's overview of figurative language, her self-assessment rubric, and the assignment for descriptions of environmental topics are included in Figure 6.8. The list of several such words, with definitions, provides an opportunity to review with students—or to introduce—the categories of "figurative language" or "poetic or rhetorical devices."

Figure 6.8 Figurative Language, page 1

Playing With Language: Using Figurative Language

The phrase "figurative language" describes the interesting turns of phrase and engaging words often used by poets as well as many other writers. When used in writing or delivering speeches, these are also called "rhetorical devices." The examples below represent different ways of using words with great effect because of their impact on readers and listeners.

After you read and discuss them, try creating some of your own. When the words that you choose to say or write can actually clarify what you mean, you have created a good example of the effective use of language.

1. **Alliteration**: Repetition of the same consonant sound in a phrase or line.

   The slow, sad murmur of far distant seas.

   Notice that "s" is a quiet sound, so the alliteration in this line makes the description sound quiet.

2. **Imagery**: Using words that create clear pictures (images) in the reader's mind.

   The fox drags its wounded belly

   Over the snow, the crimson seeds

   Of blood burst with a mild explosion.

   The contrast of the fox's crimson blood against the snow strengthens the image for the reader. The addition of "burst" and "explosion" increases the effect of the image.

3. **Irony**: Using one or more words to say the opposite of what the words actually mean.

   Two weeks here in the sun and air

   Through the charity of our wealthy citizens

   Will be a wonderful help to the little tots

   When they return for a winter in the slums.

   The irony strengthens the point—it makes the reader pause and consider the writer's meaning.

4. **Metaphor:** Referring to one thing as something else to suggest or describe it.

   The voice of the last cricket

   Across the first frost

   Is one kind of good-bye.

   The poet refers to the cricket's sound as a "voice" saying goodbye to autumn.

5. **Simile:** a comparison using *like* or *as,* and sometimes *"than"*

   Your voice sounds like a scorpion being pushed through a glass tube.

   This is much more interesting than saying, "Your voice is annoying."

Figure 6.8 Figurative Language, page 2

6. **Onomatopoeia:** the sound of the word(s) imitates the meaning, like sound effects

   The Watch

   O Death, come quick, come quick, come quick.

   Come quick, come quick, come quick, come quick.

   Notice how the repeated words "come quick" sound like a ticking watch.

7. **Personification:** giving a human quality to concepts, animals, or other elements in nature.

   November

   He has hanged himself—the Sun

   Personifying the sun creates a mood of mourning the loss of autumn.

8. **Oxymoron:** using words together that have opposite meanings.

   The father's eyes glared with loving strictness.

   Although the father may be angry, he is acting out of love.

Write about one of the environmental topics, in a way that uses one of the rhetorical devices.

Figurative Language/Rhetorical Devices	Environmental Nouns as Topics
1. Alliteration	1. Rain
2. Imagery	2. Lake
3. Irony	3. Sun
4. Metaphor	4. Sky
5. Simile	5. Moon
6. Onomatopoeia	6. Spring
7. Personification	7. Forest
8. Oxymoron	8. Mountains

Self-Assessment Rubric—How did you do?

4 I'm a star!	3 I've got it!	2 I'm almost there.	1 I'll keep at it.
· My examples are original. They help clarify my meaning and make it more memorable.	· I have managed to create my own examples that nobody else would have heard before.	· I was able to write examples of the devices, but they sound too familiar. (He was as busy as a bee.)	· Maybe I don't quite understand the different devices yet.

Add your favourite examples to your Gem Words Journal.

- Have students create their own poetic phrases using figurative language and the environmental nouns.
- Have students share their creations, and think about whether the device enhanced the meaning of their terms.
- Allow students to record any gems in their journal.
- Discuss the self-assessment rubric of writing poetry (Figure 6.9). Then, allow students to create their poems, thinking back to how the poem "Nature" highlighted something unique about the speaker's home.
- In responding to the students' poems, keep in mind the questions *What should you keep doing?* and *What should you try next time?* as you write your comments.

Figure 6.9 Self-assessment rubric for poetry

What does a good poem look like?

4 I'm a star!	3 I've got it!	2 I'm almost there.	1 I'll keep at it.
· This poem means a lot to me. · My imagery and figurative language help make what I'm saying even more meaningful.	· I care about this poem, but in places, it isn't quite "catchy." · I've used some imagery or figurative language, but the words are not always precise.	· My poem makes sense, but it isn't really anything I care about. · I've tried to use some imagery or figurative language, but the words sound familiar.	· I have too many unnecessary words. · This could be a paragraph, not a poem. · I didn't try any imagery or figurative language.

Science

New Vocabulary

Science is rich in new vocabulary. To help students master the terms, have them personalize their response to each term, rather than just copying the definitions. Over the course of the unit, students will become familiar with the accepted definitions of the scientific terms, and be able to use them in other contexts.

Key Vocabulary for the Unit

biodiversity	capillary action	convection current	current
aquifers	water cycle	water table	ground water
sediment	weathering erosion	deposition	floodplain
precipitation	saturated zone	dikes	delta

- Choose one word and model how to write a personal definition for it, how to create a simile using it, and how to create a graphic representation for it.
- Ask students to work in groups of 2 or 3 to practise three more words.
- For each remaining term, have students write a definition in their own words, create a simile, and create a graphic representation (Figure 6.10).

Figure 6.10 Vocabulary template

Vocabulary Template

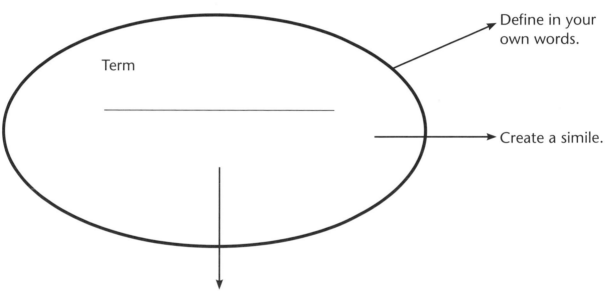

Term

Define in your own words.

Create a simile.

Draw a graphic representation.

- Throughout the unit, ask students to add to their vocabulary lists when new words are introduced to the class (Figure 6.11).

Figure 6.11 A portion of a student's illustrated vocabulary list

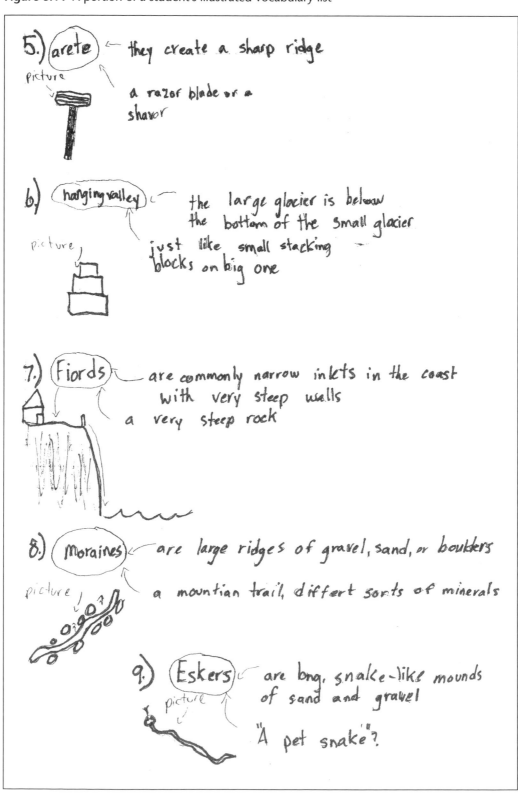

Lesson 4—Rationale

This lesson expands on the themes found in "Nature" through a piece of non-fiction writing. It provides a good tie-in to the Science unit, while still supporting the goals of the English unit. The connecting strategy, the Anticipation Guide, prepares the students for the reading by focusing on the author's intentions and their background knowledge. It also supports students with key statements to guide them as they read and after they've read.

English

Anticipation Guide, Nonfiction Writing

- Copy and distribute the Anticipation Guide (Figure 6.12) for the article "Why We Grow Insensitive to Dangers" by David Suzuki, and have students complete it (see *Crossroads 10*, p. 330).
- In a class discussion, have students explain their pre-reading answers and justify their thinking.
- As students read the article, have them confirm or adjust their thinking, citing examples from the text. Students should also note any gem or treasure words or phrases in their journals.
- Have students discuss their thinking, and invite them to share any connections they may have made between this article and the work being done in their Science class.

Science

Anticipation Guide, Weathering and Erosion

The guide for "The Power of Water" assesses students for background knowledge about weathering and erosion before they begin reading. It also helps motivate the students as they read and gives them a purpose for reading. Students become more aware of how this helps them read for specific information so they become more actively engaged in the reading. Using an anticipation guide supports students in using their knowledge of how the landscape is shaped.

The Power of Water

- Hand out 2 pieces of paper—green for "I agree" and red for "I disagree" —to each student.
- Ask students to respond to the statements—as you read from the guide (Figure 6.13)—by holding the green or red paper in the air to show their agreement or disagreement.
- When you discuss the topic with the class, ask students to explain why they agree or disagree. Be careful to not evaluate their answers but rather highlight and comment on their reasoning process.
- Ask students to read the related text to build on the earlier class discussion and verify or adjust their understanding of the topic.

Figure 6.12 Anticipation Guide — Suzuki article

"Why We Grow Insensitive to Dangers" by David Suzuki.

Before you read the article by David Suzuki, mark your response to the statements in the Yes or No column for first (1st) reading, and briefly justify your response.

After discussing your responses as a class, read the article. Then, repeat your response and reason in the second (2nd) column.

Treasure words: insensitive, exuberant, extraneous, cacophony, habituation, diminishes

Statements of Ideas + My reason for agreeing or disagreeing	1st Yes	1st No	2nd Yes	2nd No
Children need adults to show them the beauty of nature.				
As times passes, society grows more and more concerned about global warming.				
It is difficult to scientifically prove that the environment is in danger.				
It would be better if more and more people went into the forests and parklands.				
People should avoid electronics like TV and computers.				
More people aren't environmentalists because they just don't care that much about nature.				

© Portage & Main Press, 2011, *It's All About Thinking: Mathematics & Science*, BLM, ISBN: 978-1-55379-269-7

Figure 6.13 Anticipation Guide — "The Power of Water"

The Power of Water

Before you read "The Power of Water" in the textbook, complete this pre-reading activity, using what you already know. If you don't know for sure, make your best guess to circle whether you agree or disagree. Then, briefly state why to support your opinion or guess. Then, read the article in the textbook to check what the authors say, and respond in the rows below.

Before / After	Statements
Before you read:	**1. Soil (dirt) has always existed on Earth.** I agree. I disagree.
After you read:	I agree because I disagree because
Before you read:	**2. Ice can make soil.** I agree. I disagree.
After you read:	I agree because I disagree because
Before you read:	**3. When soil is moved (naturally), the Earth's surface may be changed.** I agree. I disagree.
After you read:	I agree because I disagree because
Before you read:	**4. Trees prevent landslides.** I agree. I disagree.
After you read:	I agree because I disagree because
Before you read:	**5. Water's power strips the land mass; it does not add to it.** I agree. I disagree.
After you read:	I agree because I disagree because

© Portage & Main Press, 2011, *It's All About Thinking: Mathematics & Science, ELM*, ISBN: 978-1-55379-269-7

Lesson 5

English—Writing Poetry

Sue has her students head out into the forested park across from the school, venturing out as poets. This activity builds on the Suzuki article and its theme of desensitization. In turn, it provides the students with a pre-writing activity for their next poem.

In my own backyard

- Students head out across the street equipped with journals and blindfolds, with the goal of focusing on one sense at a time. This is a process with five steps:

    1. Blindfolded, listen to the sounds of the park for one minute. Remove your blindfold and describe the sounds and any connections these sounds may hold.
    2. Blindfolded, have a partner place something from the park in your hands. Feel it for one minute. Remove your blindfold and jot down your thoughts about how it felt, including any connections.
    3. Blindfolded, think about the smells of the park. Is it a dry, warm day or a cool one, a damp or dry day? Remove the blindfold and describe the scents and their connections.
    4. Look for something that you did not notice initially. Attempt to be very specific—ask if anyone knows the name of something in your surroundings; don't just say "tree." Observe for a minute, then jot down descriptions and connections. Feel free to sketch.
    5. Reading over your observations, look for any new understandings you may have reached. Do you have a new way of thinking about things?

- Upon their return to the classroom, ask students to create a new poem based on their experience in the outdoors.

Science—Weathering and Erosion

A Local Stream

In this activity, students further apply the concepts learned in lesson 4 to a local stream. Students transform their knowledge through identifying areas of weathering and erosion. This activity shows students how their learning in the classroom is applied to the outside world and to a local, familiar place.

Park Activity

- Ask students to pair up, and share what they learned in the last class about weathering and erosion.

- Choose several students and ask them to describe their conversation about weathering and erosion as a way to review the concepts before going outside.
- Go to the local park and observe weathering and erosion at a stream.
- Ask students to identify areas of erosion, deposition, weathering; then ask them to compare these three concepts in a Venn diagram.

Lesson 6

English

Pre-reading a Poem

In order to elicit students' prior knowledge and to build their curiosity about a poem, re-introduce "graffiti," the connecting strategy they used in Science Lesson 1. In this English lesson, ask students to apply the strategy to their poetic thinking. This prepares them for the reading of the poem, values their thinking, and is social. The ensuing class discussion, using their graffiti chart paper, invites all students in, as the graffiti directs the conversation. It also prepares them for a literature circle that, in turn, serves as a "pre-write" for their next poem.

My Favourite Journey

- Select a few phrases from the poem "To Colombo" by Michael Ondaatje (1982) and write them on chart paper, placed about the room. Ask students to circulate in groups (different coloured pens assigned to each group is a helpful way to be sure that each group is given credit for their thinking) and respond to the phrases—predicting, connecting, questioning, explaining—with support for their thinking. As the comments build, invite the students to also respond to others' responses.
- Collect the charts and assemble them to use in a class discussion.
- Have students read and respond to the poem "To Colombo."
- Have students take a moment to add any gems to their journals before joining their groups to discuss their responses.
- Have individuals take the time to self-assess their responses and the class discussion according to the rubrics used previously (Figures 6.3 and 6.4).
- Have students sketch a scene from their favourite journey, thinking about strong memories and associations this trip might hold for them.
- Have students write their poems and share them in a writers' workshop.

Science—Rationale

There is an indoor and an outdoor component to the human impact activity. This allows the students to reflect locally (at the park) and then to broaden their reflections globally (through station work). Both components of the activity encourage critical thinking and use students' prior knowledge. In turn, students consider the ethics of environmental stewardship.

Park Activity: Human Impacts

Take students to a local park and ask students to record positive and negative human impacts on the park and to predict future outcomes based on their observations. These may be recorded as 2-column notes: Observations and Predictions. Their observations may include notes, sketches, or mind maps.

- Ask students to complete the activity on their own.
- Bring students back to the class and discuss the students' reflections on the human impacts in the park. Brainstorm as a class what they can do to minimize the human impacts on the park.
- Have students self-assess their journal entry, using the rubric provided, making note of what they should continue to do and what they should work on for next time (Figure 6.14).
- Show several relevant pictures or graphics that feature positive and negative human impacts. Select a graphic that relates to the students' lives and, together, create questions for them to explore.
- Have the students create stations of newspaper articles describing environmental events that have positive and negative human impacts.
- Briefly introduce each newspaper article. Have students choose the article they wish to read and move to that station.
- Ask students to answer personally relevant critical questions from the station of their choice or from one of the graphics. For example, reflecting on the article on the Great Pacific Garbage Patch, think of a situation you may have noticed that is similar; explain how it is similar and its possible impact on your local environment.

Figure 6.14 Self-assessment rubric for students' Science Journal

How do I keep a Science Journal?

4 I'm a rock star!	3 I've got it!	2 I'm almost there.	1 I'll keep at it.
· This science journal has many inspired observations of both positive and negative impacts. · The predictions are realistic and are clearly based on the observations.	· This science journal has some thoughtful observations of both positive and negative impacts. · The predictions are realistic and based on the observations.	· This science journal has some observations, many of them obvious, of both positive and negative impacts. · The predictions are somewhat based on observations.	· This science journal has a few obvious observations of both positive and negative impacts. · The predictions may not be realistic or clearly based on the observations.

Lesson 7—Defending Opinion

English

Students take a stance and support it with their thinking—from their own world as well as from lessons in Science class. This focused discussion builds motivation and helps students use their growing background knowledge in preparation for reading a related short story. After students discuss the story in the context of its theme, the teacher models the skill of creating a "found poem" and invites the students to experiment with deleting and including words, discussing the impact of various choices. Found poetry emphasizes the skills of being succinct and subtle.

Found Poetry

- Ask students how they would answer the question: Have we conquered Nature, or does Nature rule us?
- Give them a chance to discuss their reasoning with those around them before engaging in a class discussion. While the discussion continues, start a list of examples from both sides of the argument. All the while, grant students the freedom to change their position as their conversation unfolds.
- Then, have students read the story "The Interlopers" by Saki (*Sightlines 9*, p. 33), underlining the examples that suggest the power of Nature and marking with a squiggly line the examples that suggest the power of humans.
- Have students share their choices in groups, adding any gems to their journals.
- Returning to the story, ask students to double-underline the words they feel are powerful and that support their point of view.
- As students share some of their word choices, make a short list on the board.
- With the students, experiment in creating "found poetry" where the words are arranged (and deleted) for impact. It is fun to show students how such editing can change the message.
- After playing a bit with the words, have students work on their own with their own list.

Science

Water Cycle

The Guess Water Cycle activity asks students to predict the water cycle with a supporting diagram. Their predictions will focus their reading about the water cycle. After reading, students should reflect and revise their original theory of the water cycle.

Guess Water Cycle

- Supply each student with an unlabelled diagram of the water cycle. (Figure 6.15).
- Ask students to write their theory of the water cycle using the labels as support.
- Students share their diagrams with partners to discuss their theories.
- Supply students with a reading on the water cycle and ask students to revise their diagram and their theory following their reading (Nicole's assigned Water Cycle reading was from *Science Probe 8*, Carmichael et al. 2006). Students should include the vocabulary learned about the water cycle with an explanation in their own words.

Figure 6.15 Water Cycle

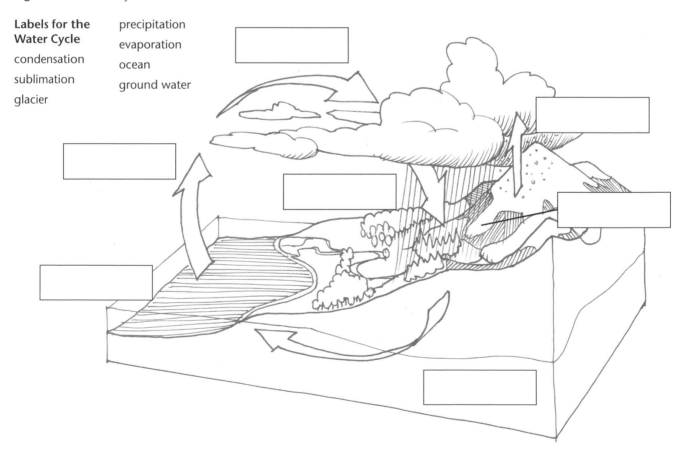

Labels for the Water Cycle

condensation
sublimation
glacier

precipitation
evaporation
ocean
ground water

Lesson 8

English—Reading Art

Sue made a PowerPoint presentation of the works of Canadian artists, using images she had collected from the Internet. This lesson highlights students' viewing skills as the PowerPoint presentation of landscapes by various Canadian artists unfolds. Art, like poetry, conveys its messages through the artists' choices—what they choose to emphasize or de-emphasize, the atmosphere they create through content and colours, the story suggested by their choices. "Reading" a painting can be a lot like reading a poem.

The Power of Viewing

- Have students respond in their journals to various Canadian landscape paintings, considering ideas such as connections, emotions, descriptive words, descriptions of the lines and colours used. Model the first one for the students, and as you proceed slowly through the slide show, invite them into the discussion.
- Have students view the paintings a second time, this time in discussion groups as they share their observations, borrowing any gems they may hear.

A Mini Studio—Time to Play

Have students select 2 or 3 words from the lists they have generated, and attempt to represent the word through an image of nature. Some may wish to draw; some may wish to select images from sites such as <www.flickr.com>. They should be able to justify their selections. Later, students can share their choices in groups and have other students guess which word they have represented. Have students self-assess and peer-assess using the rubric in Figure 6.16.

Figure 6.16 Self-assessment rubric for effective representation

What does effective representing look like?

4 I'm a rock star!	3 I'm there.	2 I'm almost there.	1 I'll keep at it.
· Made original and complex choices to enhance the meaning.	· Made interesting and somewhat original choices to enhance the meaning. · There is some degree of complexity.	· Made obvious choices to enhance the meaning.	· The choices are simple, and don't do much to enhance the meaning.

Science

Note-Making

The Trash or Treasure strategy is an exercise in note-making. The strategy focuses on learning a skill that can be used in all courses and that helps students learn content focused on the water table by making notes in a new format.

Trash or Treasure: Water Table

- Model how to make Trash or Treasure notes on the water table. Create an overhead of the reading (Carmichael 2006, 199) for the students. Read through the first paragraph out loud with the students.
- As a class, decide on the main concept of the paragraph, and write the main concept in a circle at the centre of a page.
- Ask the students to state the supporting points—also out loud. Decide how to write the supporting points around the circle (the main concept), using the least number of words possible. The words that students keep are "treasure," and the words that they abandon become "trash."
- Tell students that they can use 15 words maximum, but that symbols are not counted.
- Ask students to make their own notes for the remainder of the reading. Figure 6.17 shows part of a student's Trash or Treasure page, with the main concepts stated as questions.

Figure 6.17 One student's Trash or Treasure note-making

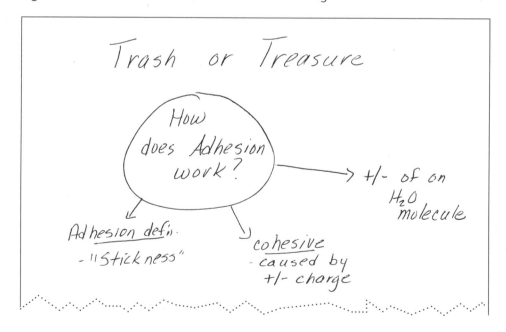

Lesson 9—Connecting

English—Connecting through Personal Artifacts

Previously in Science class, students brought in artifacts that connected them to water. Ask them now to bring in an artifact to represent their favourite place. This lesson uses the artifact as inspiration for a poem and incorporates it into a pre-write as well as a topic for their poem. Their story about their artifact allows students to further share who they are with their classmates.

A Memoir Poem

- For 2 minutes, have students tell their partner about their artifact and their favourite place. Students then switch roles, allowing their partners to tell their story.
- Have students take 3 minutes to sketch their favourite place, considering their artifacts.
- Select a poem about the author's favourite place to read aloud to your students, or choose a descriptive song lyric to play for the class.
- Ask students to jot down as they listen any gem words described in the poem or song, and to sketch the favourite place described.
- Have students take a few minutes to discuss their sketch, in turn, with their partner. *Are there any similarities or differences between the speaker's place and your place? Are there any similarities or differences between your sketch and your partner's?*
- Have students create a poem about their own favourite place, suggesting why this place is special to them.

Science—Rationale

As a follow-up to Trash or Treasure, give students a fairly open template for this activity to help them make notes on currents and tides. This activity provides structure, but encourages them to decide for themselves what the important supporting details are. Because this is a new format for the class, gradual release of responsibility helps everyone be successful.

Guided Note-Making: Currents and Tides

- Model how to complete the first frame of the template in Figure 6.18.
- As a class, complete the second frame.
- For the third frame, have students work with a partner or, if they wish, on their own.
- All students complete the final frame on their own. Move among the students as they work independently, giving descriptive feedback and providing support as needed.

Figure 6.18 Template for Guided Note-Making

Guided Note-Making
What influences water currents?

Point 1: _____ Details:	Point 2: _____ Details:
Point 3:_____ Details:	Point 4:_____ Details:

Lesson 10—Rationale

English

When Nicole's Science class is studying biodiversity and the various ecosystems found underwater, she usually takes the students on a field trip to the Vancouver Aquarium. On this trip, however, she asks the students to observe both like a scientist and like a poet. Because the unit thus far has been primarily about exploring what goes unnoticed amid the familiarity of our surroundings, this trip provides the occasion to look at the exotic in the unfamiliar. We so infrequently appreciate what we have that we grow to not notice it, no matter how strong its influence upon us. To reinforce this idea, it is worthwhile to look at something a bit more unfamiliar to us, in order to refocus.

Field Trip: The Foreign World of the Aquarium
"The Shark" by E.J. Pratt

- Have students read "The Shark" (*Crossroads 10*) while standing in front of the aquarium's shark tank. Considering both the poem and the real-life fish, have students underline the lines that resonate the strongest with them and explain why. Ask:
    - *What precisely about a shark do people find exotic and compelling?*
- Then, have students choose a creature from the aquarium that is not familiar to them and study it for 2 minutes, noting its appearance, behaviour, and any connections to them.
- Have students compose a poem that highlights what they find intriguing about this creature.

Science—Rationale

A municipal aquarium is a good way to expand the connections between our content and the real world. It takes students beyond the backyard of the park and into the larger world. It enables students to compare British Columbia's marine life to other areas of the world. On such a field trip, students will be able to understand how different *abiotic* factors (*non-living*; physical rather than biological factors) affect the species distribution.

Field Trip: Biodiversity and the Aquarium

- Have students compare the different areas within the ecosystems of the aquarium, and write their observations in their science journals. Model the process for them, and include in the modelling how to find the necessary information and different ways to record this information.
- To better understand biodiversity, students should observe two different tanks. They can then record the number of different species, look at salinity and temperature, compare producers and consumers, and make observations about the substrate to determine the factors that impact biodiversity.
- Have students practise their observation skills at two tanks with a partner.
- Then, have them observe at two more tanks and, finally, complete two on their own. From their observations, have them complete a Venn diagram, comparing and contrasting what they see in the two tanks.
- Have students self-assess their journal entries, using the same rubric as before (Figure 6.14) and adding notes of what they are doing well, what they should continue to do, and what they should work on.

Lessons 11 and 12—Representations

English—Rationale

The activity invites the students to further explore the skills of responding and representing. It provides them with a chance to further experiment before the final project, in particular, to look at the impact of the choices they make.

Representing Poetry

- Provide students with a mini-anthology of poems relating to nature. Invite them to select a poem and find a way to represent it in a powerful manner. Give them freedom to experiment—making a PowerPoint presentation, drawing, making a collage, reading poetry aloud. Have students consider their word choices that will enhance their poem.
- Show students an example of a PowerPoint presentation and ask them to discuss the choices made and their effectiveness, using the same criteria from Figure 6.14.
- Have students meet in groups to discuss a poem, according to their choices.
- Give students time to experiment with different ways to represent their work, including choice of font, images, and music, and ask them to justify their choices.

Science—Mind Maps

By creating a mind map at the end of the unit, the students transfer their knowledge from the entire unit. They connect the content in their individual and unique ways and write down their thinking processes. The students can use this mind map to organize their thinking for their final project. Figure 6.19 is a student sample.

Mind Map

- Model how to create a mind map using a subject the students have already learned in class. Have students write "Water" in the centre of a piece of paper. Allow them to select 15 terms from the unit and connect them with arrows, explaining their connections. Stress that students must explain how the concepts are related, not simply provide definitions.
- Examine the rubric, Figure 6.20.
- Show several examples of mind maps, and ask students what is good and what is lacking in the mind maps.
- To begin their own mind maps, students can use their word walls as a vocabulary list. Remind students that they are not writing definitions on the mind map, but showing how they think the concepts are connected. Each mind map should be different and show some unique connections.

- Ask students to self-evaluate their mind map, using the rubric provided (Figure 6.20).

Figure 6.19 Student sample of a mind map

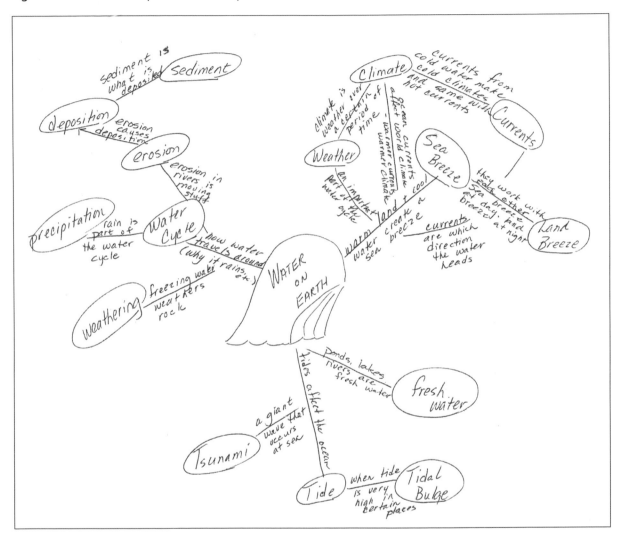

Figure 6.20 Rubric of criteria for a mind map

How do I create a mind map?

4 I'm a rock star!	3 I've got it!	2 I'm almost there.	1 I'll keep at it.
· This mind map contains many inspired connections that are clearly explained.	· This mind map contains some thoughtful connections, many of which are clearly explained.	· This mind map contains some obvious connections that are explained.	· This mind map has a few obvious connections that may not be explained.

Final Lessons — English and Science

Rationale

In keeping with the Backward Design model, students return their focus to the final project, highlighting the strong work they've done throughout the unit. The project intentionally offers choice, but with limitations. It is specific in its requirements, and requires students to use the skills and knowledge focused on throughout the lessons. Students submit one project for both courses, noting both the criteria that will contribute to the English mark and the criteria that will contribute to the Science mark. Through this project, students will be able to demonstrate their learning of the science concepts as well as their skills in writing and representing in English.

The Final Project

Sue and Nicole like the idea of the students submitting one project between the two courses. Students were given the choice of presenting information through a scrapbook, a slideshow, or an option of their choice, if approved by the teacher. Students returned to the question, "How are we connected to our environment?" To answer this question, they needed to think like a scientist as well as like a poet. In Science, because they had had feedback throughout the unit, the students revisited the major concepts of the unit in their portfolios (water cycle, erosion, human impacts) and related them directly to their local environment. The intention was to illustrate that science is more than a series of facts, and the environment does hold personal relevance for all of us. For example, as part of their project, students could write a magazine article about the effects of erosion in the local stream, or create a comic strip about how the local dump impacts the water cycle.

Alongside their science work, students showcased their own poetry, now that they had also received feedback. Being mindful of the power of words and the power of images, students chose their favourite selections from their portfolios. If the science ties the students more personally to the content, the poetry simply deepens this connection. Our environment helps shape who we are and holds a special significance for all of us. Figure 6.21 is the scoring rubric for the final project. Students had this in hand as they worked.

Although the combination of English and Science may at first appear to be an unusual choice, the fit was more natural because both units stressed the students' environment and their personal connections. As the unit closed, students held brief individual conferences with Sue and Nicole to explain how, in their opinion, the two different viewpoints on the environment were linked.

Students' responses came in varied formats — scrapbooks, PowerPoint presentations, drawings, and magazines among others. Nicole and Sue both noted the increased student enthusiasm and pride in their projects. Not all students were able to transfer their understanding to this new format — some replicated the information directly from the textbook with unrelated pieces

Figure 6.21 Assessment of Learning: Scoring Rubric for Final Project

	5	4	3	2	1
Science: Concepts x 2	Displays excellent knowledge of concepts.	Displays strong knowledge of concepts.	Displays satisfactory knowledge of concepts.	Displays unsatisfactory knowledge of concepts.	Displays poor knowledge of concepts.
Science: Transforming x 2	Effectively applies concepts in various contexts.	Appropriately applies concepts in various contexts.	Applies concepts in various contexts.	Attempts to apply concepts in various contexts.	Shows understanding of concepts in obvious contexts.
English: Ideas	Poetry has a message and is complex or creative.	Poetry has a clear message and is original in parts.	Poetry expresses common ideas.	Poetry is direct.	Poetry is simple and obvious.
English: Style	Precise language with carefully chosen words. Description and figurative language are clever.	Interesting word choices. Tries to use description and figurative language for impact.	Clear, with some interesting word choices.Tries to use description and figurative language.	Direct with common word choices. May attempt description and figurative language.	Plain vocabulary without much description or figurative language.
English: Representing	Original, complex choices were made to enhance meaning.	Some interesting choices were made to enhance meaning.	Obvious choices were made to enhance meaning.	Some simple choices were made to enhance meaning.	Little done to enhance meaning.
English: Convention	Few errors in complex matters.	Some errors in complex matters.	Some errors.	Noticeable basic errors.	Frequent basic errors.

of poetry alongside. However, an impressive number of students were able to successfully transfer their understandings, and their projects showed a personal connection to their environment. All in all, Nicole and Sue felt the unit was more authentic and meaningful, perhaps because it combined two curricular topics in a way that, at first, did not seem obvious, but grew to be apparent. Best of all, this unit is based on the students' worlds—in the biggest and smallest contexts.

Reflections from Nicole and Sue

This is not our first collaboration. We look for opportunities to work together and always feel rejuvenated by the process. Admittedly, Science and English are not the most conventional pairing, but we are always impressed with the similarities we are able to uncover, and are able to learn a great deal from the inherent differences between the two courses. Best of all, collaboration appears to be contagious. The enthusiasm we take away from working together often spreads to other colleagues who are interested in hearing about what we've done. They, in turn, take something away and make it their own. Initially, it may appear that collaboration is more time-consuming and troublesome; however, we find that because the projects on which we have collaborated are so much stronger, they endure. The new My Space in the Classroom project is, in fact, an evolution of our other collaborations. Because we have enjoyed working together, it seems we look for excuses to continue.

Chapter 7

Diversity of Life

Grades 5/6/7—Science

Assessment FOR Learning

- Who Am I? Profile
- Performance-based assessment
- Class profile
- Class-developed criteria
- Self-assessment and goal-setting

Gradual Release of Responsibility

- Connecting, processing, transforming/personalizing lesson structure
- Targeted, extended strategy instruction

Inquiry

- Weekly inquiry questions
- Essential questions

Differentiation

- Multimodal representation
- Common learning outcomes, varying levels of support
- Descriptive feedback
- Open-ended strategies

Assessment OF Learning

- Performance-based assessment
- Essential question
- Authentic task

The Collaboration

Nicole Widdess is a grade 6/7 teacher who is passionate about developing thinking skills in her students. Over the course of her teaching career, she has been a classroom teacher, learning resource teacher, and literacy mentor. Nicole and Leyton Schnellert first worked together when Leyton was a district inclusion-support teacher and Nicole was a new elementary resource teacher. As they worked together, their focus shifted from planning for individual students to planning units of instruction in ways that included, celebrated, and supported all learners. Looking back over the last 10 years of their collaboration, Nicole and Leyton have combined their interests in literacy, fine and performing arts, and holistic learning as they planned many units of study (Schnellert and Widdess 2005). Leyton, now based at Simon Fraser University, finds that working with Nicole helps him stay connected to a classroom community.

In this chapter, Nicole planned collaboratively with Leyton the development of a unit to help students inquire into science content while simultaneously targeting and building their reading and thinking skills. They designed an inquiry unit to meet learning outcomes from both the science and language arts curricula and to engage their students with questions that required them to learn through reading. As they developed the learning sequences for this unit, they kept both student learning profiles and science learning outcomes in mind.

The next year, Lori Davis used the unit with her grade 5/6 class, and helped to elaborate the persuasive writing lessons. Lori is passionate about children's literature, connecting content with the real world, and reflecting on her practice. While Lori taught the unit, the three teachers met to reflect on the lessons and make changes based on their insights. Nicole and Leyton were able to use what they developed with Lori in their new ecology unit (Schnellert, Datoo, Ediger, and Panas 2009).

The Context

Although this chapter is for a December to March unit, Nicole and Leyton began their planning by reviewing the class profile compiled in September, which summarized the strengths, stretches, interests, and fears of the diverse group of students in the class. Nicole and Leyton refer to and update their class profile as they plan new units. The Who Am I? Profile (Figure 7.1)[1] is just one of the ways they gather student information.

Nicole and Leyton had also completed a performance-based assessment (PBA) (Figure 7.2) during the fall, but they wanted to re-assess the class to see what gains the students had made during the first term. They prepared a second PBA on informational reading (see chapter 2) to determine what reading strategies the students still needed to develop. Their analysis of the descriptive coding in the PBAs helped them establish new goals for the class.

1   See Chapter 5 in Brownlie and Schnellert, 2009, for another example of this profile in use.

They coded their PBA with the BC Performance Standards for Reading Information <www.bced.gov.bc.ca/perf_stands/reading.htm>, which provides baseline data to direct their planning. This assessment-to-instruction cycle allows them to plan and teach with specific reading and thinking skills in mind. When planning science units, Nicole and Leyton choose two or three thinking skills to develop over the course of the lessons—thinking skills that are important for learning in science and across the curriculum, both inside and outside school. As part of their unit planning, they also develop a PBA to use as a summative assessment to monitor students' growth in using the targeted reading and thinking strategies by the end of the unit.

Key Structures

Open-Ended Strategies

- Connecting, processing, and transforming/personalizing lesson sequences
- Strategies organized by purpose:
    - connecting—with background knowledge and with others
    - processing—interacting with new material
    - transforming and personalizing—showing what you know in a new and personal way

Lesson sequences may take more than one class period. In this case, begin the next lesson, in the same phase (connecting, processing, transforming/ personalizing) by looking at the previous day's question (e.g., How can scientists work together effectively?).

Note-Making Strategies

- magnet notes
- two-column notes
- sketching and labelling
- Venn diagram
- mind maps
- reciprocal teaching
- Wonder books
- graphic organizers

Assessment for Learning

- Who Am I? Profile
    - The more teachers know about the individuals within the class, the more they can focus their teaching and their support on a daily and weekly basis.
    - The Who Am I? Profile serves as formative assessment. By identifying students' styles and preferences, teachers can tailor instruction, activities, and performance tasks.

- ✦ Developing independent and confident learners involves building on strengths and extending each student's abilities.
- PBA for reading information and targeted reading and thinking skills
  - ✦ The formative reading assessment (see chapter 3) is used to develop a class profile that identifies class and individual strengths, stretches, interests, and goals. When students feel welcome and have opportunities to make connections between prior knowledge and course content, they will share more of what they know about topics, issues, and ideas as well as of themselves as learners.
- Class Profile
  - ✦ Teachers communicate to students that they come with strengths and abilities; every student needs to know that their prior experiences, abilities and knowledge will be honoured.
  - ✦ Students are more capable of engaging in a unit of study when they have opportunities to use both their prior knowledge and the skills they already have.
- Class-Developed Criteria
  - ✦ Students help develop the criteria by which their work will be assessed.
  - ✦ Increases engagement, self-awareness and helps students take the perspective of a scientist.

Self-assessment and goal-setting

- Students have an opportunity to reflect on and set goals about their learning. They personalize the use of strategies.

Gradual release — targeted, extended strategy instruction

- Thinking skills identified in the formative assessment are addressed within the unit.
- Within the integrated unit, these skills are reinforced as "what scientists do."
- Teachers model the skills during think-alouds, then students have a chance to use them with partners and, ultimately, independently.

Differentiation

- In various lessons, students have opportunities for multimodal representation. This might involve offering them a choice of words, images, charts, or diagrams to show their learning within a lesson or choice of which question or form of representation they use for the summative assessment.
- With open-ended teaching (see chapter 4), everyone is taught a particular thinking strategy, then given opportunities to apply it.
- Everyone works toward common learning outcomes, but some students may require more practice, more support, or more time in order to achieve the outcomes.

- Individual students are at different places in their skill development and learning journey, and the teacher's descriptive feedback on shared criteria enables individual development.

Inquiry

- Weekly inquiry questions guide students to the big ideas in Science, which also provide a weekly teaching and learning focus.
- An essential question frames one of the summative assessment tasks so that students are focusing on core outcomes and yet can draw in a variety of information and perspectives.

Assessment of Learning

- Authentic task (persuasive writing) that includes an emphasis on people's responsibility to the environment
- Performance-based informational reading assessment

Big Ideas in Science

- Living things have similarities and differences.
- Classifying things helps us understand the diversity of life.
- We are part of ecosystems.

Figure 7.1 Who Am I? Profile

Who are you as a person and a learner?

Words that describe me:	My favourite books/stories:	Things I like to do when I'm alone:
Things I'm very good at or interested in:	Things I like to do with my family:	Things I like to do with my friends:
Things I'd like or need you to know about me:	My hopes and dreams for myself:	The easiest way for me to show what I know is:

Things I would like to get better at in this class are:

THIS IS ME! ←

© Portage & Main Press, 2011, *It's All About Thinking: Mathematics & Science*, BLM, ISBN: 978-1-55379-269-7

Figure 7.2 Comparing performance in fall and winter

Reading for Information
Grade 6 & 7, 2006–2007

Results	
Performance Scale (4 pts.)	**27 Students**
Scores remaining the same on both PBAs (Sept/Feb)	4
+0.5	11
+1.0	6
+1.5	2
+2.0	2
Missing writing one PBA	2
Students Meeting or Exceeding Minimum Expectations on the Performance-Based Standards	
September 2006	February 2007
10/25	19/27
40%	70%

Lesson Sequences

Analyzing the two formative assessments helped Nicole and Leyton prepare a class profile of their students' strengths (attentive, good listeners, willing to ask for help, prefer real-life examples and applications, visual and hands-on learners, effectively use text features, and are positive toward each other) and their stretches (generating their own strategies, determining importance, discussion, self-monitoring, and accessing prior knowledge). Their interests included socializing, sports, performing arts (dance and drama), social networking, and reading. Nicole and Leyton compiled this information on one page for quick reference as they were planning (Figure 7.3).

Based on the assessment data they had collected, Nicole and Leyton established unit goals for their students, as follows:

- Determining importance (distinguishing main ideas from details)
- Applying their learning across the curriculum
- Planning and self-monitoring the strategies they use
- Using their thinking strategies and content knowledge when engaging in an authentic task
- Transforming what they learned into a persuasive piece by using their research skills

Figure 7.3 Class Profile for quick reference

Class Profile

Classroom Strengths	Classroom Stretches
• attentive	• generating their own strategies
• good listeners	• determining importance
• ask for help	• discussion
• like real-life examples/applications	• self-monitoring
• visual, hands-on learners	• accessing prior knowledge
• good with text features	
• positive toward each other	

Interests: socializing, sports, performing arts (dance and drama), MSN, reading

Goals	Decisions
• Making connections	• Connecting, processing, transforming, personalizing lesson structure
• Determining Importance	• Targeted, extended strategy instruction
• Applying their learning across the curriculum	• Multimodal representation opportunities (differentiation)
• Developing planning and self-monitoring strategies	• Planning activities, metacognitive steps in lessons
• Writing a persuasive piece using research skills	

Individual Concerns

Medical	Language	Learning	Socio-Emotional	Challenge
Nate: (ADHD) difficulty with staying focused	Peter: ESL 2	Nate, Jason	Nate: tunes out, seeks attention, few friends	Izzy, Keisha, Brittney, Glen
	Cory, Doug, & Allie: ESL 3 6 other students: ESL 4 and 5.	Lars: frontload, key ideas, adapt outcomes, reduce workload		
		Nate: Alphasmart		

Although the Integrated Resource Package (IRP) for Grade 6 Science provided the overarching topic, Diversity of Life, Nicole and Leyton also looked at related outcomes in the IRPs for grades 5 and 7, which included an emphasis on people's responsibility to the environment. Using the learning outcomes, Nicole and Leyton determined that they could focus their unit and student learning around three big ideas:

1. Living things have similarities and differences.
2. Classifying things helps us understand the diversity of life.
3. We are part of ecosystems.

Knowing the big ideas, the class profile, and the targeted reading and thinking skills, Nicole and Leyton developed open-ended strategies for the unit.

This 14-week unit incorporates inquiry and reading/thinking strategies. Each sequence spanned two to three 40-minute lessons. Nicole and Leyton developed weekly inquiry questions to guide students to the big ideas of the unit, which also provided a weekly teaching and learning focus (Figure 7.4).

Lesson 1—Fiction Versus Nonfiction

The inquiry question for this lesson— *What tools do scientists use when reading?*—leads students to connect reading for information strategies with learning in science.

*   Ask students to think about what tools scientists use when reading. Have students jot their thinking down on a piece of paper, then ask them to share their thinking with a partner.
*   Provide each desk group with a bin of nonfiction materials (books, magazines, newspaper articles). Ask the group to look through the books and record what they notice on chart paper. Then have one student from the group report their ideas to the class.
*   Invite the students to create a master list of what features they notice in nonfiction materials.
*   Students should begin to notice such features as headings, subheadings, and diagrams. Using a T-chart, work with them to name and record the text features and their purpose.
*   Ask students to create a mini-book that acts as a text features guide to one of the items in their nonfiction bin. Their guide should include a title of the text feature, a visual to represent the text feature, and a sentence to explain the importance of the text feature (see Figure 7.5).

Figure 7.4 Diversity of Life, Unit Overview, page 1

Science 6/7 Unit Overview
Diversity of Life

Big Ideas	1. Living things have similarities and differences. 2. Classifying things helps us understand the diversity of life. 3. We are part of ecosystems.
Thinking Strategies	Main Ideas & Details, Accessing Prior Knowledge, Synthesizing, Persuading, Questioning

December

Week	1	2	3	4
Essential Questions	What tools do scientists use when reading?	How are living things related to one another?	What do living things need to survive?	What tools and approaches can I use to study organisms?
Lesson Topic	Fiction vs. Nonfiction	Characteristics of Living Things	Needs of Living Things	Diversity of Life
Thinking Strategy	Using Text Features	Determining Importance	Determining Importance	Determining Importance Planning
Teaching Strategy	Mini Text Features Booklet	Magnet Notes	3 Key Points	Storyboard Speech / Thought Bubble

January

Week	1	2	3	4
Essential Questions	How can we use tools to observe and better understand living things in our world?		How does the way things are classified help us to learn about them?	What do scientists do to examine the similarities and differences between organisms?
Lesson Topic	Thinking like a Biologist Use of Microscopes		Classification: In the home and in the world	How scientists classify living things: · unicellular vs. multicellular · plants vs. animals
Thinking Strategy	Determining Importance Questioning Demonstrating a Rule		Main Idea / Detail	· Determining Importance · Compare/Contrast
Teaching Strategy	Criteria Building Microscope Diagram Wonder Books		Mind-mapping Categorizing	Magnet Notes Venn Diagram

© Portage & Main Press, 2011, *It's All About Thinking: Mathematics & Science*, BLM, ISBN: 978-1-55379-269-7

Figure 7.4 Diversity of Life, Unit Overview, page 2

Science 6/7 Unit Overview
Diversity of Life

Big Ideas	1. Living things have similarities and differences. 2. Classifying things helps us understand the diversity of life. 3. We are part of ecosystems.
Thinking Strategies	Main Ideas & Details, Accessing Prior Knowledge, Synthesizing, Persuading, Questioning

February

Week	1	2	3	4
Essential Questions	How does the way organisms are classified help us to learn about them?	How can scientists work together effectively?	Should governments pass laws to protect living things?	Should humans be able to alter the world of living things?
Lesson Topic	Five Kingdoms Model	Five Kingdoms Model Project	Persuasive writing, based on inquiry questions	· Students do independent research on their organism · Students write their draft
Thinking Strategy	* Determining Importance * Categorizing * Questioning	* Determining importance * Synthesizing * Planning	* Determining Importance * Questioning * Synthesizing	* Determining Importance * Questioning * Synthesizing
Teaching Strategy	* Magnet Notes * Wonder books	Team decision: poster, rap, skit	Model with 1organism	Student choice note-making/ Research strategy

March

Week	1	2		
Essential Questions	How do scientists convince others?		How do scientists communicate their findings and opinions?	
Lesson Topic	Draft continues		Polished report & small group share	
Teaching Strategy	Peer-editing and conferencing		Say Something	

Spring Break ☺

© Portage & Main Press, 2011, *It's All About Thinking: Mathematics & Science*, BLM, ISBN: 978-1-55379-269-7

Figure 7.5 Student sample of mini-book

Text Feature	Visual Representation of the text feature	Important function of the text feature
Table of Contents	**contents** In This Issue crime busters . . . . 2 clues from the past . . . . 10 body of evidence . . . . 14 Common scents 18	At the front of the book that allows the reader to find their topic faster
Heading	**Body of Evidence**	Identifies the major topic in which you will be reading about
Subheading	HAIR	Identifies the smaller topic of interest that falls under the heading
Caption	HAIR Did you know that people shed up to a hundred hairs a day? Examining a single hair can tell scientists a lot about...	Notes what the photo is about in the text
Diagram	Great Moments in Forensic Sci	An image that often sums up several sentences through an organizer such as a flow chart or Venn diagram
Bold-face words	The science of **toxicology** is developed by Spanish chemist Mattieu Ortila.	Words that appear bold are important words to know and understand
Glossary	**Glossary** arsonist Someone who lights fires cast a mould made...	At the back of the book, where you can find the meanings to bold words

Lesson 2—Characteristics of Living Things

"How are living things related to one another?" is the inquiry question for this topic; the thinking skill is "determining importance" and the "magnet strategy" (a strategy for determining importance) is introduced. This strategy is adapted from the work of Doug Buehl (2009). By modelling and gradually releasing the strategy, the teacher gives students an opportunity to see this thinking skill in use. Although the goal is for students to find and develop strategies of their own, introducing one method offers students both an example and a tool that they can later select, use, and adapt. We like to have two teachers in the classroom when we introduce a new strategy. Leyton co-taught this lesson with Nicole in year one; Nicole co-taught this lesson with Lori in year two.

Connect

- Introduce the unit to the class by asking them to think about what living things are. Record some of their thoughts on the board.
- Ask students to individually record their thoughts about: *How are living things related to one another?* or *What do all living things have in common?* Encourage students to make a "best guess" because you value their current understandings.
- After students have had enough time to record their own thinking, ask them to work in partners to interview each other about their responses, using the questions: *What do you know?* and *How do you know this?* Have the interviewing student use a web to record their partner's thinking.
- Ask students to share some of their partner's ideas with the rest of the class.

Process

- Ask students to look at a text related to the qualities of living things. Nicole and Leyton used pages 6 and 7 from *BC Science Probe 6* (Doyle, Bowman, and Vissers 2005).
- Ask them to notice natural paragraph chunks on these pages. Display these two pages. Use a think-aloud to model for students what you notice about these two pages.
- Note explicitly how there are small chunks to work with when looking for main idea and details.
- Introduce the "magnet strategy." Provide students with an organizer like Figure 7.6A and sticky notes. Ask students what they know about magnets. Share or demonstrate two magnets attracting each other.
- Mark paragraph chunks of the text shown on screen. Model the magnet strategy with the first paragraph.

- Read the chunk aloud and ask the students to find one word that they think is the most important. This word becomes the magnet word that they record in the centre of their sticky note. It is important to note at this point that students may not choose the same magnet word, and this is okay.
- Reread the paragraph and ask the students to look for 4 to 6 important words that attract to the magnet word, and to record those around the magnet word on their sticky note.
- Next, ask the students to review what they wrote and create a simple sentence that uses all the words on the sticky note. The students have just found the main idea and details to that chunk and summarized it. Students can copy your model.
- Continue to model the same approach with the next paragraph..
- Then, ask students to work on paragraphs 3 and 4 with a partner, while you move around the room and facilitate their work, as needed. See Figure 7.6B as a student example.

Figure 7.6A Graphic organizer for magnet notes

Characteristics of Living Things

Connect	Interview Questions:
	What are the characteristics of living things? OR
	What do all living things have in common? (Use your best guess, if you are not sure.)
	Use a web to record what you learned from your interview with your partner.

Process	Chunk 1 Paragraph Heading:
	Chunk 2 Paragraph Heading:

Characteristics of Living Things

Process	Chunk 3 Paragraph Heading:
	Chunk 4 Paragraph Heading:

Transform/ Personalize	Show what's important to know about the characteristics of living things though drama (i.e., bableau, dialogue, series of images, hot seat, etc.)
	A. Our Plan
	A. Reflect on your performance

Figure 7.6B Student sample of magnet notes

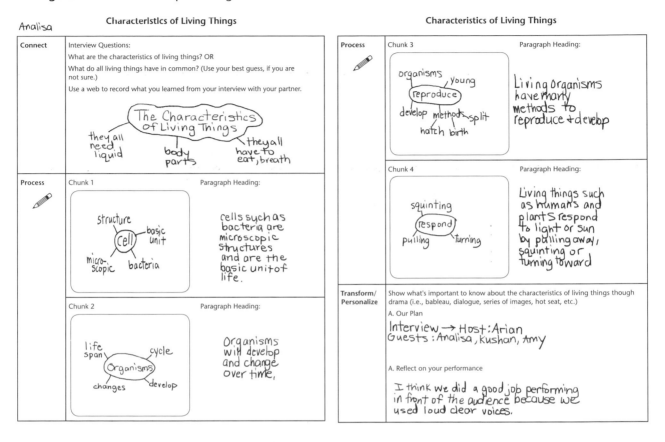

Transform/Personalize

- Have students work in groups to show through dramatic processes what's important about the characteristics of living things. Nicole's class had already been introduced to Tableau, a series of images, and Hot Seat as examples of dramatization from which they could choose.

- Using their magnet notes to aid their thinking, students drafted a plan on paper.

- After the groups have practised and presented their work, ask each person in the group to reflect on the performance. Suggest that they might include what they want you to notice about their performance or what they noticed about other group performances (see Figure 7.7).

Figure 7.7 Example of student dramatization

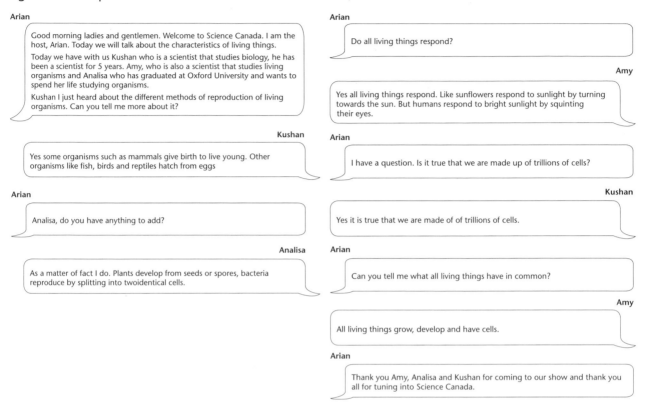

Arian

> Good morning ladies and gentlemen. Welcome to Science Canada. I am the host, Arian. Today we will talk about the characteristics of living things.
>
> Today we have with us Kushan who is a scientist that studies biology, he has been a scientist for 5 years. Amy, who is also a scientist that studies living organisms and Analisa who has graduated at Oxford University and wants to spend her life studying organisms.
>
> Kushan I just heard about the different methods of reproduction of living organisms. Can you tell me more about it?

Kushan

> Yes some organisms such as mammals give birth to live young. Other organisms like fish, birds and reptiles hatch from eggs

Arian

> Analisa, do you have anything to add?

Analisa

> As a matter of fact I do. Plants develop from seeds or spores, bacteria reproduce by splitting into twoidentical cells.

Arian

> Do all living things respond?

Amy

> Yes all living things respond. Like sunflowers respond to sunlight by turning towards the sun. But humans respond to bright sunlight by squinting their eyes.

Arian

> I have a question. Is it true that we are made up of trillions of cells?

Kushan

> Yes it is true that we are made of of trillions of cells.

Arian

> Can you tell me what all living things have in common?

Amy

> All living things grow, develop and have cells.

Arian

> Thank you Amy, Analisa and Kushan for coming to our show and thank you all for tuning into Science Canada.

Lesson 3—Wonder Books

"Wonder books" is a strategy that Nicole and Leyton have adapted from *Strategies that Work: Teaching Comprehension to Enhance Understanding* by Stephanie Harvey and Anne Goudvis (2000). They provide students in the middle years with mini-booklets in which to record any questions they have during a unit. This strategy helps students devise their own inquiry questions and sets the stage for expanding their own thinking later in the unit. Once a week or so, the class discusses what they have been wondering about, what they have learned so far in response to these questions, and what new questions are emerging. The page set-up is shown in Figure 7.8. Provide time to record questions and remind students to use their books.

Figure 7.8 Wonder book format

What I Wonder	Where I Can Find the Information	What I've Learned and/or New Questions that I have

Lesson 4—The Needs of Living Things

The inquiry question for this lesson—*What do living things need to survive?*—builds on both the content and the thinking skills of the previous lesson. The strategy emphasized continues to be "determining importance," but students are introduced to a second strategy for determining importance—two column notes, and images are used as the visual modality to help students connect to and process content.

Connect

- Collect a variety of images of living things in their natural surroundings to display for and discuss with your students.
- Ask:
  - *What might each photo represent about what living things need to survive?*
  Again suggest that making a best guess is okay for now.
- Encourage students to talk with partners during this stage, then report back to the class.
- In preparation for the personalizing activity, use images from your collection to prepare a model response on a copy of the 2-page graphic organizer, or template (Figure 7.9A).

Process

- Nicole and Leyton used pages 8 and 9 in *BC Science Probe 6* to have students examine images and related text.
- Whether using this or a different text, ask students to examine an image and its neighbouring paragraph.
- After reading the paragraph, ask students to come up with one key word to identify the "need" represented by the photo and three supporting points from the text.
- Have students work in pairs to identify at least three needs and related details.
- Share out. Students should come up with terms like *water, oxygen, habitat, food,* and *light.* The variety of terms offered can lead to excellent discussion about the needs of living things.

Transform/Personalize

- Provide a variety of resources (books, magazines, Internet access) for students to look for images that show what humans need to survive.
- Distribute copies of the template entitled "The Needs of Living Things" (Figure 7.9A) for the students. Then discuss your model with students, asking for their suggestions about how they might choose to demonstrate what they have learned in this lesson. Figure 7.9B represents how one student, Belinda, used the organizer and images from her research.

Figure 7.9A Graphic organizer, page 1

The Needs of Living Things

Connect	Look at the following images. In your opinion, what need does each photo represent for what living things need in order to survive? (Use your best guess if you are not sure.)

Process	Image/Need	3 key points from the text

© Portage & Main Press, 2011, *It's All About Thinking: Mathematics & Science*, BLM, ISBN: 978-1-55379-269-7

Figure 7.9A Graphic organizer, page 2

The Needs of Living Things

Process	Image/Need	3 key points from the text
Transform/ Personalize	Find images by looking at a variety of resources (books, magazines, internet) to show what humans need to survive. Cut and paste your images below or draw them.	

Figure 7.9B Student work using graphic organizer, page 1

Belinda

The Needs of Living Things

Connect	Look at the following images. In your opinion, what need does each photo represent for what living things need in order to survive? (Use your best guess if you are not sure.)

water

air

habitat

nutrients & energy

Process	Image/Need	3 key points from the text
	Nutrients & energy	−Need to keep healthy and grow −Found in soil and food −Need to grow, develop and reproduce
	Water	−Main ingredient of cells of all living things −Humans made of 2/3 water −Without water you can only live for a few days

Figure 7.9B Student work using graphic organizer, page 2

The Needs of Living Things

Process	Image/Need	3 key points from the text
	Oxygen	- get oxygen from air - get oxygen from water (fish) - carbon dioxide, water, sunlight, food, oxygen (plants)
	Habitat	- has living place and right conditions - shares a habitat - habitat provides energy/ nutrition, water, air, temperature
Transform/ Personalize	Look through a variety of resources (books, magazines, internet) to find images that show what humans need to survive. Cut and paste your images below, or draw them.	

Earth

Food

Oxygen

Habitat

Sleep

zzzz

Water

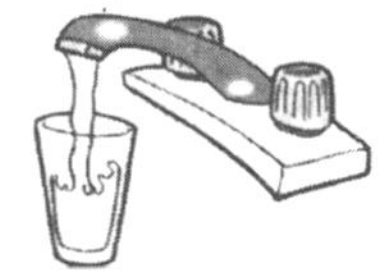

Lesson 5—Thinking Like a Biologist

The lesson inquiry question—*How can we use tools to observe and better understand living things in our world?*—invites students to explore and identify how a microscope can be used to learn about living things. The focus is on process in this lesson, that is, making and recording observations, asking relevant questions, and formulating a principle or hypothesis. By the end of the lesson, students are involved in developing the criteria for what biologists might value when making, recording, and sharing their observations.

Connect

- Introduce microscopes at this point, but first hold up an object (sugar, cork, carrot, hair, ditch water) that students will be analyzing under the microscope and ask them what they will have to do to analyze the parts of the object. Encourage discussion within their desk groupings.
- Ask students to choose one person per group to share what the group decided.

Process

- PART I: Provide students with the parts of the microscope sheet (Figure 7.10B) and label it together. Ask students to think about how these parts are going to help them learn to use a microscope. Partners can discuss this and record it on their organizer. Have pairs report back to the group.
- PART II: Demonstrate how to use a microscope. Then, have students choose 4 of the objects to examine under the microscope, draw them, and label their findings.
- This is often the students' first experience with a microscope and with drawing and labelling observations. If so, stop at various points during the lesson, and discuss what and how the students are drawing. However, do not teach a "right" way.
- PART III: After the class has had a chance to use the microscopes and become more familiar with them, ask students to help generate criteria for a Thinking Like

Figure 7.10A

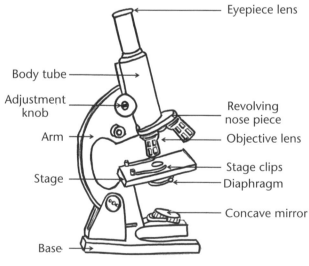

Eyepiece lens

Body tube

Adjustment knob

Arm

Stage

Base

Revolving nose piece

Objective lens

Stage clips

Diaphragm

Concave mirror

Figure 7.10B The compound microscope

The Compound Microscope

a Biologist organizer. Build these criteria into a rubric, useful for students in determining what works in their note-taking and what's next. Set out a table with 4 stages across the top and two stages down the left side like Figure 7.11, an example of a completed table of criteria (a rubric), compiled by one of our classes.

- The process just described is complex and requires practice. Nicole, Lori, and Leyton worked with their students to create the You Did It column first, because this is what they want all students to aim for, recognizing that some will exceed. Once these achievements are clear, the other columns can be described. As students describe each aspect, record their thinking on the overhead. The final rubric with all four columns can be used to give descriptive feedback to the students as they work, and later to provide a summative assessment.

Figure 7.11 Class-generated criteria for assessing Thinking like a Biologist

	Not Quite Yet (2)	Good Start (3)	You did it! (4)	Wow! (5)
Information *relevant *accurate *key/important	Rarely uses microscopes and equipment accurately Shares very few and/or inaccurate observations and/or questions in discussions or writing Records some data; may be inaccurate or missing key information	Sometimes uses microscopes and equipment accurately Notices observations but may be vague or lack key details; asks yes/no questions Data is generally accurate; diagrams include labels and some details	Uses microscope and equipment with accuracy Makes descriptive and accurate observations (spoken/and written) and asks relevent questions Records data accurately; diagrams include relevent labels and details	Uses microscopes and equipment with precision Makes descriptive and insightful observations (i.e., notes relationships) and asks relevent questions that show an understanding of key ideas Records data accurately; diagrams include relevent labels and key details
Thinking Process *logical inferences *explanation *understands concept *clear	Does not attempt to formulate a "law"	Proposes a "law" that is not yet fully developed	Formulates a "law" that is clear and logical	Formulates a "law" that is clear and logical; uses evidence to justify it

Transform/Personalize

- After students have viewed their organisms and captured them in an image, ask them to devise a rule, law, or principle that would show their understanding of the use of a microscope.
- Be prepared for this task to challenge your students, and scaffold their search by reminding them of other rules and principles they know, such as those in math.
- Ask students to bring something in that they, their family, or someone they know uses to classify and understand things in the world. Nicole's examples were an agenda to organize her time and a utensil tray to organize her forks, spoons, and knives at home.

Lesson 6—How Scientists Classify Living Things

The inquiry question is: How does the way things are classified help us to learn about them? In this lesson, we emphasize main idea and detail, using mind-mapping as a strategy for categorizing.

Have students get organized in a circle, then ask each student to share their object used for classifying and understanding things in the world. After the class has finished sharing, ask students to create a mind map (a web with categories) grouping the kinds of objects brought and described by their peers and naming the categories in which they can be classified (Figure 7.12) .

Connect

- Ask students to discuss in partners what scientists do to examine similarities and differences between organisms. Ask them to record their thoughts and report back.
- Encourage students to add ideas to their list when others share back.
- Encourage partner talk and allow time for a report back.

Process

- PART I: Offer students reading material related to plant and animal cells. Nicole and Leyton used page 28 in the Nelson science text. Ask them to use the magnet strategy to identify the main ideas and details about unicellular and multicellular organisms. Encourage them to do unicellular organisms with a partner and multicellular organisms on their own. Ask them to create a sentence summary for each. Model this. Share sentence summaries in a whip-around.
- PART II: Have students now look for information about the similarities and differences between plant and animal cells. Demonstrate how to record 2-3 similarities and differences on the Venn diagram. Have students finish independently.

Figure 7.12 Student mind map of how things are classified

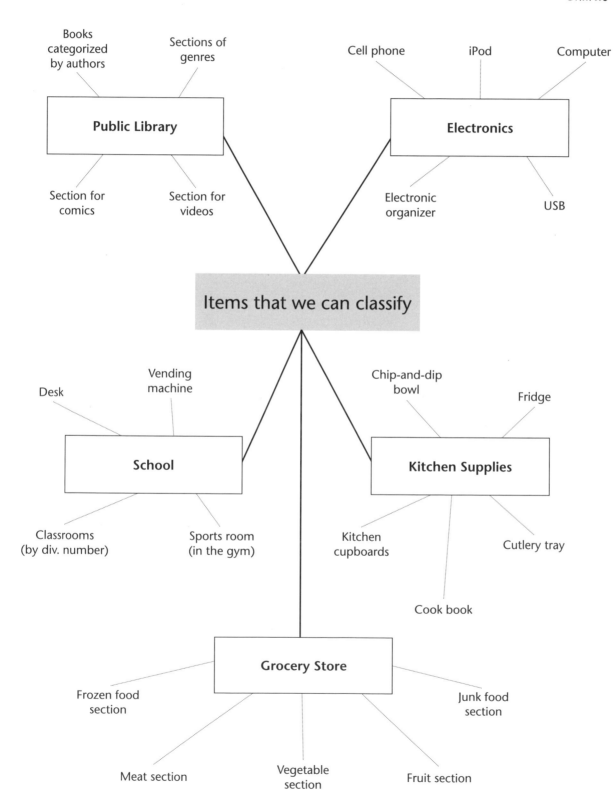

Charlie

- Encourage partner talk and allow time for a report back. Record student thinking on a master Venn diagram. Master sheets completed by the teacher to summarize the class's thinking can always be used as support for notes for students who need them—due to absences, learning English, or a challenge with written output.

Transform/Personalize

- PART I: In groups, ask students to discuss and record how they believe biologists classify living things, by using their discoveries in class to date.
- Ask groups to report back; record their thinking on a master chart.
- PART II: Students will soon be choosing an organism that they wish to study in more depth as part of an inquiry project. To prepare for this, ask students to think about how they might use what they've learned so far to do research and present information to others.
- Ask students to use 5 to 7 minutes of quiet think time on their own to formulate where they might decide to go with this project. Then encourage talk to expand individual thinking.

Lesson 7—Five Kingdoms Model

The inquiry question is—*How does the way organisms are classified help us learn about them?* We want students to learn that organisms are classified by qualities that they have in common. These classifications build on the information of the last several lessons. This is the last lesson where all students work with a single text to build background knowledge. Within two lessons, students will be forming opinions in order to write persuasive pieces about living organisms. In this lesson, reciprocal teaching helps students summarize, clarify, and ask questions as they read together.

Connect

- Ask students to privately record their thinking about the different ways that we can categorize living things. Then ask 3 or 4 students to share with the class.

Process

- Have students choose a partner, then provide them with textual information about how organisms are classified into kingdoms. Nicole, Lori, and Leyton used page 30 in the *Science Probe 6* textbook.
- Ask students to divide the text into sections for note-making. Sections are not usually more than two or three paragraphs.
- Introduce the reciprocal teaching strategy where students summarize, clarify, and ask questions as they read together.

- Partner One reads the first chunk of text, then explains it to Partner Two, saying what he thinks the big idea is and why (summarizing).
- Partner One asks "Did I miss anything?" (clarifying)
- Then one partner asks the other, "What are the most important details?" Students are invited to record their notes in any way that works for them as they are now familiar with magnet notes, two-column notes, webs, and mind maps.
- The process is repeated with Partner Two reading the next chunk of text and Partner One clarifying.
- Finally, each pair adds any new questions to their Wonder books as part of the question stage of reciprocal teaching.

Transform/Personalize

- Allow students some reflection time to think about which kingdom they are most interested in, remembering that each kingdom has subcategories.
- Then ask them to privately record one organism or kingdom that interests them, explain why, and show a representation of it.
- You may want to model this first by describing a kingdom of interest to you.
- Encourage them to talk and share ideas.

Lesson 8—Five Kingdoms Project

This activity provides students with an opportunity to choose how to apply what they have been learning about classification and living things. Making a choice tends to have students engage with, personalize, and synthesize content at a more sophisticated level. We ask the question "How can scientists work together effectively?" to engage students in a conversation about collaboration and group work, both of which are highly valued skills in scientific communities.

- Provide students with a copy of the assignment (Figure 7.13). Talk to them about the task, about how to "unpack" the assignment, and about what they have to do.
- Discuss the rubric in Figure 7.14. It is an example of a class-generated rubric, which can be used in other classes. Alternatively, generate a new rubric with your students before they prepare their projects. The rubric can be used to guide their work and help inform their learning. This is a group project, so each group of students will have to develop a plan.
- Figure 7.15 is a student example of a Five Kingdoms Project.

The Five Kingdoms Team Project

Your Task	To create or design a team poster, game, skit, comic strip, rap song or _____ to explain the Five Kingdoms
How?	Read pages 34–45 (omit pages 38 & 41) from your textbook. You may also want to use *The Tree of Life: The Incredible Biodiversity of Life on Earth* by Rochelle Strauss (2004) and other resources to help you gather your information.
	Divide the work among your team members.
	Make a plan to show how you will divide the work up within your table group. (Complete the chart [Figure 7.14] on the back of this page.)
	Remember: TEAM WORK! TEAM WORK!

For each of the five kingdoms, use the following questions and instructions to plan your project:

1. What specific details do scientists use to place an organism in this kingdom?

2. How do scientists divide up organisms in this kingdom?
   Find a way to show what this looks like or how this is done.

3. Use the criteria that we created together to check if you have all of the information that you need.

4. Practise for your presentation.

Figure 7.14 Class-generated criteria for Five Kingdoms Project

The Five Kingdoms Team Project

Our Team Name: _____

Member's job	What to do	How to do it	When to do it by
Name:			
Name:			
Name:			
Name:			
Name:			

Comments: _____

_____

_____

_____

© Portage & Main Press, 2011, *It's All About Thinking: Mathematics & Science*, BLM, ISBN: 978-1-55379-269-7

Figure 7.15 Example of one student group's Five Kingdoms Project

Lesson 9—Persuasive Essay: Protecting Living Things

Having built background knowledge related to the diversity of living things, we wanted to explore some of the students' questions from their Wonder books. During both years that we taught this unit, students had questions about ecosystems and sustainability. The next several lessons gave us an opportunity to explore our final big idea—humanity's relationship to and responsibility for ecosystems.

Connect

- Form an opinion line based on the statement or question—*Governments should pass laws to protect living things* or *Should humans be able to alter the world of living things?*
- Ask those who strongly agree (SA) to stand in a group in one corner of the room while those who strongly disagree (SD) group in the opposite corner of the room. The students who are not sure, are undecided (UD) or are in-between can then place themselves anywhere between the two corners. There are no wrong answers.

- Have students share their ideas and thinking to defend their place on the line. Teacher in role of a reporter holds a "microphone" up to students so that they will project their voices (use highlighter pen for a microphone).
- Ensure that the students recognize that they are building an argument to convince the other side why their point of view is a good one.
- Share the experiences of most students who placed themselves in the strongly agree zone. Figure 7.16 captures the opinions of one class.

Figure 7.16 Class opinions on statement

Opinion Line

Governments should pass laws to protect living things.

What they said:

Rebecca: (SA) "Living things have a right to be free."

Caterina: (SA) "We shouldn't kill animals which might kill a species."

Angela: (UD) "If you don't cut down trees we won't have furnitures."

Tony: (UD) ESL 2 "Some countries, they kill a lot but still have a lot and still have to protect."

Karina: (SA) "If we chop down trees to make houses and furniture it is affecting us because trees produce oxygen and we can't live without oxygen.

Alan: (SA) "We need to protect all animals, it's like killing all of us."

Betsy: (SA) "We shouldn't have zoos because animals need freedom too."

Brian: (SA) "Gov't. should protect living things because living things are already decreasing & if they keep decreasing there won't be anymore."

Angelica: (A) "If we lose part of living things, you lose food, so laws should be limited."

Arian: (SWA/UD) "…we cut down so many trees we should only cut 50% of what we usually do."

Kushan: (SA) "If we kill trees then animals don't have a habitat & they will be homeless."

Tiffany: (SA) "…because animals are getting lesser and lesser."

Joshua: (SWA/UD) "Like the bald eagles are almost extinct & the more the trees get cut down our community won't be the same."

Legend:
SD: Strongly Disagree   UD: Undecided   SA: Strongly Agree
SWD: Somewhat Disagree   SWA: Somewhat Agree
D: Disagree   A: Agree

- Introduce the idea that, in order to persuade someone to adopt your point of view, you need to back up your ideas with evidence or some form of proof.
- Have the class read two pieces that show different sides of an issue.
- Use the overhead to share the two pieces, one For and one Against. Lori used two pieces from *Should there be zoos?* by T. Stead (2000).

Transform/Personalize

- Have students work in groups to discuss what they notice about the two pieces and record what persuasive writing looks like, sounds like, feels like. Share out their responses in the class. Figure 7.17 is a sample of one class's list of qualities.

Figure 7.17 Qualities of Persuasive Writing

What Does a Good Piece of Writing Look Like?

Look like?	Feel like?	Sound like?
· Text features	· Convincing	· Written in 3rd person
· Visuals (photos, graphics)	· Honest	· Uses specific words
· An opening statement to capture the reader's attention	· Personal thoughts/ experiences	· Stays on topic
· A hook to keep the reader's attention	· Exciting writing	· Convincing
· An opening quote	· Questions that make you think	· Research has been done
· Asks questions and provides answers	· Entertaining but stays on topic	· Written in own words
· Research has been done	· Team work	· True facts
· Facts/data		· Catchy words
· Previous knowledge		· Accurate information
· Written in own words		· Persuasive
· Incorporated text features		· Sophisticated and detailed
· Ending statement/ concluding the topic		· Honest
· Gives examples		· Questions were answered
· Sentence variety		· Peoples' opinions based on research/ facts
		· Connecting words (for example, additionally, as you can see, however)

Lesson 10 — Seeing All Sides

- We want students to look at issues from more than one perspective. At the same time, taking one side can help them to research and write with purpose and passion. This lesson helps them to do both.

Connect

- Lori asked her students to take a minute to think about how they felt about the statement: Governments should pass laws to protect living things.
- Review the attributes of persuasive writing, and invite students to take a side on the issue of whether or not governments should have laws to protect living things.
- Ask them to write down whether they strongly agreed, agreed, were undecided, disagreed, or strongly disagreed. Figure 7.18 provides a graphic organizer for students to record their thinking.

Process

- Brainstorm examples that might have people on both sides of the issues; for example, a local bog, a new housing development, bodies of water where ships carry possible pollutants in their cargo.
- Record the possibilities and encourage students to think from both sides of an issue.

Transform/Personalize

- Ask students to record what they know, then brainstorm what they still have to find out.

Lesson 11 — Supporting a Point of View

We like to spend one to three periods in the library collecting information. By the time they are working on this lesson, students have learned several note-making strategies. Still, a graphic organizer supports students when collecting their ideas. Students are not required to synthesize information in this way, but some students need and like this kind of support. Another way to provide more support is to locate shorter pieces of engaging texts ahead of time. There are many issue-based texts on the National Geographic Kids website <kids.nationalgeographic.com/kids/> and that of the National Geographic Explorer <magma.nationalgeographic.com/ngexplorer/index.html>, and the writing offers a range of reading levels. Other online resources like Boldprint <www.boldprintbooks.com/> focus on issues in two or three pages of text and include a lot of visual elements.

Figure 7.18 Student organizer for thoughts and facts about living things

Thinking about Living Things

Connect	Take a minute to think about how you feel about the statement below. There is no wrong answer. What makes you feel this way? **Governments should pass laws to protect living things.**
	I strongly agree. I agree. I am undecided. I disagree. I strongly disagree.
	I feel this way because …

Process	I know...	My Evidence...	What I need to know...	How do I find out?

Connect

- Invite students to form groups of two or three—or you may want to organize groups ahead of time. These groups are to look for examples of why a government should or should not create laws to protect living things.
- Ask groups to make a plan about how they will collect information.
- Have groups share their plan with another group to give each other more ideas.

Process

- Review Figure 7.19 and offer it as a way for students to collect information from a resource. Some groups will get through several resources while others tackle only one or two.

Figure 7.19 Student organizer for supporting a point of view

Examples used to prove my point

	Evidence: What's important (quotes, pg #'s, facts, etc.)	Why is this important? OR How does this support my point of view?	So what does this make me think of or wonder about?	Next Steps ...
Source #1				

Transform/Personalize

- Ask groups to take a side on the issue. Then ask them to brainstorm what the other side might say and how they could respond. Figure 7.20 can help students organize this information.

Figure 7.20 Organizer for considering another point of view

What might someone say to disagree with me?	What will my answer be?
✓	✓
★	★
→	→

Lesson 12—Rationale

We have found it helpful to have guest speakers come into class to show the less popular side of an issue. An outside point of view helps students consider another perspective and bolsters those students who have taken the "road less travelled." Students often decide, after this lesson, to switch perspectives in order to stretch their viewpoint. Inviting someone in also introduces students to new resources. Ask the guest to bring brochures, newspaper articles, YouTube clips, and personal vignettes. Finally, this is a chance to have students practise the thinking skills that you have been targeting: determining importance, asking questions, taking multiple perspectives, and note-making.

Connect

- Have students share with a partner what was most helpful from the last class, what they have learned about the issue, and what they still want to find out.

Process

- Invite a guest speaker. Our speaker was Rosalind Poon, our district science helping teacher. She gave her presentation in four chunks. She took the Against stand on our statement: Governments should pass laws to protect living things. For each chunk, she gave some information and showed a visual, then stopped.
- Have students use the magnet strategy to record the main idea and supporting details. Figure 7.21 is our recording form..

Transform/Personalize

- Ask students to write a paragraph to their research partners summarizing what they learned from the guest speaker and how it relates to their research so far.

Lesson 13—Rationale

Connect

- Ask students to share with a partner what was most helpful from the last class and how it relates to the persuasive piece they are working on.

Process

- Invite a second speaker.
- Our second guest speaker was a colleague, Kevin Lyseng, who took the position For. Kevin made his presentation in three chunks, and provided us with information and some articles.
- The students used the graphic organizer, Figure 7.22, during his presentation. After each chunk, the speaker stopped so students could record the main idea and supporting details. If your students so choose, they could use the magnet strategy or any other note-making strategy they have learned, rather than the strategy of Main Idea and Supporting Details.

Figure 7.21   Guest speaker notes, Magnet Strategy

Governments should pass laws to protect living things

Connect	Strongly Agree	Agree	Undecided	Disagree	Strongly Disagree
	Guest Speaker:				
Process	Chunk 1	Sentence:			
	Chunk 2	Sentence:			
	Chunk 3	Sentence:			
	Chunk 4	Sentence:			
Transform/ Personalize	Thinking about everything we have learned from our guest speaker, write a paragraph to our research partner about what you learned.				

Figure 7.22 Guest speaker notes, Main Idea and Supporting Details

Governments should pass laws to protect living things

Connect	Strongly Agree	Agree	Undecided	Disagree	Strongly Disagree
	Guest Speaker:				

Process	Main Idea	Supporting Details

Transform/ Personalize	Think about what we have learned from our guest speaker, and write a persuasive paragraph to someone who believes something different about the issue. You might want to think about the following: **What roles can we as individuals play to effect change?**

Transform/Personalize

- Ask students what would make a powerful persuasive paragraph. They might come up with criteria like these: a hook, an opening statement, and evidence or proof to back up statements or opinions.
- Ask them to review their notes and write a persuasive paragraph to someone who takes a different point of view, using what they have learned. If some students would like a prompt, suggest the topic: "What we can do as individuals to effect change."

Lesson 14—Rationale

Connect

- Have students share with a partner what was most helpful from the last class and how it relates to the persuasive piece they are working on.

Process

- Ask students to organize in small groups and complete reasons For and Against on a T-chart (modelled on Figure 7.23) to summarize what they have learned about why governments should pass laws to protect living things. This helps all students clarify their thinking
- For many students, it will be just at this point that they firm up a position and even an understanding of the issues.
- For students who have been clear about their position for some time, this sharpens their thinking and helps them to consider more sides of the debate.

Figure 7.23 T-Chart Summary for Issues

Governments should pass laws to protect living things.

Reasons for	Reasons against

Transform/Personalize

- Have small groups share their thinking in a large group while one teacher records/combines their thinking on a chart.
- This process fuels interesting discussions on what students agree or disagree with and helps them formulate or further clarify their thinking for their persuasive piece.

Lesson 15—Persuasive Writing and Beyond

Connect

- Have students choose partners and begin to plan their writing (title, hook, quote, paragraphs, graphics) and think about sentences—variety, length, questions/answers. Use the graphic organizer provided (Figure 7.24) to scaffold student thinking.

Process

- Students can write alone or in pairs—or trios, if this works for them.
- Meet with students around their draft.
  - Give descriptive feedback related to the headings in Figure 7.24.
  - Remind them to write, edit, write, edit, write, edit, proofread.
  - Have students share drafts with partners and then with other students in the class. Continue to use Figure 7.24. for peer feedback.

Transform/Personalize

- Share students' persuasive writing in large groups. Figure 7.26 is a student sample that was published in a local newspaper. Celebrate the students' writing.
- Provide time for the students to self-assess and reflect on their work (Figure 7.25).

Assessment of Learning

- Use the BC Performance Standards: Writing to Communicate Ideas <www.llbc.leg.bc.ca/public/pubdocs/bcdocs/357503/writeg6.pdf> for summative assessment.
- Reference the students' self-assessment and reflections on their work (Figure 7.25).

Figure 7.24 Graphic organizer for persuasive writing feedback

Writing is Thinking: Persuade 'Em

What is my point of view on the issue?	
Why do I think this is the most important thing for people to know? (the big idea)	What evidence will I use?
Hook the Reader	**Powerful Ending**
How will I begin? ☐ Question ☐ Quotation ☐ Story or example ☐ Wake-up call	How will I wrap things up? ☐ Circle back to the beginning ☐ Possible solution ☐ Restate and emphasize thesis ☐ Further questions to talk about
Mechanics	
Tight writing: ☐ Sophisticated language ☐ Sentence variety ☐ Transitional phrases	Ideas

© Portage & Main Press, 2011, *It's All About Thinking: Mathematics & Science*, BLM, ISBN: 978-1-55379-269-7

Figure 7.25 Organizer for students to reflect on persuasive writing

Persuasive Writing Reflections

Date: _____ Name: _____

Partner(s): _____

How did I contribute to our partnership? Did I do my share of the work? What was easy or difficult?

How well did my partner and I work together? Why?

What did I learn from working with a partner(s)?

Reflections:

What I noticed was...

What I did best was...

Goals: What might I do the same or differently next time?

© Portage & Main Press, 2011, *It's All About Thinking: Mathematics & Science*, BLM, ISBN: 978-1-55379-269-7

Figure 7.26 Student letter published

The Richmond News   June 27, 2008   **A11**

No New World to be had

The Editor,

Obviously, you do not have to think about it! Of course we have to protect living things. This is called conservation. Many living things in the whole world are getting extinct. Can you believe it? We really wish humans would do the right thing We should throw garbage in the garbage can, compost, use hybrid cars, recycle, stop factories from dumping bad contents in the rivers that will affect the fish, cut down less tress so the squirrels, birds and raccoons can live. If animals go extinct, this will affect our meat needs.

For example, if all salmon go extinct, what about the animals that eat salmon? They will probably go extinct too. Remember... if we lose our world, we cannot get a new one.

Gwen Tam and Katie Ngai
Both 11 years old
Richmond

Reflections

We have found that we can help our students to read, write, and think more like scientists. The focus on inquiry questions, scaffolding, and thinking skills has made this success possible for both students and teachers alike. The assessment cycle of using formative assessment to help guide instruction has made our teaching of skills more explicit.

We conducted our third PBA at the conclusion of this unit, and found that most students were fully meeting or exceeding expectations, and that the others were at least minimally meeting them. We believe our collaboration played a significant role in developing lessons that engaged and supported our learners. Involving students as meaning-makers and authors has shifted our science unit away from individual lessons that focus on teaching information and toward class investigations. Inquiry is at the heart of the discipline of science, and we find the students are particularly engaged when they are writing and sharing their persuasive pieces.

Being collaborative gave us confidence because science is a content-based subject requiring background knowledge that, like many elementary teachers, we do not have. Our three-way collaboration has increased our confidence in planning thoughtful and engaging science units. We now have a working framework. Finding ways to make new units engaging while also exploring key concepts to build thinking skills has now become a fun challenge!

Chapter 8

Authentic Research

Grade 10—Science

Assessment FOR Learning
- Learning intentions
- Descriptive feedback
- Self-assessment

Gradual Release of Responsibility
- Background information
- Internet searching
- Questioning

Inquiry
- Essential questions

Differentiation
- Diverse texts
- Collaborative teaching

Assessment OF Learning
- Research response logs
- Exit slips
- Brochure

The Collaboration

Kristi Johnston is a teacher-librarian in a suburban secondary school for grades 8 to 12. One of the roles that she enjoys most is collaborating with teachers to develop inquiry-based library research units. She believes that we need to reignite the curiosity of secondary school students and that the school library, where students are surrounded by a variety of resources, can spark a question that will eventually lead them to research.

Over the past couple of years, Kristi has collaborated with Tracy Snipstead, head of the English Department, on developing strategies for student research. They have been keenly interested in incorporating more assessment-for-learning strategies into their practice to improve student achievement. They began by devising inquiry questions and related learning intentions. They then revised a note-taking strategy that would help guide students as they refined their research skills. Tracy and Kristi believed this strategy would also reduce students' reliance on copying directly from their sources without acknowledgment—plagiarism, in a word. Many teachers had been hesitant to take their students into the library to complete a research assignment because they expected to receive only reports that were cut and pasted from websites that popped up on a Google search.

Tracy and Kristi believed that, if students had a clear understanding of the essential questions and the learning intentions, their content knowledge would improve. They implemented a note-taking strategy that required students to pose "thick questions" and interact with a variety of texts in order to find the answers. They found that their students, after researching their own questions, took more in-depth research notes, and began to develop critical research skills, multiple literacies, higher order thinking skills, and metacognitive behaviours. As a result, the students' final work was not just "click, cut, and paste." Instead, their research reports demonstrated deep thinking, reflection, and synthesis. At the end of each library day, Tracy and Kristi provided descriptive feedback on their students' research notes, and were very pleased with the positive impact their feedback had on the students' subsequent note-taking.

Kristi and Tracy shared their strategies with educators in other departments, and now the strategies have become common practice for library research in their whole school. This unit on biomes is a collaboration with Jeremy Ellis, who has been teaching junior science, physics, and computer programming for 20 years. Recently, Jeremy has been working to incorporate more assessment-for-learning strategies into his practice. Because this is Jeremy's first collaboration with Kristi on a research project, Kristi often takes the lead, modelling what she has learned and developed with Tracy and other teachers. It has become an "infectious" process, quietly rippling throughout the school and resulting in increased numbers of teachers and students researching in the library.

The Context

This chapter's focus on biomes—large areas of Earth that have characteristic climate, plants, animals, and soil—and how communities of flora and fauna adapt to particular climatic conditions began with Jeremy and Kristi having an initial chat in the photocopy room. Jeremy had heard from the Science 8 and 9 teachers about the research process in the library, and decided to introduce his class to inquiry-based research while incorporating AFL strategies. Kristi, who had been reading Jeffrey Wilhelm's book *Engaging Readers and Writers with Inquiry* (2007), was inspired to continue shifting her library research practice toward inquiry. She and Jeremy decided on two essential questions to direct the unit of study. From these questions, the students would develop personal questions to guide their research process.

Jeremy and Kristi wanted the students to write from a point of view that was authentic and relevant, which they believed would increase student ownership of the learning process. Because the essential questions centred on climate change, they wanted the students to take a stance and create a product that would be relevant to their lives. In one sense, the students would be addressing the question *Why should we care?* One of the prescribed learning outcomes (PLOs) in the Science 10 Integrated Resource Package (IRP) is scientific literacy; one of the achievement indicators is the capacity to explain how science and technology affect individuals, society, and the environment. Jeremy and Kristi decided that, for their end-of-unit assessment, the students should take the point of view of Greenpeace, and create a brochure to educate the public about the impact that temperatures continuing to increase and rainfall to decrease would have on their biome. Most importantly, they wanted the students to understand and explain the consequences if their biome ceased to exist.

Essential Questions

- How will a particular biome be affected if its temperature increases and its rainfall decreases?
- How will the world be affected if a particular biome ceases to exist?

Key Structures

Gradual Release of Responsibility

- Background knowledge development by science teacher
- Model and practise note-taking strategies using text features (bold headings, maps, diagrams, photographs, and captions)
- Internet searching
- Posing thick questions

Diverse Texts

- Science 10 textbooks
- Websites

- Variety of nonfiction books
- Specialized encyclopedias
- Videos

Assessment for Learning

- Content learning intentions (matched to the learning outcomes in the Science IRP)
- Research learning intentions (matched to the research continuum for grades 8 to 12)
- Descriptive feedback
- Self-assessment matched to learning intentions
- Exit slips

Assessment of Learning

- Research response logs
- Compelling brochure

The Planning Sessions

When a teacher wants to take a class into the library for research, Kristi arranges at least two planning sessions with the teacher to establish a framework for the research. These planning sessions are critical to the success of the unit because they ensure that adequate resources are available for the students and that the process of research does not turn into an exercise in plagiarism. To get ready for the planning sessions, Jeremy was asked to think about two things—the skills of his students and the end-of-unit project he wanted them to produce. In turn, Kristi familiarized herself with the Biomes section of the Science 10 IRP and reviewed the resources in the library, both print and non-print.

Planning Session #1

When planning for a collaborative unit, the tasks of the science teacher and the teacher-librarian are to:

- review the Science 10 IRP
- highlight the learning outcomes to be addressed while the students are in the library
- co-create content learning intentions based on the learning outcomes in the IRP
- identify and connect research learning intentions to the content learning intentions
- co-create essential questions, and consider what is important for students to know and understand by the end of the unit
- gather and review the print resources to ensure a sufficient variety to meet the needs of all the students

By the end of their first planning session, Kristi and Jeremy had established their essential questions and learning intentions in both the content area and the development of research skills. These essential questions and learning intentions will guide student learning throughout the research process.

Planning Session #2

- Revisit the essential questions and the learning intentions to make any necessary revisions.
- Teacher-librarian models the note-taking strategy for the science teacher so he, in turn, can model it with his class before the students come into the library.
- The two teachers together co-create the research criteria.
- They also design performance tasks for the culminating project, and consider how students can demonstrate their learning.

Brochure as Culminating Project (AOL)

Kristi and Jeremy decide that their students' culminating project should be the creation of a brochure, and they prepare the following instructions:

1. Create a compelling brochure.
2. Writing from the point of view of Greenpeace, clearly articulate why the survival of your biome is important to the rest of the world.

Figure 8.1 presents the research criteria and scoring guide co-created by Kristi and Jeremy during planning session #2. Then, during the first class in the library, they reviewed the details with Jeremy's students. Figure 8.2 is the template for a note-taking sheet on which the students can record their questions and their research.

Figure 8.A Inside cover page of student Research Folder

Essential Questions and Learning Intentions

Essential Questions

- How will a particular biome be affected if its temperature increases and its rainfall decreases?
- How will the world be affected if a particular biome ceases to exist?

Content Learning Intentions

- I can locate my biome on a map of the world.
- I can create a climate graph depicting rainfall and temperature.
- I can describe the physical features of my biome.
- I can describe one animal's adaptation to the biome.
- I can describe one plant's adaptation to the biome.
- I can explain the consequences of climate change on my biome.

Research Learning Intentions

- I am able to create a "thick" question from the main idea.
- I am able to find 3 to 5 supporting details for each question.
- I am able to use key words and to paraphrase ideas for my notes.
- I am able to use text features as a source of information.
- I am able to use valid sources.
- I am able to use several types of information sources.
- I am able to complete a bibliography.

© Portage & Main Press, 2011, *It's All About Thinking: Mathematics & Science*, BLM, ISBN: 978-1-55379-269-7

Figure 8.1 Sample structure for research criteria and scoring guide

Research Criteria and Scoring Guide

Research Criteria	Comments	Scoring Guide
Research Process · Writes up daily research log (Figure 8.3). · Selects relevant and reliable websites.		10
Note-Taking · Sets goal of 3 or 4 "thick" research questions per day. · Uses 5 to 7 key words and paraphrased ideas from research sources. · Confirms accuracy of information by checking more than one source. · Provides minimum of 3 supporting details to fully answer each question.		50
Reference List · Prepares initial list of possible sources/ resources as working document. · Assembles minimum of 4 sources/ resources per question. · Prepares and edits final reference list.		.20

Figure 8.2 Sample note-taking sheet

Note-Taking Sheet

Topic:	Date:
Question 1: Notes	
Question 2: Notes	

Library Day 1—Posing Questions

In each of the lessons in this unit, the role of lead teacher is shared, that is, the science teacher and the teacher-librarian alternate as lead teacher and take responsibility for moving the learning forward. The unit's essential questions, as the framework for the students' research, are addressed and reflected on during each library research session.

Materials

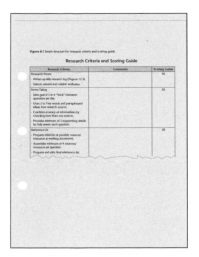

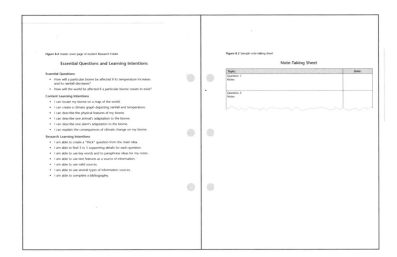

To introduce the research unit, prepare enough 3-hole punched research folders for the students in the class, and make sufficient copies of the materials listed below. During the first lesson for this unit of study, distribute the folders and copies and ask students to include them in their folder:

- As the cover, insert Figure 8.1 (Research Criteria and Scoring Guide).
- As the left page of the next 2-page spread, insert Figure 8.A, the Essential Questions and the two lists of learning intentions, both content and research.
- As the right page of the spread, insert the first blank template (Figure 8.2) of the Note-Taking Sheet.
- Provide students with sufficient copies of Figure 8.2 for the duration of their research.

Tell students that you want them to keep their research notes in these folders and hand them in at the end of each library day for your feedback.

Setting the Stage

- Introduce the unit by explaining and discussing the two essential questions, the content learning intentions, and the end-of-unit project for assessment.
- Lead a group discussion about the essential questions. Have the students brainstorm a list of possible answers to the questions.

- Pose the key question:
  - *Why should we care about the biomes of the world?*
- The most important word in this question is *care* because it establishes the relevance to students' lives. Their engagement with the research on a personal level will make their assignment more compelling than a simple report on the destruction of the rainforest.
- Encourage students to respond thoughtfully to the questions and to bring some of their prior knowledge to the discussion.
- To activate students' prior knowledge, have them choose a biome, then ask:
  - *What do you already know about your biome?*
  - *Record your ideas.*
- Help students connect with another classmate who is researching the same biome. Have them share their prior knowledge and add new ideas.
- Then, have students brainstorm in pairs to list the questions they hope to find answers to during their research.

Share and Compare

- Do a quick sharing session to allow students to hear others' ideas. Kristi and Jeremy call this "sharing and borrowing." As students share their questions, others may "borrow" one of their questions and add it to their list. Although the biomes that they study are different, the research questions can be the same or similar.

> **Supporting student learning**
>
> The process of having students brainstorm a list of questions before they start gives them a focus for their research. It is an effective confidence-builder because most students are able to brainstorm at least 10 questions before they even start looking at resources.

- During this sharing and borrowing session, review with the students the difference between "thick" questions and "thin" questions:
  - Thick questions require answers with at least three details in order to be considered a full answer.
  - Thin questions need only one-word answers.

  With each question ask: Thick or thin?
- One pair of students posed the following question: *Are there different kinds of grasslands?* The class decided that this was a thin question because it could be answered with either yes or no.
- The pair had to rephrase the question so that it could be answered by at least three research facts. Their revised question became three: "*What types of grasslands are found in the world? How are they alike? How are they different?*" Submitting this thick question to peer review led to much richer research.

> **Importance of feedback**
>
> The share-and-compare component of this lesson is critical. It reinforces the types of questions that the students should pose for their research. As students propose their questions, they get immediate feedback from their peers and their teachers, which helps them refine and focus the questions for their research.

- Students are more likely to engage with the main ideas of the lesson when they pose a thick question. Thick questions demand more thoughtful research and require students to make connections between ideas.

Connecting to the Learning Intentions

- Emphasize that the day's work has been focused on the following content learning intention: "I can describe the physical features of my biome."
- Add the following research learning intention: "I am able to create a thick question from the main idea."

Beginning the Research

- For work in the library, divide the class into two groups — one group will use the Internet for research, the other group will use the varied print sources.
- Review with the students the research criteria and the research learning intentions in their folders.
- Before the students begin their research, have them identify which content learning intentions they plan to work on and record them. Figure 8.3 is an example of a research log, another record that students should keep in their research folder. You might choose to make a template initially for this log and provide copies for students.

Figure 8.3 A sample research log

Research Log	Name:	
Day and Date	Content learning intention in focus today	Interesting facts or additional questions

Mini-Lesson on Evaluating Websites

Too often, those who research online do not take time to evaluate the information they find. As the teacher-librarian, Kristi wanted the students to develop as critical thinkers and readers, in particular of online informational text, and she taught them to subject a website to a set of criteria. Her lesson sequence went as follows:

- For this lesson, Kristi projected on screen some material from a website about the Pacific Northwest Tree Octopus, found at <zapatopi.net/treeoctopus/>. This website is actually a hoax about a fictitious endangered species; however, to most students, it looks on first glance like a credible website.

- Kristi asked the students first to look over all elements on the website, then, as a group, to consider the following questions for evaluating it:
    - *Who has put this information on the Web?*
    - *What is the expertise of the individual or group that created the site?*
    - *When was the site last updated?*
    - *Is the information believable?*
    - *Does the content appear to be fact or opinion?*
    - *Can the information be verified in books or other sources?*

To do this with your own class, you might choose a different website, but ask the same questions. Ask your students to share their thinking with a partner, then ask them to contribute their findings in a whole-class discussion. Focus the conversation on the notion of the validity of this website as a source of information. Emphasize that appearances do not necessarily tell the whole story. As a point of future reference, students might be interested in a website such as <www.snopes.com/> as a source for verifying "incredible" stories.

A WINDOW IN: What the students did

Through the discussion of these questions, Kristi's and Jeremy's students realized that the site was a hoax. Although it had all the components of a valid website and it looked real, the information contained in it was false.

Students were surprised that a website like this was on the Internet at all. Many asked, "Why would someone put a fake website on the Internet?" Kristi's response was: "Because they can. Anyone can publish on the Internet, much more easily than publishing a book. There are no common criteria for publishing on the Web." Students must recognize that skepticism, too, is an "essential understanding" for becoming a critical reader of websites.

Connecting to the Learning Intentions
Note with the students that the day's work has been focused on the following content learning intentions:

- I can locate my biome on a map of the world.
- I can describe the physical features of my biome.
- I can explain the consequences of climate change on my biome.

Add the following research learning intentions:

- I am able to create a thick question from the main idea.
- I am able to check for valid sources.
- I am able to use several types of information sources.

Assessment for Learning

- At the end of the class, have students fill out their research log by writing down an interesting fact they learned or a question that arose from their research. Doing so serves as their exit slip for the day.

- Ensure that students leave their research folders for your review as they leave the library.
- As you review your students' research logs and questions, put a checkmark in the "Interesting facts or additional questions" column if the students have filled out their research log thoughtfully.
- Using the "Research criteria and scoring guide," review your students' note-taking. Put a check mark beside the work that meets any criteria, and highlight the criteria they missed.

From Assessment to Instruction

Use this information gained from the review of students' research folders to frame the lesson for the next class. Consider the following in planning:

1. *What are students doing well?*
   - Begin the next class by giving them positive feedback.

2. *What are students struggling with?*
   - Identify areas of concern within the whole class as well as for individual students.

3. *What can we plan to address these concerns?*
   - The answer to this question can form the mini-lesson for the next day.

Library Day 2

When the students return to the library for their next research class, explain the coding system used for your descriptive feedback in their research folders. Explain that a checkmark says: "*Thumbs up — you are meeting the criteria for note-taking.*" A highlight says: "*You are not meeting this particular criterion. I am drawing your attention to a skill you need to work on and improve.*"

- Remind students to compare their highlighted notes against the criteria and try to revise them. By doing so, they learn to monitor their own learning, keeping in mind the set of learning intentions. Figure 8.4 is a sample of Maddi's research. Notice that she is struggling with two items — using only 5 to 7 key words as notes, and paraphrasing ideas embedded in longer sentences or descriptions.

Figure 8.4 Highlighted criteria in Maddi's research record

Name: Maddi

Biomes Research Assignment

Biome: Grasslands

Research Process · Research Logs · Relevant and Reliable websites have been chosen		10
Note Taking ✓ · 3–4 "thick" research questions per day ✓ · Minimum of 3 supporting details under each question · 5–7 key words and paraphrases ideas are consistently used ✓ · Information is accurate ✓ · Supporting details thoroughly answer each question		50
Bibliography · Working Bibliography · Minimum of 4 sources · Final Bibliography follows APA style		20
Final Product · Brochure		50

Mini-Lesson: Note-Taking

After the first research session, Kristi and Jeremy noticed a trend in their feedback on the students' note-taking in their research folders—most were not picking out key words as supporting details, nor were they paraphrasing ideas. After pointing this out to the class, Kristi and Jeremy invited the students to review their marked pages and assess to what degree this was true for their own work. Then, the teachers again modelled how to make notes, using the research criteria for note-taking: "minimum of 3 supporting details" and "5 to 7 key words and paraphrased ideas." They prepared the following teaching notes for a mini-lesson on note-taking:

- Present an example of a thick question (one that requires several responses):

    What are the physical features of tropical grasslands?
    - The land in tropical grasslands is mainly flat.
    - The soil in tropical grasslands is less rich because nutrients are removed by heavy rains.
    - In hot tropical grasslands, grass fires are common.

- Ask the students to give some feedback on the answers to this question, by referring to the note-taking criteria on the front of their folders. *Students will notice that answer notes are longer than 5 to 7 key words.*

- Ask students which words in the responses are not essential. As they answer, cross the words out, as follows:
    - ~~The~~ land ~~in tropical grasslands~~ is mainly flat.
    - ~~The~~ soil ~~in tropical grasslands~~ is less rich ~~because~~ nutrients ~~are~~ removed by heavy rains.
    - ~~In hot tropical grasslands~~ grass fires are common.

- Have students turn to their own sheets and review their notes to reduce full sentences to key words by crossing out non-essential words. Encourage students to use this note-taking strategy for each day's research (see Figure 8.5).

Figure 8.5 Maddi's edited notes, key-word responses to research questions

Grassland (Temperate and Tropical)

Biomes

Question #1 Where are Grasslands located?

- ☐ ~~found~~ above 23.5° north latitude (Temperate)
- ☐ ~~found~~ below 23.5 South latitude (Temperate)
- ☐ ~~found from~~ 5° to 20° north and south of equator (Tropical)
- ☐ ~~called~~ Prairies in North America
- ☐ ~~called~~ Savannas in Africa, South America, northern Australia

Question #2 What is the climate of Grasslands?

- ☐ Precipitation 25cm - 100 cm annually (Temperate)
- ☐ ~~hot~~ summers of 30°C ~~and cold~~ winters ~~below~~ -10°C   (temperate)
- ☐ Precipitation 50cm - 130cm annually (Tropical)
- ☐ daily temperatures 20°C to 30°C (Tropical)
- ☐

Question #3 What are the physical features of Grasslands?

- ☐ land mainly flat, ~~is~~ (temperate and tropical)
- ☐ Soil ~~is~~ rich ~~and~~ fertile ~~in~~ (temperate ~~grasslands~~)
- ☐ nutrients removed by heavy rain ~~in~~ tropical ~~grasslands~~
- ☐ Precipitation ~~occurs~~ late ~~spring~~ Summer /early spring, followed by dry period
- ☐ grass fires common ~~in~~ (tropical) ~~grasslands~~

Question #4 How do plants adapt in Grasslands?

- ☐ both types, trees scarce ~~because of~~ limited rainfall
- ☐ Fire ~~and~~ grazing animals kill tree seedlings
- ☐ blue grama ~~and~~ buffalo grass adapt ~~well~~ to drought
- ☐ plants ~~with~~ well-developed root systems, regrow after fire
- ☐ Flexible stalks ~~enable~~ grass ~~to~~ bend, without breaking ~~in wind~~

Back to the Research

In the library after the mini-lesson, the two teachers exchange student groups, observing and supporting a different group from the one they worked with in the previous library session. First, have students revisit the content learning intentions and identify the one(s) to focus on for their research that day. Remind the group of students who were researching on computers last day to keep in mind the six questions for checking website credibility. You might post the list of questions (Figure 8.6) next to the computer stations for the students' reference. For those students doing research from print media, Kristi and Jeremy provided a mini-lesson on how to use text features to prepare their thick questions.

Figure 8.6 Questions to consider when evaluating a website

Questions for Evaluating a Website

- Who has put this information on the web?
- What is the expertise of the individual or group who created the site?
- When was the site last updated?
- Is the information believable?
- Does the content appear to be fact or opinion?
- Can you verify the information in a book or other sources?

Mini-Lesson for Text Features in Print Media

Jeremy had students open their science textbook to the section on biomes, and asked:

- *How many of you read just the printed text and ignored the photographs, diagrams, and graphs?*

Most students raised their hand, saying they thought the information they needed was in the written text and that the other "stuff" was just extra.

Working with students as a group, Jeremy discussed the range of "stuff" called *text features* that support and clarify informational text in print. Then he asked them to pick one text feature and explain why they selected it. During their discussions, the students selected a "climate graph" as a text feature, recognizing that "understanding climate change is one of our content learning intentions" and "reading a climate graph is critical to understanding the climate of a biome." Jeremy asked:

- *What information is presented in this text feature?*

"The average precipitation and the average temperature over the 12 months of the year."

- *What thick questions can we ask about the information in this text feature?*

At their tables, the students devised the first question that arose from "reading" a climate graph:

- *Which months have the most precipitation?*

Jeremy then challenged them to develop at least two questions in their journals from other text features and identify the feature in parentheses.

As he circulated among the students, giving feedback and coaching as necessary, Jeremy observed that, although the students began to examine other text features more closely, many still did so on a surface level, simply describing the animals and plants native to their biome. They did not address the concept of "adaptation," another one of their content learning intentions.

Jeremy stopped the class and explained that, in addition to describing the animals and plants that were part of their biome, the students should also describe the adaptations they made to survive in the biome. When it became clear to him that the majority of students did not truly understand the meaning of "adaptation," he developed notes for another mini-lesson that would help students in their research.

Mini-Lesson on Adaptation

Ask the students to visualize a polar bear, then pose these questions:

- *Why does a polar bear have such a thick, white coat?*
- *How do polar bears move over ice?*

Confirm that the polar bear's thick coat of fur keeps it warm and that its white coat blends in with its snow-covered environment. Emphasize that the term *adaptation* describes modifications to an organism (or its parts) that enable it to live in its particular environment. Extend student thinking. Ask:

- *What would happen to a polar bear if it were transplanted into the desert?*
- *What modifications would make it more fit to live in that particular environment?*
- *How would it adapt to life in the desert?*

Focus on the adaptations that the polar bear would have to make to survive in this new environment. Remind students that understanding adaptation is one of the content learning intentions for this unit.

Connecting to the Learning Intentions

Highlight that the day's work has been focused on the following content learning intentions:

- I can create a climate graph depicting rainfall and temperature.
- I can describe the physical features of my biome.
- I can describe one animal's adaptation to the biome.
- I can describe one plant's adaptation to the biome.

and the following research learning intentions:

- I am able to find 3 to 5 supporting details for each question.
- I am able to use key words and paraphrase ideas for my notes.
- I am able to use valid sources.
- I am able to use text features as a source of information.

Teacher Reflections on Intervention with Mini-Lesson

This mini-lesson on adaption came at a critical time. By observing our students as they worked, we were able to judge when they had not grasped key understandings. Doing a mini-lesson as an intervention meant that students were able to refocus on the learning intentions and make important connections between the environment and the plants and animals in it.

After our discussion about adaptations, we circulated to see if students were making the necessary changes and/or additions on their note-taking sheets. We could tell that students were thinking about the concept of adaptation as they were reading because we could hear the conversations about the types of fur or the ability to swim or fly that signal modifications of an organism. Students were then able to apply their understanding of the adaptations of animals to that of plants, discussing and asking questions about size and the textures of leaves and root systems, for example.

Assessment for Learning

At the end of each research class, have students complete their research log by reflecting on what they learned about their biome, and by checking off the learning intentions that they have understood, then hand in their folders. Review students' folders again, this time using a different colour highlighter. The process of highlighting takes about thirty minutes, but it is thirty minutes well spent. When you note similarities in the students' notes and reflections that indicate a trend, use that observed need to guide your instruction for the following day.

Self-Monitoring

Having the students check off the learning intentions that they complete each day keeps them accountable for the content they must address while they are researching. It is also a quick indication to you which students are well on their way and which ones need a little more guidance and support.

Reflection Midway through the Unit

The process of giving descriptive feedback to students was new to Jeremy, but he was pleased by the results and impressed by the quality of the students' questions. Overall, he was happy with the amount and depth of the science content they were covering. He was surprised by the number of students who were internalizing the feedback he and Kristi had given, as evidenced by the revisions they made on their note-taking sheets. After the mini-lesson, he could see how well the students had handled the idea of adaptation, and he was pleased to see how much they were learning.

As the teacher librarian, Kristi appreciated the chance to review the students' work and to assess how well they were meeting the criteria and paying attention to the teachers' feedback on their previous day's work. She, too, was able to monitor the effect of the mini-lessons on student work, and was able to assess whether students were taking the six questions into account when they evaluated the websites.

Kristi and Jeremy saw that the mini-lessons had made a difference. By the end of the session, students were using only key words in their notes and had begun describing adaptation in reference to the animals and plants in their biome. It was clear that the students were beginning to think about their research questions, to be critical readers of online text, and to consider text features as an important source of information. They were making connections between content learning intentions, and they were beginning to address the research learning intentions. The project—and the students' thinking—were evolving.

Library Day 3

- Hand research folders back to students and give them about five minutes to review the feedback.
- Share your observations about student growth with the whole class. Such positive feedback will reinforce the behaviours you want to see repeated.
- Remind students of the essential questions for the unit, the questions that frame their research.
- Pose the following questions to the group:
  - *Consider what you know so far about your biome. How would your biome be affected if its temperature increased and its rainfall decreased?*
  - *What predictions can you make? How do you know?*
  - *What questions do you still have?*
- Give students an opportunity to discuss what they know so far. Encourage them to share their reasoning with their peers, referring to the research they have done to this point.
- Bring students together in small groups. Have a student from each table share their predictions and their questions. Record students' thinking, and include any supporting evidence they offer. List the new questions students now have. Explain that these new questions can help them refine their research and give them a new focus for their critical readings.

The value of feedback

As an experiment, Kristi and Jeremy decided to not give any feedback to three students at the end of day 2. One student had worked hard to revise her questions, which the teacher had highlighted the day before, but her revised work had not received checkmarks despite all her effort. The teachers waited to see if these students would notice the oversight.

After a few minutes, their hands were up, and Kristi and Jeremy had to confess to the experiment. The students were unhappy that their work had not been assessed or re-assessed. They wanted to know that they had met the criteria, and they felt let down when the teachers had not responded to their work! The students' comments reinforced for the teachers that students had been paying attention to the feedback, that they wanted confirmation that they were meeting the expectations for the unit.

Focusing on Consequences

- Discuss the last content learning intention, the most challenging one for the students: *I can explain the consequences of climate change on my biome.* Focus on the word *consequences* in the statement and have students highlight or circle it so they know that it is an important one.
- Return their attention to their research folders and their own responses to the essential questions. Ask:
  - *Which of the ideas you have recorded could be considered a consequence?*
- As students give their input, underline each point that they believe to be a "consequence." This helps to define and explain the word's meaning and provides a model of the kind of supporting evidence they must identify as they address this learning intention.
- In order to identify a consequence of climate change on a biome, students will need to make connections and draw inferences from their research. This is a critical thinking skill, and one that requires that students think deeply and reflect on the content of their research to make conclusions.

Back to the Research

- Have students revisit the content learning intentions and identify the one(s) they will focus on for their research that day. Emphasize the importance of focusing on "consequences" in their research.
- In the library, ask the two groups of students to exchange resources—those who have been researching on the computers will switch to text-based research; those who have been researching from books will go online to research.
- The teachers, too, should exchange student groups, observing and supporting a different group from the previous class.
- Repeat the mini-lesson on evaluating websites with this new computer-based group. Consider using different websites, perhaps one drawn from content that students are already familiar with—even from another subject area.
- Repeat the mini-lesson on using text features with this new group. Choose a different website for students to analyze.

Connecting to the Learning Intentions

Summarize that the day's work has been focused on the following content learning intentions:

- I can locate my biome on a map of the world.
- I can describe the physical features of my biome.
- I can create a climate graph depicting rainfall and temperature.
- I can explain the consequences of climate change on my biome.

Add the following research learning intentions:

- I am able to use valid sources.
- I am able to use text features as a source of information.

Assessment for Learning

Exit Slip

At the end of the class, have students complete their research log. Instead of writing down an interesting fact or question, have the students write down a possible consequence if their biome ceased to exist. This is their exit slip for the day.

Teachers' end-of-day reflections

Each time we go through the folders, the process goes more quickly. For one, we are getting used to the process of referring to the criteria. More gratifying, though, is that we are recording more check marks and doing far less highlighting. The students are getting it!

Library Day 4

- Distribute the research folders, and ask students to consider their feedback, then revisit the content learning intentions and identify which they will focus on for their research.
- Have students return to the stations they occupied in the previous class.
- Monitor student progress by observing students while they work and asking good questions. Work with small groups, as needed.

Small Group Instruction

Just-in-Time Learning

By reviewing folders on a regular basis, Kristi and Jeremy have noticed that a couple of students are struggling with the research aspect. They become a focus for the teachers, and Kristi sits with them for about twenty minutes, working on the specific skills they need to move forward in their research. These students needed more instruction on how to use a book's index and how to use text features to create questions. While Kristi is working with these students, Jeremy continues to circulate.

Jeremy has noticed that very few students are asking for clarification on how to do research. Because the descriptive feedback is directly related to the criteria, the students know how to correct the areas that have been highlighted and if they don't, they seek help from a peer.

As he moves about the room, Jeremy notices one student whose website looks a little suspect. Although the set of questions for establishing the validity of a website included identifying an author of the information, this student could not see an author at the top of the site, and had chosen to ignore that question. Jeremy encouraged her to scroll down to the bottom of the site—another place where the author might be listed—and the student saw, to her dismay, that the site was part of a grade 6 class project on biomes.

In response to Jeremy's asking why she hadn't looked elsewhere, she replied that, unable to find the author at the top of the page, she thought that there wasn't an author. She added that the information seemed to be OK because it was information she had seen in print texts in her previous research.

This assumption is a common error that inexperienced students make, not looking at a whole website before drawing information from it. Most read the first couple of lines, believe it "sounds good enough," and then begin note-taking. This particular student learned a valuable lesson that day; in turn, her teachers were reminded how important it is to engage students in thinking critically about what they read. Because Jeremy was observing students while they worked and asking good questions, this student had been re-directed in her research.

Assessment for Learning

- At the end of the class, have students complete their research logs as their exit slip, and hand in their folders.
- Review and assess the additions to students' research folders. Focus on the extent to which they are addressing the content learning intentions in deep, meaningful ways.

Library Day 5

- Distribute the research folders, and allow time for students to consider their feedback.
- Then, have students revisit the content learning intentions and identify which they will focus on during their final day for completing their research on their essential questions.
- Use this as a work period for all students, leaving them free to research either on computers or in other resources, including books.
- Facilitate their learning and provide assistance when necessary.
- Circulate and look at the research learning intentions, ensuring that by the end of the class the students have addressed all of them.

Assessment of Learning

Whip-Around

- At the end of the class, have each student share with the rest of the class one consequence of their biome ceasing to exist.
- This sharing session allows the teachers to quickly assess whether the essential questions have been addressed. It also gives the students a chance to listen for similarities and differences between the different biomes selected by their peers.

- Remind the students of how they are expected to compile their research.

> 1. Create a compelling brochure.
> 2. Writing from the point of view of Greenpeace, clearly articulate why the survival of your biome is so important to the rest of the world.

- Lead a discussion of the term *compelling*. Bring in or have students generate examples of compelling advertising and its effects: *What are the qualities of a compelling advertisement?* Ask why the brochure they develop should be compelling, and discuss the students' responses.

In the Science Class

- To complete their brochure, the students use their research about biomes and the consequences of any changes to their own biome.
- Collect and make available examples of brochures so that students can see how a professional brochure is set up. Examining examples of compelling brochures allows the class to generate criteria for how a brochure should look and what content it should include.
- Generate criteria for an effective and compelling brochure with the class. Explain that the brochure itself is to be written from the point of view of Greenpeace, with the intent of increasing awareness of the consequences of climate change on biomes.
- Explain that student work will be assessed according to this set of criteria.
- Encourage students to use technology to complete their brochures. Several word-processing applications (Microsoft Word and Pages) include templates that are easy to use, and that allow students to drag and drop their thoughtful content into pre-set formats.
- Figure 8.7 presents the criteria set by the class for a compelling brochure.

Figure 8.7 Criteria for a compelling brochure

	Criteria	Mark
Presentation	· Presentation includes credible information drawn from a range of sources.	10
	· Sources are referenced and included in a bibliography or list of references.	5
	· Presentation is visually pleasing and includes features like charts, images, graphs and climatographs.	10
	· Is concise and easy to read, and includes text features like bold print, arrows and captions	25
Content	· Clearly addresses the content learning intentions	25
	· Clearly answers the essential questions	25
	TOTAL	100

Kristi's Reflections

About a week after the research was complete, Jeremy came into my library office feeling extremely pleased with the students' brochures. He said, "They are all excellent. Given the criteria, I think the majority of the class will get at least a B (75%) or higher." This was very gratifying for me to hear because it confirmed that the learning intentions and the descriptive feedback had had a positive impact on student achievement. He also mentioned that by bringing in examples of professional brochures, the students had gained a better idea of the layout of a brochure and how to put visual images and text together to create their own professional-looking product. The students definitely addressed the essential questions in their brochure and incorporated their research facts into their write-ups. In the end, their brochures were informative and thought-provoking. There was no evidence of "click, cut, and paste"—instead, there was evidence of application, synthesis, and evaluation.

Jeremy's Reflections

The structure and organization of the student research folders kept all students on track. Because the process is introduced in grade 8, the majority of students recognized the handouts in the folders, which meant that very little time was needed to explain the process. The criteria sheet on the front of the folder gave students a constant reminder of the expectations for their research. It also served as a daily communication tool that allowed the teacher to "talk" with the students. The learning intention sheet that was taped to the inside cover served as a constant reminder of what the students were expected to learn from both the research perspective and the science perspective.

The daily feedback from teacher to student through the use of highlighter check marks for "achieved" and highlighter lines for "areas needing improvement" was very powerful for both the students and me. I was able to see very quickly who was progressing well and who needed more support. In addition, each library mini-lesson was developed and based upon the work of the students from the previous day. It gave Kristi and me something to focus on. By examining the students' work after each lesson, each successive lesson was tailored to fit the needs of the students. I was surprised at how quickly students became accustomed to teacher feedback through the use of highlighters, and how eager they were to look for their check marks. The learning intentions and criteria provided learners with the opportunity to achieve to the best of their abilities. The students were proud of their brochures, and I was encouraged by their high quality and by the amount of thought and effort each student put forth. I will definitely be back in the library to do more research.

Chapter 9

Thinking about Polynomials Concretely, Pictorially, and Abstractly

Grade 9—Mathematics

Assessment FOR Learning

- Quick-writes
- Peer-mediated conversations
- Midway check-in
- Criteria-setting
- Use of student exemplars
- Co-created rubrics
- Peer-assessment and self-assessment

Open-Ended Strategies

- Connecting, processing, transforming/ personalizing lesson structure
- Critical thinking
- Problem-prompts

Differentiation

- Open-ended strategies
- Use of manipulatives
- Extensions/adaptation provided

Assessment OF Learning

- Unit Test
- Vocabulary
- Visual representations
- Multiple ways of showing

The Collaboration

Katie Wagner is a teacher of secondary mathematics who works in a large suburban school in Richmond, BC. Katie uses constructivist teaching methods in her classroom and devises assessment-for-learning strategies as a regular part of her instructional plan. When the new BC math curriculum for grades 8 and 9 (2008) required the use of manipulatives to teach most learning outcomes, Katie saw the approach as an opportunity to promote strategic thinking and understanding of mathematics concepts in her students.

For this lesson sequence on polynomials, she worked with Carole Fullerton to design, teach, and assess students' mastery of the algebra concepts presented. Together they planned lesson sequences that focused on communication and connection-making, on modelling and representing strategic thinking.

The Context

The curriculum unit on polynomials is one of the "make it or break it" units in secondary mathematics, a cornerstone of formal algebra. Traditionally, the introduction of polynomials and operations on them has been presented in an abstract and linear way—with students having to learn rules for addition, subtraction, multiplication, and addition of polynomials and then recall those rules to apply throughout a series of practice problems. For many students, this exercise in memory work—organizing discrete procedures to be recalled and applied—means that they lose the opportunity to develop their conceptual understanding of the operations and the subsequent relationships between the variables.

Katie was not satisfied to teach this unit in an abstract way. Drawing on the prescribed learning outcomes (PLOs) in the new curriculum and on the work of John Van de Walle (2006), a mathematics educator and author, Katie and Carole designed a lesson sequence that put conceptual understanding at the forefront of student learning and that, with a lesson sequence about relationships, patterns, and visualization rather than about memorization, could transform the dreaded polynomials unit.

Katie taught the lesson sequences outlined in this chapter with each of her three blocks of grade 9 math students. Approximately 20 per cent of the students in Katie's classes were ESL (English as a second language) learners who demonstrated a range of proficiency in English. Peer tutors—students in grade 12 participating in a school-based leadership program—provided support for students in all three of Katie's Math 9 classes; many of these tutors actually learned math along with their grade 9 charges, particularly when the math was presented in a hands-on context.

Notably in this unit of study, students did not use a math textbook. Instead, the teacher posed open-ended problems to the whole group, and teacher and students used algebra tiles (see "Algebra Tiles—A Primer," pages 236 to 238) as both the context and the model for learning important concepts.

Students were also encouraged to use virtual manipulatives (see page 238) at home to practise and hone their skills and understandings. This allowed them to consolidate their thinking and to explore the relationships presented in a different context—online.

Big Math Ideas

- We can model and solve polynomial equations using concrete materials and pictorial representations.
- Algebra tiles provide a concrete example of why we group like terms in polynomial expressions.
- We can use what we know from integer operations to help us simplify polynomial expressions.
- Mathematicians simplify expressions before they apply mathematical operations on them.
- We can show addition of polynomial expressions with algebra tiles.
- We can show subtraction of polynomial expressions with algebra tiles.
- Zero pairs can be used with x^2 and x tiles to show the difference.
- Mathematicians use an area model to show multiplication and division of polynomials.
- Creating a rectangular array helps us describe the relationships when we multiply or divide polynomials.

Key Structures

Open-Ended Strategies

- Using problem-prompts, such as asking *How can you…?*, focuses student attention on developing competence in applying strategies.
- Manipulatives highlight different strategies for arriving at solutions, that is, different ways to arrive at the same answer.
- Games for practice allow students to vary the complexity of their work.

Connecting, Processing, Transforming

- Prior knowledge warm-up: Getting re-connected activities
- Math-to-math connections
- Sequences focused on big math ideas
- Summary discussions
  - connects—focus on transforming student learning
  - quick-writes to highlight enduring understandings at the end of each lesson

Assessment for Learning

- Quick-writes
- Peer-mediated conversations (partner interviews)
- Midway check-in—demonstrating understanding by using numbers, pictures, and models (algebra tiles)

- Model it—show what you know
- Peer-assessment, self-assessment

Differentiation
- Manipulatives used during lessons allow students to access the math in different modes or styles of learning.
- Extensions/adaptations provided—"Go Deep" tasks and questions

Criteria-Setting/Use of Student Exemplars
- Criteria-setting: What makes a good piece of math writing?
- The Conceptual Thinking Pentagon (5 ways to show that you get it)
- The Good, Satisfactory, Not Yet (G/S/N) assessment rubric co-created with students

Overview of the Lessons

Before beginning this unit, the class had been studying *integers* and *operations on integers*. Katie had used colour tiles in her work with integers to help her students make meaning of the patterns within the operations while they were learning strategies for representing multiplication and division of integers. They had also learned about *powers* and *bases*, so they understood the meaning of the x^2 label for the product of two x terms.

Students should understand how to model operations with integers using either 2-sided counters or algebra tiles, and they should be comfortable with the *zero principle*. They should also have had experiences with area models for multiplication and be able to describe relationships between factors and products in this way.

The classroom time for the lessons in this chapter was 75 minutes in length, but the lessons can easily be implemented in shorter blocks, allowing one day for exploration and consolidation and a second day for reconstruction and deepening of concepts. The work of John Van de Walle framed not only the content of our lessons but the 3-part lesson model we planned and implemented.

Figure 9.1 Webs of understanding

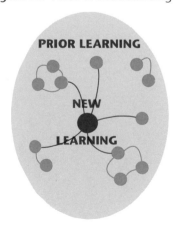

PRIOR LEARNING

NEW LEARNING

BEFORE THE MATH: Get re-connected

This part of the lessons "re-connects" students to prior learning or to a related idea that will set them up for success.

The quick warm-up task is *not* designed to tell students how to solve the day's problem but rather to help them recall the prior knowledge they might find useful in the new context. John Van de Walle talks about the power of "webs of understanding"—the learners' capacity to make sense of new mathematical concepts by connecting them to previously learned concepts. His graphic (Figure 9.1) suggests that the more connections made, the deeper the learning, and that there are many relationships between strands in mathematics.

DURING THE MATH: Learning math by doing math

The problem, or the problematic task of the day, is framed as an open-ended question. Although many of the tasks presented in this unit had one right answer, just asking the students how they could solve the problem left the choice of strategic approach open-ended. Each day's problems were constructed to engage students in the big math ideas for the lesson. A well-crafted constructivist math lesson must have tasks that are complex enough to engage all learners, the math must be central, and the task itself must not be one that students know immediately how to solve. This may sound strange, but it is by reasoning and problem solving through these complex tasks that students "learn math by doing math"—their struggle is an appropriate part of a math lesson and leads to their deep learning of content. While they work to make sense of the task, whether alone or as partners, teachers move around the room, asking questions to keep students focused on and thinking about the math:

- *What are you doing?*
- *Why are you doing it?*
- *How does it help you?*

By moving about the classroom and asking questions, teachers have opportunities to assess how the students are doing in the throes of the math task, and to extend or adapt the task for individuals or pairs, as needed. This instructional flow is used in each of the lesson sequences outlined in this unit.

AFTER THE MATH: Highlighting and consolidating

The conversation guided by the teachers at the end of each math lesson is the most important phase of the learning sequence. The students have the opportunity to share what they have discovered during the exploration portion of the lesson as well as to hear from their peers. Peer-to-peer learning is very powerful, particularly in middle school and secondary school classrooms, because all of the voices and perspectives and all of the strategies used by the students to problem-solve make up this essential "summary conversation." The teachers, as they observe and listen to their students exploring the math, can choose individual students to share their thinking, and to draw compelling or efficient strategies from the group. Chapin, Canavan Anderson, and O'Connor (2003) outline five strategies (see chapter 3, 42–43) that teachers might use in guiding these classroom discussions toward statements of enduring understandings. Of these five strategies, we use four strategies—re-voicing, re-phrasing, adding on (extension), and wait-time—to engage as many student perspectives as possible in the conversation.

Practice makes up an important component of any mathematics lesson. We believe practice must be meaningful and be used to build students' capacity for thinking and to consolidate their understanding of the important math concepts.

For us and for our students, games can also be meaningful and provide a fun way to engage with the big math ideas; as well, they provide different opportunities for teachers to assess students' mathematical thinking while they are strategizing and playing to win.

Lesson 1—Modelling Polynomials and Grouping Like Terms

BEFORE THE MATH: Get re-connected

- "Algebra Tiles—A Primer" on pages 236 to 238 provides an introduction to the use of algebra tiles in mathematics classes.
- Start with a simple integer sum on the board $(+3)+(-5)$. Ask students to describe how they might model this sum with 2-colour tiles.
- Use the overhead or magnetized colour tiles to show the sum. Focus on the creation of zero pairs with the materials (a negative tile and a positive tile together).
- Explain to students that the strategies they used to find the sum or difference of integers will help them in their explorations of polynomials.
- Deconstruct the word *polynomial*—a mathematical expression with more than two terms.

> **Math-to-math connection**
>
> Integers and polynomials can be modelled using algebra tiles.

DURING THE MATH: Learning math by doing math

- On the overhead, show students a single positive unit algebra tile. Name it a "unit tile" or a "positive tile." Both the base and the height of this tile is 1, so its area is 1 unit squared (1^2).
- Next, show the x tile. Explain that, although we know its base is 1 unit, we do not know its height so we label its area x, meaning *unknown*. Its area, then, is $1 \times x$ which is rendered as x.
- Finally, introduce the x^2 tile. Have students predict its name, given what they can determine from its base and height, both of which are x.

> **Think about it**
>
> Note that the colour of each algebra tile tells its sign. Red indicates a negative value; the other colours indicate positive values.
>
> Algebra tiles are available in a range of different styles, single-sided or double-sided, and in different colour combinations as well.
>
> We used overhead sets for all the students. Blue was the colour for positive terms, and red was the colour for negative terms.

Figure 9.2 Positive and negative algebra tiles

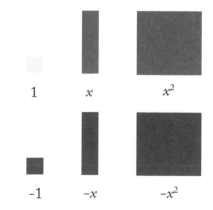

1 x x^2

-1 $-x$ $-x^2$

- Hand out sets of algebra tiles to your students. Have them explore the pieces in their set. Observe as they sort and order their pieces.
- Ask:
  - *What are you finding out about your tiles?*
  - *What do you think your discovery means?*
  - *What connections can you make?*
- After sufficient exploration time, pose the first problem of the lesson.

Problem: What polynomials can you make with your algebra tiles? What are their names?

- Have students select tiles from their set, place them on their tabletop, and name what they have built. Ask them to compare with a partner and discuss how their sets are the same and how they are different.
- As you observe the class work, select students who have modelled expressions with one, two, and three or more terms. To help address the first big math idea, have these students come one by one to the overhead or magnetized white board to show what they have built.
- Invite a second student to label the terms in the expressions.
- Use these samples as a way of deriving the key math vocabulary for the lesson — *term, monomial, binomial, polynomial.*

Key Vocabulary

A *term* is a signed number or variable used in an expression.
x, $2y$, $3m^2$, -5

A *polynomial* is an expression formed by adding or subtracting terms.
$2x^2 - 3x + 5x + 7$

A *monomial* is a polynomial expression with just one term.
x, $3x$, -5 or $2x^2$

A *binomial* is a polynomial expression with 2 terms, each of which has a different power.
$x + 4$; $3x - 2$; $-5 - x^2$, or $2x^2 + x$

- Next, tell students they are going to play a game. They are to grab as many algebra tiles as they can from their set, organize them on the table in front of them, then name the set they have created, and describe all the terms.

Figure 9.3 Lucas organized his tiles as shown below. Then he expressed the math shown by the tiles.

> **Math-to-math connection**
>
> We can simplify polynomials by using the idea of zero pairs. When a positive unit tile and a negative unit tile are added, the result or sum is zero.

$$+2x^2 - 1x^2 + 2x - 3x + 3 - 4$$

Lucas's expression has 6 terms, and is called a *polynomial*.

- Highlight in students' work where their groups of algebra tiles are the same size and shape as one another. This is what mathematicians call "grouping like terms." On paper, we do exactly the same thing as we do with algebra tiles on the tabletop—we group x^2 terms, x terms, and units, and we order them in that way.
- Tell students that, by recording all the terms in their handful of algebra tiles, they have described what mathematicians call an *expanded* polynomial expression.
- Ask:
  - *Is there another way to describe your expression?*
  - *How can you make it simpler?*
  - *How can you use what you know about integers to help you?*
- Students work to apply their prior knowledge about positive and negative integers to this new context. Using the concept of zero pairs, students should be able to apply the same thinking to the algebra tiles, which include positive and negative x and x^2 tiles.
- Have students create a visual representation of the tiles and an expression to match both their expanded and their simplified polynomials, as in Figures 9.3 and 9.4B.

Big Math Idea
- Algebra tiles provide a concrete example of why we group like terms in polynomial expressions.

Figure 9.4A Lucas recalled what he knew from work with integers and set aside the zero pairs as in this figure.

$+\ x^2 - x^2 + 2x - 2x + 3 - 3$

Each red tile of the same size and shape "zeroed" the corresponding blue algebra tile. The whole set was simplified to zero.

Figure 9.4B After Lucas had simplified his expression by removing all the zero pairs, he was left with the tiles in this figure.

$+1x^2 - x - 1$

His new expression has 3 terms, so it is a polynomial, too, but a *simplified* polynomial.

AFTER THE MATH: Highlighting and consolidating

- Bring students together and ask them to compare their expanded and simplified polynomials with a partner.
- Direct students to share how they grouped their tiles, then simplified the expression. Some may have grouped them by size and shape, then found zero pairs; others may have found zero pairs first, then organized their remaining tiles to show the simplified expression.
- Focus on these or other strategies used by your students to highlight the big math ideas of the lesson:

Big Math Ideas

- We can model and solve polynomial expressions using concrete materials and pictorial representations.
- Algebra tiles provide a concrete example of why we group like terms in polynomial expressions.
- We can use what we know from integer operations to help us simplify polynomial expressions.

Assessment for Learning

- Build a polynomial expression on an overhead projector using algebra tiles.

Figure 9.5 Agree or Disagree Task

This set of algebra tiles shows $2x^2 - 3x^2 - 2x + 5x + 1 - 1$

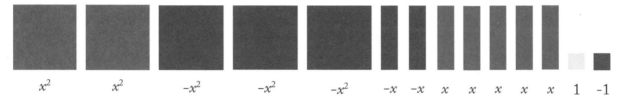

| x^2 | x^2 | $-x^2$ | $-x^2$ | $-x^2$ | $-x$ | $-x$ | x | x | x | x | x | 1 | -1 |

- Write the simplified expression underneath the group of labelled tiles (Figure 9.5). Make an intentional error in grouping like terms, and record the incorrect answer underneath the set of algebra tiles. Consider something like $-3x^2 + 5x + 5$ as a possible incorrect expression.
- Ask students whether they agree or disagree with the simplified polynomial. Have them record their reasoning in numbers, pictures, and words. If they believe there is an error, they should correct it.
- Gather the students' writing samples at the end of class. Encourage your students to use tiles to model the correct simplified expression in addition to writing about it.

This assessment strategy allows students to represent the key mathematical idea in 4 of the 5 possible ways suggested in Figure 9.6, John Van de Walle's "Conceptual Thinking Pentagon" (2006, p. 10, Figure 1.5). As you assess student work, pay attention to examples of the key words of the day—*polynomial, binomial, monomial, term, simplified, expanded.*

Figure 9.6 Conceptual Thinking Pentagon

Five different representations of mathematical ideas. Translations between and within each can help develop new concepts.

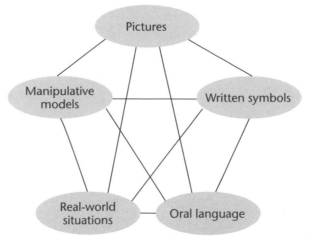

Alternative Assessment for Learning

Have students record, in a 2- or 3-minute quick-write, what they learned about subtracting polynomial expressions. Encourage them to include examples (sketches and numbers) in their writing to explain their thinking. Look over the students' work, in particular for their understanding and application of zero pairs.

The three samples below provide evidence that these students understood the big math ideas of the lesson. When you ask students to be brief (as in a quick-write), place the emphasis in your assessment on the quality of their ideas, not on sentence structure or neatness.

Figure 9.7 Three sample student responses on the quick-write assessment

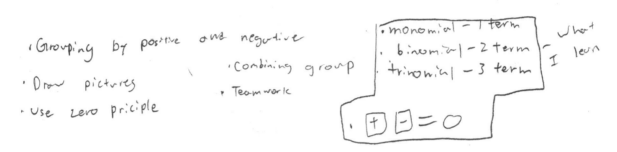

Go Deep

As an extension task, provide students with a simplified expression like $-3x^2 + 5x + 5$. Have them model and record as many different *expanded* expressions as they can. For example, the original expression could have been $5x^2 + 2x^2 - x + 6x + 3 + 2$ or many others. Because there are many possible answers to the question, this open-ended task provides opportunities for students to apply what they have learned, and gives you an indication of how well they understand the key concepts.

Lesson 2—Adding Polynomials

BEFORE THE MATH: Get re-connected

- Write an expanded expression on the overhead, white board, or SMART board.
- Ask students to build it using their tiles, then to model how they would simplify the expression.
- Ask them to recall how zero pairs can help simplify a polynomial expression.
- Tell students that, while they work with polynomials, they will make connections to what they already know about modelling similar operations on integers.

DURING THE MATH: Learning math by doing math

- Ask each student to select a handful of algebra tiles and record a polynomial expression for what they have modelled.

Problem: Work with a partner. How can you find the sum of your two polynomial expressions?

- Observe students as the partners combine their algebra tiles to show the total. Do they use zero pairs? Do they simplify their expressions first before adding? Can they explain their process?
- The student work samples in the three figures below show clearly that the student was removing sets of zero pairs before adding the expressions together, as indicated by the arrows.

Figure 9.8 Three sequential samples of the partners' responses

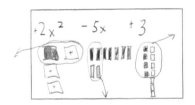 + 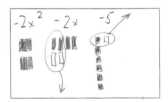 =

Your polynomial expression   +   Your partner's polynomial expression   =   Combined and simplified polynomial

- Have students repeat this process, this time adding their combined sum to that of another pair of learners. Have them record the addends and sum.
- Ask:
  - *How can we be sure that the final sum is correct?*
- When they suggest it, assign a value to x to verify the solution.
- Have students evaluate their original expanded polynomial expressions (their original handful of algebra tiles), then verify that the combined sum is the same as the value of the final simplified expression. See Figure 9.9.

Figure 9.9 Example of students' individual and combined work

Annie	Bruce
$3x^2 - 1x^2 + 3x - 2x - 4 + 2$ $3(3)^2 - 1(3)^2 + 3(3) - 2(3) - 4 + 2$ 19	$1x^2 - 2x^2 + 4x - 2x - 2$ $1(3)^2 - 2(3)^2 + 4(3) - 2(3) - 2$ -5

Christie	Donna
$5x^2 + 1x - 2x - 7 + 1$ $5(3)^2 + 1(3) - 2(3) - 7 + 1$ 36	$-3x^2 + 2x^2 + 4x - 4x - 5 + 6$ $-3(3)^2 + 2(3)^2 + 4(3) - 4(3) - 5 + 6$ -8

The sum of Annie, Bruce, Christie and Donna's expressions is:

$(3x^2 - 1x^2 + 3x - 2x - 4 + 2) + (1x^2 - 2x^2 + 4x - 2x - 2) + (5x^2 + 1x - 2x - 7 + 1)$

$+ (-3x^2 + 2x^2 + 4x - 4x - 5 + 6)$

or $5x^2 + 2x - 9$

And when we evaluate the expression we get

$5(3)^2 + 2(3) - 9 = 42$

which is the same as the sum of their evaluated expressions.

$19 + (-5) + 36 + (-8) = 42$

AFTER THE MATH: Highlighting and consolidating

- Bring students together and ask them to explain what they discovered when they added their polynomial expressions. (The final sum was the same as their partial sums combined.)
- Talk about why mathematicians simplify expressions before they add, and how this step helps to avoid errors.

Big Math Ideas

- Mathematicians simplify expressions before they apply mathematical operations on them.
- We can show addition and subtraction of polynomial expressions with algebra tiles.

Assessment for Learning

Interview Cards and Partner Interview

Because it is difficult to observe each of 30 students carefully while they use manipulatives to apply strategies and learn new concepts, Katie asks them to engage in partner interviews. These partner interviews put assessment for learning—and meaningful practice—in the hands of the learners. For the lesson on polynomial addition, Katie wanted to be sure her students had grasped the concepts and that they could successfully model an addition sentence with algebra tiles, then simplify the sum. Using her strategy in your classroom is quite simple:

- First, create three to five 2-sided cue cards with a question on the front and the answer on the back for partners to use with one another. You might draw the questions for these tasks from a traditional text, but the questions should require students to model the question and answer with manipulatives in order to demonstrate their understanding of the concept.

Figure 9.10 Sample of 2-sided question-and-answer cue card

Model the polynomial sum shown below using algebra tiles. $\left(-3x^2 + 4x - 3\right) + \left(4x^2 - x + 2\right)$ Write the simplified polynomial for the sum.	Simplified polynomial 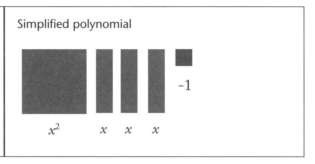

- During the interview, one student poses the question on their cue card to their partner, and uses the answer on the back as a guide for their assessment. Students may give anecdotal feedback to their partner or give their partner's response a score out of 3, depending on the task.
- When they share their work with you, encourage them to highlight any clarifications needed and any misconceptions or creative solutions that they might have encountered through the interview process. This strategy helps both students because they must understand not only their own thinking but also the thinking of their partner and others.
- This peer-assessment strategy allows you to gather assessment data on the entire class within a very few minutes, while also observing individual students while they work together. We have found that students enjoy the partner interviews—they appreciate the opportunity to work together and enjoy supporting one another. The strategy itself breeds independence and teaches study skills when used as a way of reviewing key concepts.

Lesson 3—Subtracting Polynomials

BEFORE THE MATH: Get re-connected

- Use integer tiles (or unit algebra tiles) on the overhead projector. Model the expression $(+4) - (-5)$
- Start by using 4 yellow tiles to model the positive 4.

Figure 9.11A

1   1   1   1

- Since we cannot subtract 5 red tiles (five -1 tiles) from the four positive 1 [$+1$] tiles in the figure above, we have to use zero pairs to create red tiles without changing the value of the modelled number. Our new model for $+4$ looks like this:

Figure 9.11B

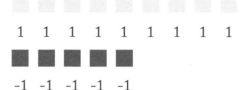

1   1   1   1   1   1   1   1   1

-1   -1   -1   -1   -1

> **Math-to-math connection**
>
> We can subtract polynomials just like we subtract integers—by using zero pairs.

- Now we can subtract, or take away, the 5 negative tiles from the modelled number. Removing these 5 negative 1 tiles leaves us with:

Figure 9.11C

1   1   1   1   1   1   1   1   1   or $+9$.

So the expression is $(+4)-(-5)=+9$.
Tell students that they will use these same strategies when subtracting polynomials.

DURING THE MATH: Learning math by doing math

Problem: Work with a partner. How can you find the difference between your polynomial expressions?

- As in lesson 2, ask students to grab a handful of algebra tiles, record the name of their polynomial, then simplify it before the next step.
- Then ask the students to subtract their partner's polynomial from theirs, and to record the difference between their expressions.
- Group each pair of students with another pair of students and ask them to subtract again, finding the difference between their expressions. Challenge students to choose partners carefully and to continue subtracting until they have only a monomial left.

Go Deep

A grade 9 math student was subtracting polynomial expressions. One of the expressions was a polynomial with 4 terms. One of the expressions was a binomial. The difference between them was $-3x^2 - 2x + 5$. What might the expressions have been? How many can you find?

- After a set amount of time, have students trade papers with a partner and evaluate one another's expressions using $x = +1$ to verify their answers.

AFTER THE MATH: Highlighting and consolidating

- Bring students together and ask them to explain what they discovered when they subtracted their polynomial expressions. (The difference could be found by using zero pairs and algebra tiles.)
- Ask them to explain how they chose partners to ensure their simplified polynomial difference was as little as possible.

Big Math Ideas

- We can show subtraction of polynomial expressions with algebra tiles.
- Zero pairs can be used with x^2 and x tiles to show the difference.

Assessment for Learning

Midway Check-In

Katie was thrilled with the progress of her students after only a very few lessons. Students had been working on a number of important concepts and procedures dealing with polynomials, and they seemed completely at ease with the content, the language, and the concepts they had discovered. In order to assess their comprehension of the big math ideas to that point in the unit, she decided to do a quick check-in.

The assessment piece was very low key, and included manipulatives, drawing, numbers, and writing—accessing 4 of the 5 representations of mathematical ideas. Katie wrote the quiz (Figure 9.12) on the overhead because her students tended to find this kind of test less anxiety-producing. The students, in addition to showing their solutions with algebra tiles, had to explain their thinking.

Analysis of responses on the quiz

- Both Jonathan and Michael show their thinking by using tiles and mathematical expressions. They demonstrate their understanding of how to create zero pairs and to remove them from an expression, denoted by the arrows.
- However, the back of the paper—where students were asked (Figure 9.12, question 5) to explain how they add and subtract polynomials— proved much more interesting. Many could do the operations with tiles and numbers, but some struggled to explain their thinking.

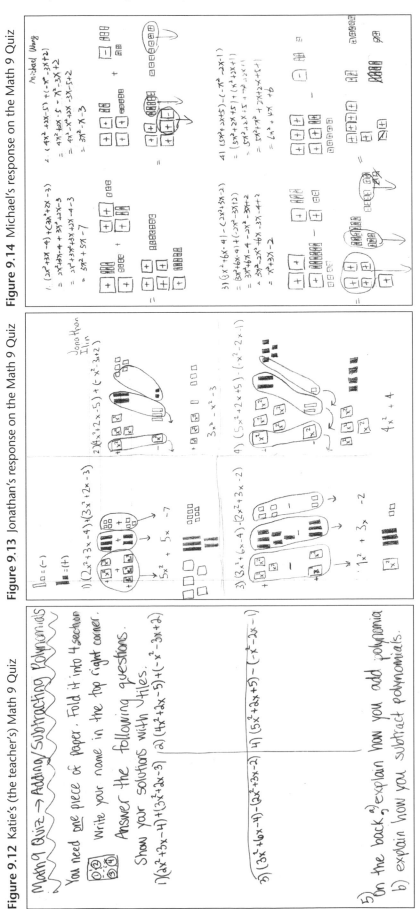

Figure 9.12 Katie's (the teacher's) Math 9 Quiz

Figure 9.13 Jonathan's response on the Math 9 Quiz

Figure 9.14 Michael's response on the Math 9 Quiz

- Michael's work (Figure 9.14) shows a competent grasp of the operations. However, his limited grasp of English is evident in his explanation on the back (Figure 9.15). Nevertheless, we can still see that he is taking a shortcut to solve subtraction problems, first multiplying the second expression by negative 1 (-1) and then adding the expressions together.

Figure 9.15 Michael's explanation

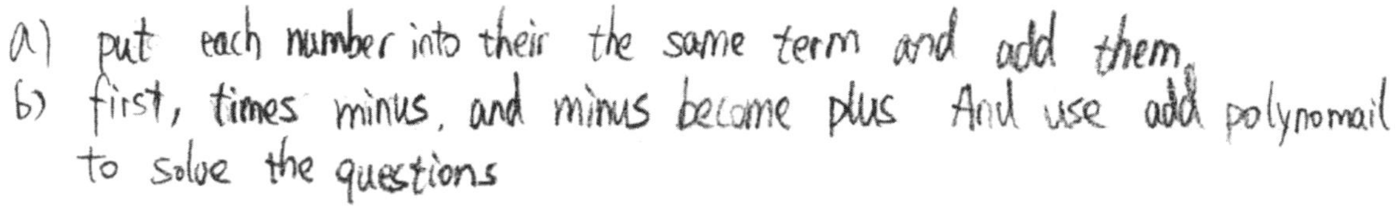

a) put each number into their the same term and add them,
b) first, times minus, and minus became plus And use add polynomail to solve the questions

- Looking at his writing sample led us to re-examine his other work. Michael approaches his solutions abstractly first, then models the solution. This is different from other students in the class, who modelled to understand the problem, then described their process.

Figure 9.16A Alex's explanation of adding polynomials

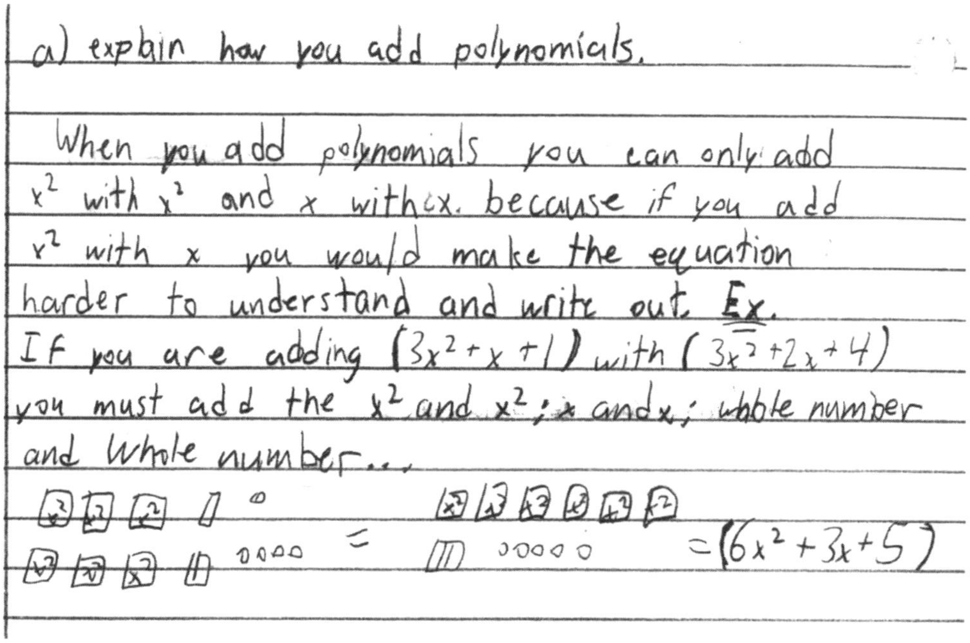

a) expbin how you add polynomials.

When you add polynomials you can only add x^2 with x^2 and x with x. because if you add x^2 with x you would make the equation harder to understand and write out. Ex. If you are adding $(3x^2 + x + 1)$ with $(3x^2 + 2x + 4)$ you must add the x^2 and x^2; x and x; whole number and whole number...

$= (6x^2 + 3x + 5)$

- Another student, Alex, explained the importance of grouping like terms in his description of how to add and subtract polynomials. In Figures 9.16A and 9.16B, he gives an example in which he shows the idea of simplifying his sums and differences, but does not mention it explicitly.

Figure 9.16B Alex's explanation of subtracting polynomials

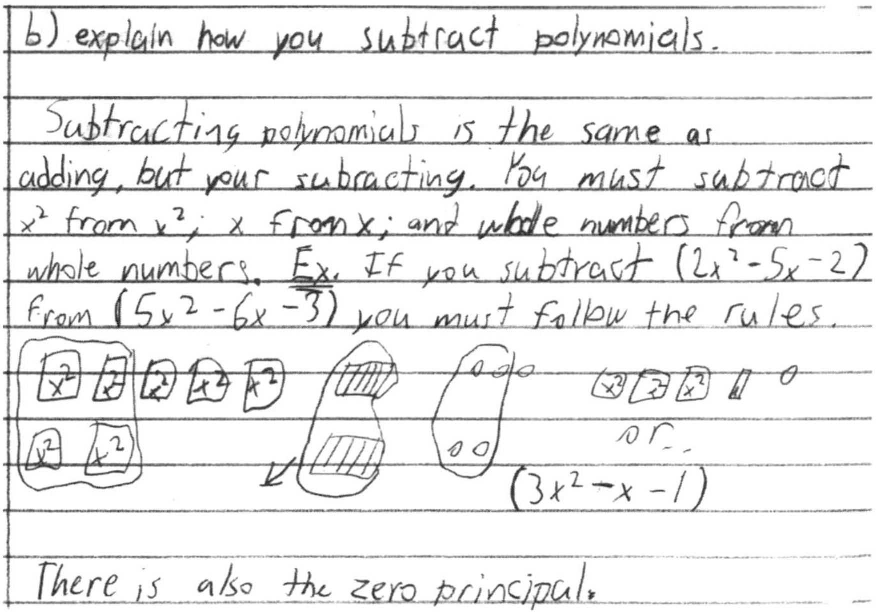

b) explain how you subtract polynomials.

Subtracting polynomials is the same as adding, but your subracting. You must subtract x^2 from x^2; x from x; and whole numbers from whole numbers. Ex. If you subtract $(2x^2-5x-2)$ from $(5x^2-6x-3)$ you must follow the rules.

$$(3x^2-x-1)$$

There is also the zero principal.

- Maya's work (Figure 9.17A) shows a deeper understanding. She describes the zero principle and gives an example in which she has grouped like terms.

Figure 9.17A Maya's explanation of adding polynomials

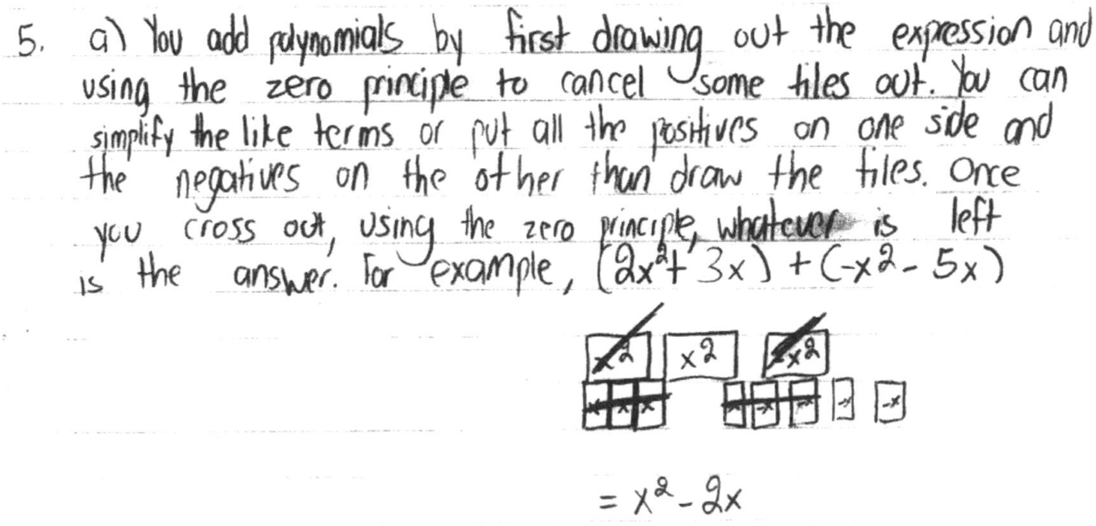

5. a) You add polynomials by first drawing out the expression and using the zero principle to cancel some tiles out. You can simplify the like terms or put all the positives on one side and the negatives on the other than draw the tiles. Once you cross out, using the zero principle, whatever is left is the answer. For example, $(2x^2+3x)+(-x^2-5x)$

$$= x^2 - 2x$$

- Maya's description of subtraction (Figure 9.17B) is even clearer; she makes connections to the strategy modelled at the beginning of the subtraction lesson using integer tiles, then adding negative tiles in order to be able to subtract them. Her writing and her example show a clear understanding of the big math ideas.

Figure 9.17B Maya's explanation of subtracting polynomials

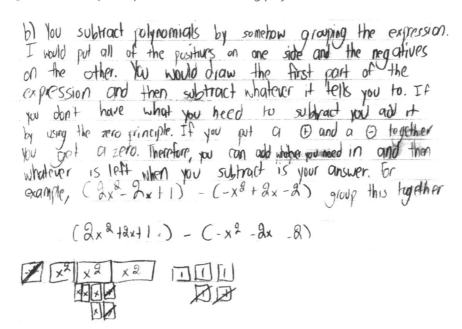

b) You subtract polynomials by somehow grouping the expression. I would put all of the positives on one side and the negatives on the other. You would draw the first part of the expression and then subtract whatever it tells you to. If you don't have what you need to subtract you add it by using the zero principle. If you put a ⊕ and a ⊖ together you get a zero. Therefore, you can add whatever you need in and then whatever is left when you subtract is your answer. For example, $(2x^2 - 2x + 1) - (-x^2 + 2x - 2)$ group this together

$(2x^2 + 2x + 1 .) - (-x^2 -2x -2)$

$3x^2 + 4 + 3$

- Most of the students in the class were able to demonstrate success in modelling, using numerical expressions, and writing about their thinking using words and examples. With our assessment-for-learning data collected in these overlapping and complementary ways, we got a clear picture of our students' understanding of the important math ideas.
- Satisfied with their progress, Katie forged ahead to multiplication of polynomials in lesson 4.

Lesson 4—Multiplying Polynomials

BEFORE THE MATH: Get re-connected

Math-to-math connection

We can multiply polynomials by using an area model.

Use unit tiles on an overhead to construct a rectangle that is 3 rows of 2 tiles. Ask students to name the dimensions of the shape (2 in height and 3 in width) as well as the area of the shape $(2 \times 3 = 6)$.

Explain that when we use tiles in this way, we are using an *area model* to show the product—a model the students will also use with polynomials.

DURING THE MATH: Learning math by doing math

- Arrange another rectangle on the overhead using six x^2 tiles, as in Figure 9.18A.

- Ask students to describe the dimensions of this rectangle $(2x$ by $3x)$. Identifying the rectangle's dimensions in terms of their linear measurement is important—students might name the factors as $2x^2$ and $3x^2$ if they are considering the area of the tile as opposed to the length of it.
- Highlight the length of the tiles by laying down *guiding tiles* along the edges of the rectangle, as in Figure 9.18B.

Figure 9.18A Six x^2 tiles   **Figure 9.18B** Guiding tiles highlight length and width

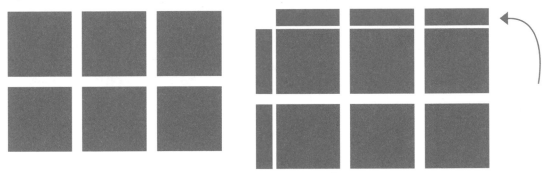

- Have students name the area of the shape $(6x^2)$. Generating the area of the shape does not require formal algebra, since students have only to "read" the blue tiles laid out.
- The dimensions of the rectangle, represented by the guiding tiles, are the factors of that product. For example, the area of the rectangle above is $6x^2$. The dimensions of the rectangle are $2x$ and $3x$, as indicated by the guiding tiles. That also means that $2x$ and $3x$ are the factors of the product $6x^2$.

Pose the following problems to the students, allowing time for them to share and explain.

- Use your algebra tiles to show 4 rows of $(x+4)$.
  - *What does the rectangle look like?*
  - *What's the area of the shape?*
- Use your algebra tiles to show $3x \times 4x$.
  - *What does the rectangle look like?*
  - *What's the area of the shape?*
- Use algebra tiles to show a rectangle with the dimensions $(x+3)$ and $(-2x)$.
  - *Do guiding tiles help you? In what way?*

AFTER THE MATH: Highlighting and consolidating

- Bring students together and ask them to explain what they discovered when they created rectangles with the dimensions you set out for them (e.g., the area could be found by creating a rectangle and naming, then simplifying the terms of the polynomial).

- Ask them to explain how they knew whether the elements of their rectangle would be positive or negative (e.g., multiplying a negative term and a positive term together results in a negative term; multiplying a negative and a negative term results in a positive term).
- In British Columbia's *Integrated Resource Package* (IRP) *for Mathematics 2008*, students in grade 9 work only with multiplication and division of polynomials by monomials. Nevertheless, it's easy to extend the concept to the multiplication of binomials $(x+3)(-2x+7)$, since students will eventually use the same process and materials to represent and construct area models for binomials.

Big Math Ideas

- Mathematicians use an area model to show multiplication and division of polynomials.
- Creating a rectangular array helps us describe the relationships when we multiply or divide polynomials.

> **Math-to-math connection**
>
> When we multiply positive and negative terms in a polynomial, we treat them the same as positive and negative integers.

Go Deep

Problem: When a grade 9 math student multiplied polynomial expressions, the product was $8x^2 - 6x + 2$. Construct a rectangle with this area. How many ways can you find to show it? What might the factors have been?

- After a set amount of time, have students compare rectangles with a partner and assess whether both are possible.

Figure 9.19 Students model the product of -3 and $x+2$, using overhead algebra tiles.

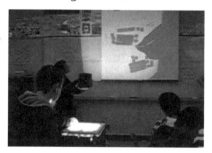

Assessment for Learning

Game and strategy write-up

- Play the game Race to 1000! with the students.
- Students should work in partners. Each pair will need a copy of the game instructions (Figure 9.20), a pencil to record solutions, and a "triple die" (or 3 dice of different colours). Students may elect to use a calculator, but it is not required for this game.
- Observe the students (Figure 9.21) while they play, first creating polynomial expressions and then evaluating them when given a value for x. To assess students' thinking about the multiplication of polynomials, ask:
  - *What are you doing?*
  - *Why are you doing it?*
  - *How does it help you?*

Figure 9.20

Race to 1000!

Roll the triple die. Use the numbers you rolled to create a binomial and a monomial.	
The blue die tells the number of x terms in your binomial. The red die tells the number of constant terms in your binomial.	 $3x$  4
Record your binomial.	$3x + 4$
The **white** die tells you the number of x terms in your monomial. *Even* numbers are positive. *Odd* numbers are negative. Record your monomial.	 $-5x$
Multiply your binomial by your monomial. Sketch the tiles you used and the arrangement you made. What's your product?	$-5x(3x + 4)$ $-15x^2 - 20x$
Now choose either $x = -2$ or $x = +3$ and solve your equation. This is your score for the round.	$-15(-2)^2 - 20(-2)$ $-15(4) + 40$ $-60 + 40 = 20$
Play again. The first one to 1000 points wins!	

Figure 9.21 Students play Race to 1000!

- When the game is finished, announce the winner, and give students a chance to write about their strategies for winning. How did they choose a value for *x*?

Lesson 5—Division of Polynomials

BEFORE THE MATH: Get re-connected

- To reconnect to what students know about an area model for multiplication of polynomials, pose the following problem to the students.

Problem: A grade 9 math student was multiplying polynomial expressions. The product was $+9x^2 - 6x$. One factor was a binomial $-3x + 2$. What was the other factor? What did the rectangle look like?

- Present the problem to the students and have them construct the rectangle to uncover the value of the missing dimension or factor.
- Students should show the missing side with guiding tiles to illustrate the factor.

> **Math-to-math connection**
>
> In an array model for multiplication, the area of the rectangle is the *product*. The dimensions of the rectangle are the *factors*.

- Explain that when we divide polynomials we can use an array model, just like we used when we multiplied monomials and binomials together.
- Emphasize that the guiding tiles represent the dimensions of the rectangle as well as the factors of the multiplication used to construct it.

DURING THE MATH: Learning math by doing math

Pose the following three problems to the class. Have them use algebra tiles to construct rectangles to illustrate each problem. Students should label the sides of the rectangle to connect concrete, pictorial, and abstract aspects together.

1. The area of a rectangle is $4x^2$. One side has a length of $4x$. What's the length of the other side? Use guiding tiles to show your answer. Record your solution in numbers. What do you notice?
2. The area of a rectangle is $-6x^2 - 2x$. One side has a length of $-2x$. What's the length of the other side? Use guiding tiles to show your answer. Record your solution in numbers. What do you notice?
3. The area of a rectangle is $3x - 6x + 9$. One side has a length of -3. What's the length of the other side? Use guiding tiles to show your answer. Record your solution in numbers. What do you notice?

AFTER THE MATH: Highlighting and consolidating

Figure 9.22 A student describes the solution with tiles on an overhead

- Bring students together and ask them to share their strategies for finding the missing factors in the polynomial problems. Ask them to share their numerical representations as well as their modelled solutions with algebra tiles (Figure 9.22).
- Highlight the ways in which the numbers (the terms of the polynomial) tell the same story as the images they created.
- Explain that when we divide polynomials, we must consider each term when partitioning it into a row.
- Consider using an error analysis task to highlight possible misconceptions, for example:
  - *A student says that $6x + 9$ is divisible by $3x$.*
  - *Do you agree or disagree? Use your tiles to prove your thinking.*

Big Math Ideas
- Mathematicians use an area model to show multiplication and division of polynomials.
- Creating a rectangular array helps us describe the relationships when we multiply or divide polynomials.

Go Deep
Have students generate a polynomial expression using a die. Have them follow these steps:

a. Roll a die. Take that number of x^2 tiles.
b. Roll the die again. Take that number of x tiles.
c. Roll the die a third time. Take that number of unit tiles.

d. Record this simplified polynomial:

Example: When I roll my dice, if I roll a 3 then a 4 then a 2, I should have $3x^2$ tiles, $4x$ tiles and 2 unit tiles on the table in front of me. Therefore, my expression is $3x^2 + 4x + 2$

Problem: How can you use the tiles you collected—or ones created using an expanded equivalent—to create a rectangle? What are the dimensions? Write a division sentence to match your modelled rectangle. Note: One of the dimensions cannot be 1!

Assessment for Learning

Problem creation and misconception check

- Give students file cards on the front of which you ask them to create a polynomial division problem for a partner to solve. Then, on the back of the card, have them write the solution by drawing a picture (with guiding tiles) and labelling the factors. They must show their answer algebraically (see Figure 9.23).

Figure 9.23 Students create peer quiz cards.

- Use the set of cards that the class has created in multiple ways. Have students quiz each other using the cards, then provide feedback to the teacher on how well they understood the concept at play in the problem/solution.
- Alternatively, have students take a card and study the question, then imagine an error that someone might make while trying to solve the problem. Ask students to discuss possible strategies and pitfalls in checking their own solutions.
- At the end of this assessment activity, have students submit their card, their partner's card, their solutions, and their comments for your review or re-use.

Assessment of Learning

Unit Test

The students created our assessment rubric (Figure 9.24.) in class as part of their preparation for the Unit Test (Figure 9.25). We used sample solutions to come to a consensus on what constituted a "Good" solution (Figure 9.26).

An AOL test should include vocabulary and the visual and algebraic representations of the operations on polynomials—what students have been learning in this unit. The instructions should allow students to show in multiple ways what they have learned. When creating the test, be sure to stress to students the importance of communicating solutions in a thorough way.

Figure 9.24 Student-created assessment rubric—Good / Satisfactory / Not Yet

Good	Satisfactory	Not yet
· Show all work (Awesome!) · Explain – visuals, code (what's +/-?) · Thought processes clear · The right answer to the question	In the middle	· No answer or wrong · Just the answer · Very little work · Blank

Figure 9.26 Student sample: Alex's scored Page 1 of the Unit Test.

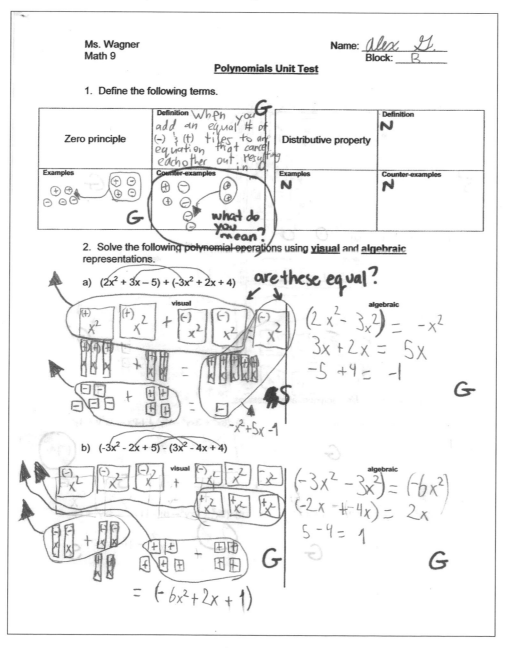

Figure 9.25 Katie's Polynomials Unit Test, page 1

Ms. Wagner—Math 9   Name: _____

Block: _____

Polynomials Unit Test

1. Define the following terms.

	Definition			Definition
Zero principle			**Distributive property**	
Examples	Counter-examples		Examples	Counter-examples

2. Solve the following polynomial operations using visual and algebraic representations.

a) $(2x^2 + 3x - 5) + (-3x^2 + 2x + 4)$

visual	algebraic

b) $(-3x^2 - 2x + 5) - (3x^2 - 4x + 4)$

visual	algebraic

Figure 9.25 Katie's Polynomials Unit Test, page 2

c) $-3y(4y-3)$

visual	algebraic

d) $(12a^2-3a)+(-3a)$

visual	algebraic

3. Simplify the following polynomial expressions.

a) $3x+5-2x+6+4x-8$

b) $(8x^2+3xy^2-4y)+(-2x-3x^2y+4y)$

c) $(2a^2-3a+8)-(-2a^2+a+4)$

d) $(9x^2+2xy^2-6)-(11x^2-4xy^2+5)$

Figure 9.25 Katie's Polynomials Unit Test, page 3

4. Simplify the following polynomial expressions.

a) $-12a(-5a^3 + 6b)$

b) $-3xy^2(5xy^5 - 7x^3y^5)$

c) $(18x^3y - 9x^6y^7) + (-3x^2y)$

d) $\dfrac{-15xy^2 + 5x^2y}{5xy}$

5. Explain how you multiply polynomials (using tiles and algebraically).

6. Explain how you divide polynomials (using tiles and algebraically).

7. The outside of a picture frame has a length that is 3 cm shorter than twice its width. The inside of the picture frame has a length that is 10 cm shorter than the outside's width, and a width of 5 cm. Determine an expression for the area of the picture frame.

© Portage & Main Press, 2011, *It's All About Thinking: Mathematics & Science*, BLM, ISBN: 978-1-55379-269-7

Katie's Reflections

I found that using visual representations to introduce polynomials was accepted as more intuitive by the vast majority of students. They had practised the zero principle using integer chips before the introduction to polynomials, so the transition to polynomials and variables was intuitive. In future when I introduce algebra tiles, I would not name the tiles for the students; rather, I would have them name the tiles using the variables of their choice. I found that when I introduced students to polynomials with variables other than · x, they hesitated to use tiles to describe what they saw. For example, if the question was $x^2 + x = 2$, they could easily model the polynomial with tiles; however $y^2 + y = 2$ caused them to hesitate.

Students were eager to use the algebra tiles to create the kind of problems that would impress their teacher and their friends. Students who picked up the concept quickly would try to create challenging problems algebraically, then model them with tiles. They developed some great questions that brought us into engaging discussions of how we could model x^3 using 3-dimensional models—and the problems that would arise if we were to attempt to model x^4. Students who needed more time to practise and engage with the material were able to take the time, and to develop their own meaning.

I found that my students were far more successful when they used multiple representations to show their understanding. Students also developed lasting understandings. When they were preparing for their midterm exams, they did not require as much review of polynomial concepts and expressed how comfortable and competent they feel with this content of this unit. As a teacher, it is especially exciting to hear my wide range of students saying that they feel comfortable with math.

Algebra Tiles—A Primer

Mathematicians and math teachers alike have used algebra tiles for years to represent algebraic relationships and to solve equations. When used to model polynomials, the operations performed on polynomial expressions are intuitive and visual. They provide an important scaffold for students who must move from concrete materials to pictorial representations and, finally, to abstract representations of this important mathematical concept.

Algebra tiles are carefully constructed sets of materials that feature important relationships between the dimensions of the pieces. These plastic tiles are commercially available, and come in a variety of forms and colours, which denote the sign (positive or negative) of each piece. Most commercially available sets are double-sided; that is, they are made of two pieces of plastic fused together, so that one side shows a positive value and the other shows a negative value. While far from consistent in their choice of colour, most tiles tend to have one side that is red—which usually shows a negative value, suggesting that being "in the red" is a negative state.

It is important that students discover the relationships between the pieces. Allowing them to explore the materials will almost certainly elicit comparison—most students tend to lay pieces on top of one another or line them up to see "which ones fit." Through this question, we can begin to elaborate on the purposeful relationships that exist. Begin by naming the smallest piece as a "unit." Explain that the piece has an area of 1 unit squared (1^2), and ask students whether they can then extrapolate to determine its width and length (1 unit and 1 unit). Over time, we refer to this piece as 1.

Figure 9.27 One tile, one unit squared

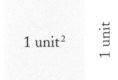

1 unit^2 1 unit

1 unit

The next piece to explore is the long one. Students will have observed that there is no linear relationship between the length of the long side of this tile and the unit tile. For that reason, we call this tile "x units long." It does, however, line up exactly along its short side with the unit tile. This means that the height of the tile is 1. The area of this tile, therefore is x units^2 since it has a length of x and a height of 1. Over time, we rename this as x.

Figure 9.28 Height of x unit tile is the same as the 1 unit tile.

The last piece is easy to compare and name. With 2 side lengths equal to the length of the long side of the *x* tile, this square piece has dimensions of *x* by *x* or x^2 units². We rename this as x^2.

Figure 9.29 The x² tile has both sides of equal length.

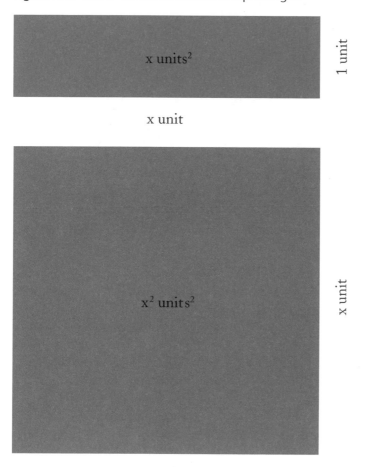

These tiles have been illustrated in 2 colours—beige for the units, green for the x tiles, and blue for the x^2 tiles. These are the colours used in one set which is commercially available, and which students may have seen illustrated in their math textbooks. The individual colours are less important that the signs—and the relationships—they represent.

A complete range of algebra tiles, then, using these colours, would look like Figure 9.30. Note that the red side shown is actually the reverse of the beige, blue, and green sides.

Figure 9.30

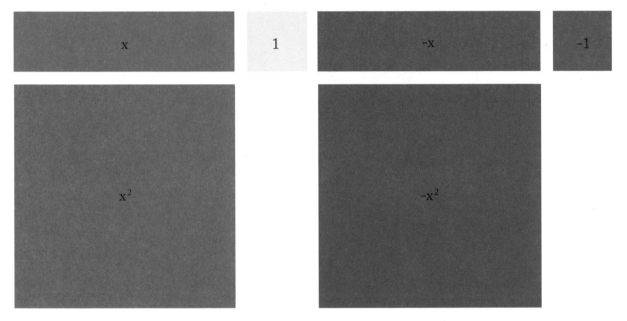

In our explorations, Katie chose overhead algebra tiles rather than double-sided ones. Overhead algebra tiles are, of course, intended for use on the overhead projector and usually are intended for use by teachers. The advantage of this particular brand of overhead tiles, in Katie's opinion, is that they come only in 2 colours, blue and red, where blue denotes a positive value and red a negative one.

The National Library of Virtual Manipulatives <www.nlvm.usu.edu> offers many online applets for exploring and manipulating algebraic concepts, among others. Approved math textbooks for students and teachers at the secondary level also provide online resources that are worth exploring. If you have access to a computer and an LCD projector, it's powerful to model these virtual materials, or e-materials, to your students. Encouraging them to use these digital tools for homework assignments is a meaningful use of technology.

Chapter 10

Thinking about Surface Area and Volume

Grade 8—Mathematics

Assessment FOR Learning

- Quick-writes
- Think-Pair-Share
- Agree or disagree tasks
- Model and build it

Open-ended Strategies

- Connecting, processing, transforming/personalizing
- Problem prompts
- Multiple solution strategies

Differentiation

- Open-ended strategies
- Use of manipulatives
- Extensions/adaptation provided

Assessment OF Learning

- Focus on problem solving
- Final performance task

The Collaboration

Carole Fullerton is often invited by teachers to collaborate with them in planning and implementing lessons in schools around the province. Working with different teachers and students in a variety of schools is a challenge she loves. The more she travels and interacts with students, the more convinced she is that they crave the same things—engaging tasks and meaningful mathematics, presented in a way that allows them to experiment and inquire.

The following set of lessons is a compilation of collaborative lessons presented around the province of British Columbia—Richmond, Campbell River, and Salt Spring Island. Strung together, they provide a lesson sequence for grade 8 measurement—and a jumping-off point for grade 9 concepts. Each lesson was tested in classrooms and all have been conscientiously crafted to respond to diversity.

The Context

Almost a third of the grade 8 math curriculum is dedicated to investigation of space and shape outcomes—ideas about Pythagoras, tessellations, and studies of 3-dimensional objects. Each of these concepts of measurement and transformation is grounded in problem solving, which is their application to real contexts. For that reason, this unit presents many hands-on investigations and explorations and engages students in thinking practically about the math. It allows students to visualize and make connections to art, to construction, and to design.

Big Math Ideas

- We can sketch a net for a 3-D object that shows what it would look like unfolded and flattened.
- Where the faces of a 3-D object connect, they form an edge.
- There are relationships between the faces of a net. When the faces are connected (e.g., on the edges), they share a dimension—a height, a width, or a length.
- On the net of a cylinder, one dimension of the rectangular face has the same measure as the circumference of the top or bottom.
- We can find the dimensions of a cylinder by first visualizing the net of that cylinder—2 circles and a rectangle—and then sorting out which dimensions are the same (e.g., the circumference of the circle and one edge of the rectangle).
- Mathematicians know that the formula for calculating the surface area of a cylinder is: Add the area of the circles (the top and bottom) to the area of the rectangle (the tube).
- We can imagine a "stack of bases" when we visualize the volume of a cylinder—or any prism.
- Mathematicians know that the volume of a cylinder can be calculated by finding the area of the circular base and multiplying it by the height of the cylinder.

- The volume of a cylinder changes when the *height* of the cylinder increases or decreases.
- The volume of a cylinder changes dramatically when the *radius* of the cylinder increases or decreases.
- Changing the radius of the cylinder has a much greater effect on its volume than changing its height.

Key Structures

Open-Ended Strategies
- Using problem-prompts in each lesson such as asking *How can you...?* focuses student attention on developing competence in applying strategies.
- Manipulatives highlight different solution strategies, different ways to arrive at the same answer.

Connecting, Processing, Transforming
- Prior knowledge warm-up: Getting re-connected activities
- Math-to-math connections
- Visualizing to draw on prior knowledge
- Predict-and-justify tasks
- Sequences focused on big math ideas help make connections
- Summary discussions focus on transforming student learning.
- Real-world problems make the math meaningful

Assessment for Learning
- Quick-writes
- Think-Pair-Share
- Agree or disagree tasks
- Model and build it—showing what you know

Differentiation
- Manipulatives used during lessons allow students to access the math in different modes or styles of learning
- Extensions/adaptations—Go Deep tasks and questions/problems

Overview of the Lessons

In the *Western and Northern Canadian Protocol* (WNCP) *Common Curriculum for Mathematics*, students engage with geometry concepts according to a developmental progression through elementary and middle school. The content addressed at each grade level is listed below. Having experienced these topics at previous grades assures success and points of connection to the new content at the grade 8 level.

Assumed Prior Knowledge
- Surface area of triangles (grade 6)
- Surface area of circles (grade 7)
- Pythagorean theorem (grade 8) C1
- Nets of 3-D select objects (grade 8) C2

Lesson 1—Nets of prisms

BEFORE THE MATH: Get re-connected

- Place a small rectangular prism on the overhead projector and project silhouettes of the faces of the prism on the screen.
- Ask students to identify and sketch the faces they see.
- Ask:
  - *Can you imagine how they are attached?*
- Explain that every 3-D object has faces that can be visualized and considered separately, but that mathematicians know that it is helpful to think of these faces as part of a connected whole.

DURING THE MATH: Learning math by doing math

- Hold up a familiar rectangular prism or box, like a box of cereal or crackers. Rotate the box as you show it to the students.
- Ask:
  - *Imagine that I unfold this box and lay it flat on the table. What will it look like?*
  - *Have students sketch the net of the box, including all the faces.*
- Cut the box along one of its edges, then another edge. Show students how the box has changed and ask them to edit their drawings, if necessary.
- Continue cutting and showing the box, allowing students to edit their drawings if they want to.
- Have students share their completed nets with a friend, comparing how their nets are alike and different. (Note that students' nets may differ from the configuration of the box you cut up, and still be correct.)
- Have students in partners compare 2 faces of their nets that are attached.
- Ask:
  - *What aspects of your nets are related?*
  - *How are the connected faces the same?*

Aғтᴇʀ ᴛʜᴇ Mᴀᴛʜ: Highlighting and consolidating

- Bring students together and ask them to compare their nets.
- Focus on the fold-lines of the nets created. These parts make up the edges of the 3-dimensional object, the prism.

Figure 10.1 Prisms

Big Math Ideas

- We can sketch a net for a 3-D object that shows what it would look like unfolded and flattened.
- Where the faces of a 3-D object connect, they form an edge.
- There are relationships between the faces of a net. When the faces are connected (e.g., on the edges), they share a dimension—a height, a width, or a length.

Go Deep

- Use unusually-shaped boxes, like a chocolate box (a triangular prism), a box from commercially produced ink (a trapezoidal prism), a box of dishcloths (a hexagonal prism), or even a fancy gift box, for an extension task. Have students repeat the task in Aғтᴇʀ ᴛʜᴇ Mᴀᴛʜ, and test their nets by cutting and assembling them.

Figure 10.2 A hexagonal (6-sided) prism

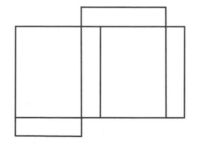

Assessment for Learning

Problem: Present a 3-D solid and a corresponding net that has been incorrectly drawn. Say that a student has drawn this net of a rectangular prism. Do you agree or disagree with his image? Why?

Figure 10.3A A rectangular prism   **Figure 10.3B** Net of a rectangular prism

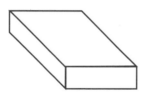

Lesson 2—Nets of cylinders

Bᴇғᴏʀᴇ ᴛʜᴇ Mᴀᴛʜ: Get re-connected

- Show some student-created nets from the previous lesson. Recall the big math ideas:
- We can sketch a net for a 3-D object that shows what it would look like unfolded and flattened.
- Where the faces of a 3-D object connect, they form an edge.

DURING THE MATH: LEARNING MATH BY DOING MATH

- Hold up a cylindrical container of potato chips. Rotate the container as you show it to the students.
- Ask:
  - *What might the net of this 3-D cylinder look like?*
- Have students draw their prediction, then sketch the net of the cylinder, including each of the faces.
- Watch for students who struggle to visualize and to draw the rectangular piece that forms the tube of the cylinder. Assist students by having cylinders of other sizes available (soup cans, tuna cans, juice cans, hockey pucks, even a roll of paper towel, with the paper towel on it) for students to rotate and deconstruct visually.
- Encourage students to run their fingers along the edges of the cylinder to locate the place where the faces meet.

Try this!

- Roll a cylinder in paint (pop cans work well for this task).
- Have students create the image of the rounded face of the cylinder by then rolling it (one full rotation) onto a sheet of paper.
- Have them compare the long edge of the painted rectangle with the circumference of the circular face on the top and bottom of the can. Ask what they notice.
- Have students share their completed nets with a partner, comparing how their nets are alike and how they are different.
- Ask:
  - *What aspects of your nets are related?*
  - *How are connected faces the same?*

A WINDOW IN: What the kids did

One student was given a can of peaches and asked to predict what the net of the cylinder would look like. He sketched the net, and was asked to explain his reasoning. The student knew that the circular edge of the can had to be related to the width of the label, so he measured the diameter of the can (Figure 10.4A) and used that measure to calculate the circumference of the top (the distance around the lid). Then he cut the label off the can (Figure 10.4B)

Figure 10.4A Measuring diameter

Figure 10.4B Cutting label

Figure 10.4C Label as rectangle   **Figure 10.4D** Comparing measures

and measured across the long edge of the rectangular label (Figure 10.4C). He was pleased to find that the measures were the same (Figure 10.4D)!

AFTER THE MATH: Highlighting and consolidating

- Bring students together and ask them to compare their nets. Focus on the relationship between the circumference of the top or bottom of the cylinder dimensions of the rectangular face.

Big Math Ideas

- There are relationships between the faces of a net. When the faces are connected (e.g., on the edges), they share a dimension — a height, a width, or a length.
- On the net of a cylinder, one dimension of the rectangular face has the same measure as the circumference of the top or bottom.

Go Deep

Problem: The radius of the top of a cylinder is 2 cm. What might the net of the cylinder look like? How many ways can you find? Draw your ideas.

Assessment for Learning

Have your students sketch the net of a tuna can, and the net of a Pringles can. Then ask them to describe how they are alike, and how they are different.

A WINDOW IN: What the kids did

For this task, we saw some interesting results. In Avneet's class, most could sketch a net that showed the similarity between the 2 cylinders (e.g., a similar-shaped base). Likewise, their drawings showed a clear difference in the heights of the cans. One student commented:

> The nets are alike because they both show rectangles and circles. The bases are almost the same size, except the tuna can is a bit bigger in diameter. The Pringles can is much taller than the tuna can, so the height is bigger. You could put about 7 tuna cans on top of each another to make one Pringles can.

In Dave's class, however, students were less inclined to make such connections. Students tended to simply enlarge the net of the tuna can or to shrink the Pringles can in their drawings. They did not account for the difference in height of the rectangular face.

The next day, Dave and I brought in from our pantries a collection of cans with paper faces, including another regular Pringles can and a collection of the shorter, snack-sized Pringles. After predicting, sketching, and comparing the nets of several cans (soup, peaches, apple juice), we presented students with the two Pringles cans and asked them to sketch and label the nets of these cylinders. With these additional experiences under their belts, students could more easily extrapolate to successfully sketch the nets, with appropriate heights and identical circular faces.

As a ticket out the door, we asked students to write down what they had learned that day, and to explain what ideas from the day's lesson they found difficult to grasp and those that were easy. One student wrote:

> Today I get how the height changes with a tall can. It's still hard to predict how long the circumference edge is going to be.

Another student wrote:

> It helped to unwrap the cans. I was surprised how much paper is used in labels!

It is important to use such information from assessment for learning to guide our instruction. Although this AFL task seemed simple, it helped us see that students in Dave's room needed additional experiences to fully understand the math. Dave kept this in mind as he introduced and worked through nets of other 3-D objects in his explorations.

Try this!

Use these interactive online applets to show how 3-D objects can be unfolded to show their nets. Students can choose the type of solid to unfold and digitally manipulate the images by rotating them.
- <www.mathopenref.com/cylinderarea.html>
- <www.uff.br/cdme/pdp/pdp-html/pdp-en.html>

Lesson 3—Surface Area of Cylinders

BEFORE THE MATH: Get re-connected

- Copy the two blackline masters for Cylinder Match-Up to project for the class. The shapes on Figure 10.5A have labels only and no measures; Figure 10.5B is a duplicate with the measures added. The shapes are to scale, so you can use Figure 10.5A again for a more challenging task.
- Project the images from your choice of the masters, on the overhead. Explain that the nets of 3 different cylinders are pictured on the sheet of paper. The task for the students is to match each base and top (1, 2, or 3) with one of the rectangular surfaces (A, B, or C). Ask students to use what they know about the relationships between the dimensions of the net of a cylinder to assemble the cylinders.

Figure 10.5A Cylinder Match-Up (without measures)

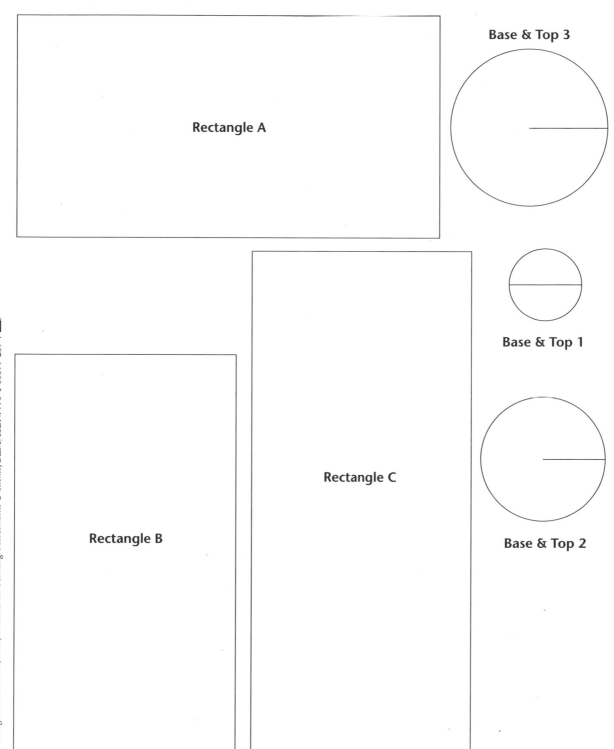

Figure 10.5B Cylinder Match-Up (with measures)

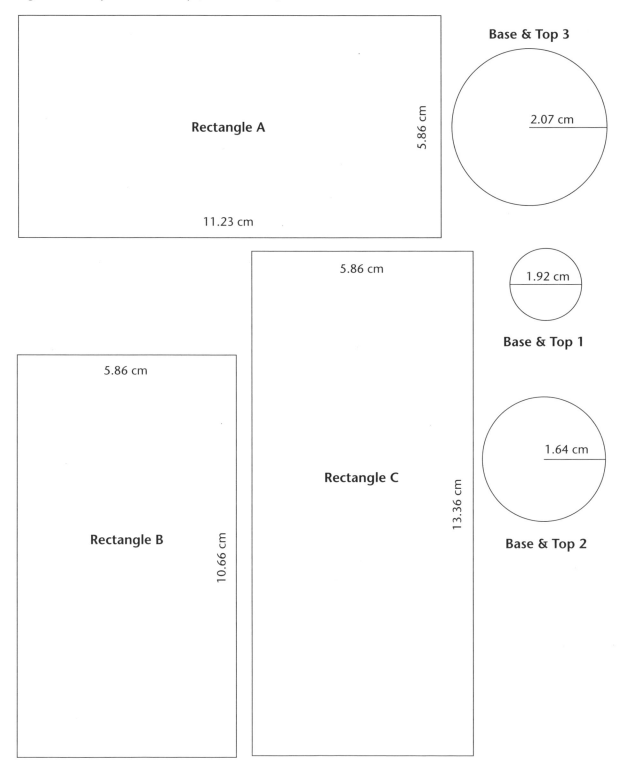

Rectangle A

5.86 cm

11.23 cm

Base & Top 3

2.07 cm

1.92 cm

Base & Top 1

5.86 cm

Rectangle B

10.66 cm

5.86 cm

Rectangle C

13.36 cm

1.64 cm

Base & Top 2

© Portage & Main Press, 2011, *It's All About Thinking: Mathematics & Science*, BLM, ISBN: 978-1-55379-269-7

- Invite student pairs to choose the level of task that best suits them. Provide copies of the appropriate BLM to the student pairs.
- When they are finished, have students share their thinking about which base and top matched each rectangle.

DURING THE MATH: Learning math by doing math

- Have students use the nets of cylinders from their initial Cylinder Match-Up task.
- Ask:
  - *Which of the cylinders uses the most paper?*
  - *How do you know?*
- Have students consider a closed cylinder—that is, one that includes both a top and a bottom circle—in their calculations.
- As students work, circulate and watch to ensure they are correctly applying the ideas of the circumference of a circle ($2\pi r$) and the area of a circle (πr^2). The students must have calculators for this task.

AFTER THE MATH: Highlighting and consolidating

- Bring students together to explain how they determined which cylinder used the most paper. Ask:
  - *How did you do your calculations?*
  - *What information and dimensions did you use?*

Big Math Ideas

- We can find the dimensions of a cylinder by first visualizing the net of that cylinder—2 circles and a rectangle—and then sorting out which dimensions are the same (e.g., the circumference of the circle and one edge of the rectangle).
- Mathematicians know that the formula for calculating the surface area of a cylinder is: Add the area of the circles (the top and bottom) to the area of the rectangle (the tube).

Assessment for Learning

Problem: Ariel says that, really, you need to know only two things to find the surface area of a cylinder. Do you agree or disagree? What might she be thinking of?

Go Deep

Problem: You have one sheet of letter-size paper, and you have been asked to make a cylinder from it. Unfortunately, you will be charged $10 per cm² of wasted paper.

- *What are the dimensions of the cylinder that costs you the least amount of money?*
- *What is the total surface area of the cylinder?*
- *How much will you be charged for waste?*

Lesson 4—Connecting Surface Area to Volume

BEFORE THE MATH: Get re-connected

- To explore relationships between the area of a circle and the volume of a cylinder, bring a supply of DVDs or CDs to class and give one to each student. Have them estimate how many CDs or DVDs they would need to create a stack 1 cm high. Use their estimates to solve the following question:
  - *How many DVDs would fit in a cylinder 20 cm high?*
- Ask one or two students to explain how they figured it out.
- Explain that to find the volume of any 3-D object, we can try to imagine stacking the shape of the cylinder's bottom, one on top of another to the height given.

DURING THE MATH: Learning math by doing math

- When we worked out how many DVDs would fit in the 20 cm high cylinder, we were measuring the capacity of it, that is, how much it would hold. We did that by measuring it in DVDs. But what if we wanted to measure the volume in cm³?
- Give each pair of students a circle with a radius of 5 cm and a handful of centicubes (approximately 100). Explain that the circle forms the base of a cylinder 25 cm tall.

Figure 10.6 One centicube has a volume of 1 cm³

> **Note**
>
> The math manipulative known as a *centicube* is exactly that—a cube that measures 1 cm×1 cm×1 cm, with a volume of 1 cm³. The unit cube in a set of base ten blocks is 1 cm³.

Math-to-math connection

Problem: If you know the surface area of the bottom of a prism and you know the height, how can you find the volume of the cylinder? How can you use materials to model your thinking?

- Watch for students who use the centicubes to cover their circle as a way of assessing its approximate surface area.
- Ask:
  - *What are you doing?*
  - *Why are you doing it?*
  - *How does it help you?*

AFTER THE MATH: Highlighting and consolidating

- Bring students together and ask them to compare their estimates of the volume of the cylinder, measured in cm³. Ask:
  - *How did you calculate?*
  - *What information did you use?*

- Focus on the idea that the centicubes allow us to measure both the surface area of the circle on the bottom by covering the bottom surface, and also to model the volume of a cylinder—if that cylinder had a height of just 1 cm. Then we can imagine 25 such cylinder slices stacked one on top of the other to calculate the volume of the cylinder itself.

Big Math Ideas
- We can imagine a "stack of bases" when we visualize the volume of a cylinder—or any prism.
- Mathematicians know that the volume of a cylinder can be calculated by finding the area of the circular base and multiplying it by the height of the cylinder.

Assessment for Learning

Cylinder Search
- Have students look in their pencil boxes, purses, and backpacks for items in cylindrical shapes (e.g., water bottles, lipstick, pencils, glue sticks). Have them choose 3 to 5 different cylinders and estimate their volume. Then ask them to calculate the volume of each one to the nearest cm³, and to submit their answers along with their reflections.
- Ask:
  - *What did you notice?*
  - *Did any cylinders with different dimensions have the same volume?*
  - *How could that be?*
- Alternatively, you might bring in a collection of items in cylindrical shapes to supplement this task (e.g., mugs, water bottles, vases).

Go Deep
Problem: The volume of a cylinder is between 75 cm³ and 100 cm³. What might the dimensions be?

Lesson 5—Surface Area and Volume

Figure 10.7 Two paper cylinders

BEFORE THE MATH: Get re-connected

- Show students two identical pieces of letter-size paper. Roll one lengthwise to form a cylinder and tape it, being careful not to overlap the paper used. Take the other piece of paper and roll it widthwise to form a second cylinder.
- Ask:
  - *Which cylinder holds more—the tall skinny one or the short fat one? Or, do they hold the same?*
- Have students record their predictions in writing.
- Then have students share their reasoning with a partner. Encourage all students to offer their prediction and their rationale.

- On a flat surface, fill the taller cylinder with counters such as rice or other loose material. After you have established that the tall cylinder is indeed full to the top, slide the short fat cylinder over the taller one until it rests on the table top. As you pull the tall cylinder up and out of the shorter one, have the students note what happens. See Figure 10.8 below showing the progression from tall to short cylinder. You might use sheets of acetate for both cylinders for greater visibility!)

Figure 10.8 Progression from tall cylinder to short cylinder

- Ask :
  - *Were you surprised? Why do you think this happened?*
- Have students record their thoughts and their reasoning about the result.

Figure 10.9 Redoing the experiment with paper half as wide

DURING THE MATH: Learning math by doing math

- Provide students with paper, scissors, tape, and counters (rice or other loose material), and copies of The Paper Problem (Figure 10.10). Ask students to explore relationships between the area and the volume of cylinders through the tasks outlined on the handout.
- Ask :
  - *What can you find out about the volume of different cylinders?*
  - *What happens when you change the width?*
  - *What happens when you change the height?*

Figure 10.10 The Paper Problem, page 1

The Paper Problem

A piece of letter-size paper is rolled lengthwise and filled with rice. Another sheet of letter-size paper is rolled widthwise and filled with rice.

Cylinder A   Cylinder B
(height 11")   (height 8.5")

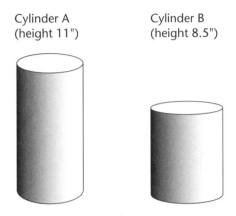

Which cylinder holds more? Or do they hold the same amount?

Make a prediction, and state why you think so.

Test your prediction by measuring and pouring loose rice into the 2 cylinders.

Were you surprised by the results when you compared the quantities? Explain the comparison, using numbers, pictures, and words to explain your thinking.

Figure 10.10 The Paper Problem, page 2

Think about it

Imagine you rolled a sheet of letter-size paper lengthwise into a cylinder, and filled it with rice. Your partner rolled a sheet of paper twice as long lengthwise into a cylinder, then filled it with rice.

How would you compare the volume of rice held by the two cylinders? Explain your thinking. Use numbers, a diagram, and words in your explanation.

Now, imagine you rolled a sheet of paper lengthwise into a cylinder and filled it with rice. Imagine your partner took another sheet of paper half as long, rolled it into a cylinder, and filled it with rice. How would you compare the volume of rice the two cylinders held? Explain your thinking.

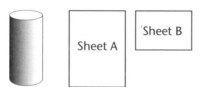

Connecting the Pieces

What relationship do you see between the **length** and the **width** of the paper rolled into a cylinder, and the **volume** of rice that the cylinder can hold? Explain why you see such a relationship. Test your explanation by thinking up other examples. Draw one or two of such examples.

© Portage & Main Press, 2011, *It's All About Thinking: Mathematics & Science*, BLM, ISBN: 978-1-55379-269-7

AFTER THE MATH: Highlighting and consolidating

- Bring students together and ask them to share what they have learned about the volume of the cylinders they constructed.
- Ask:
    - *What dimensions did you use in calculating the volume of your cylinders?*
    - *How did changing the height affect the volume of your cylinder?*
    - *How did changing the radius of the cylinder affect the volume?*
    - *Which had the greater effect?*

Figure 10.11 Comparing cylinders when the height is doubled

Although students may not be ready to make connections between the ratio of the height of a cylinder and the square of its radius (or the relative effect of changing either one), they should be able to grasp the big math ideas of the lesson.

Big Math Ideas

- The volume of a cylinder changes when the *height* of the cylinder increases or decreases.
- The volume of a cylinder changes dramatically when the *radius* of the cylinder increases or decreases.
- Changing the radius of the cylinder has a much greater effect on its volume than changing its height.

Figure 10.12A Students worked hard to sort out why the volume wasn't the same

Figure 10.12B Students debate and explain their reasoning

A WINDOW IN: What the kids did

Students enjoyed this task a great deal. The cognitive dissonance that occurs when students see that cylinders with the same surface area can have a different volume raises all kinds of questions. The conversations and debates that happen as a result of this unease are rich and important examples of mathematical reasoning.

Asia wrote:

> I was very surprised that the fatter cylinder was able to hold more rice. I figured that if the pieces of paper were the same, they would be able to hold the same quantity of rice.

Ryan wrote:

> I think this happened because of the circumference and volume. I think when you add up the numbers to get the volume, the circumference makes a difference.

Rosalie built on Ryan's thinking, and added diagrams to explain her reasoning, as in Figure 10.13.

Figure 10.13 Rosalie's solution

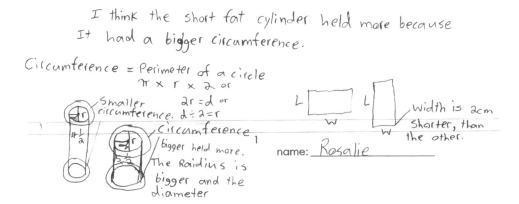

Michael used the materials to explain why doubling the radius of a cylinder causes the volume to quadruple. He built a cylinder with the larger radius, then constructed four cylinders and inserted them into the larger one. Not satisfied with the way they fit, he created rectangular prisms of the same height and inserted them into a rectangular prism with double the width. His demonstration was far clearer than anything we tried to explain by using the formula for the volume of a cylinder.

Figure 10.14A Inserting 4 small cylinders into the larger one

Assessment for Learning

Quick-Write Task

You can double just one dimension of your cylinder. Which one will increase the volume the most? Give an example to show how you know.

Alternative Assessment for Learning Challenge

Problem: Pose The Paper Problem (Figure 10.10) to your parents, siblings, or friends. What did they predict would happen? Write a note to explain why it happens.

Figure 10.14B Michael represents the solution visually

Assessment of Learning

We focused on four concepts in this unit— nets of 3-D objects, nets of cylinders, surface area of cylinders, and volume of cylinders. The most important thing is to support the students in connecting these concepts to one another and then to apply them in problem-solving contexts.

We strove for ambiguity in each of the problem-solving contexts that we set for the students, particularly in The Paper Problem. Students engaged with complex mathematics, accessed the language necessary to describe their thinking, and were required to visualize while they sketched nets and constructed cylinders from paper. While we were observing students as they worked through the problems posed throughout the unit, it became clear to us that most students had mastered the big math ideas of the unit.

Final Performance Task

- Because The Paper Problem asked students to bring all their knowledge of nets, area, and volume of cylinders together, consider using it as the final assessment for the unit, rather than a more traditional assessment or test.
- If you elect to do a more formal assessment, Figure 10.15 provides another one. It is short and focused on problem solving, with questions similar to those given during the course of the unit.
- Consider choosing only those questions that you believe will provide you with missing pieces of assessment data—you don't have to assign all the questions!

Figure 10.15 Assessment of learning for the unit, page 1

Cylinder Assessment

1. Sketch the net of the cylinder in the image.

2. Sketch the cylinder that matches this net. Label the dimensions.

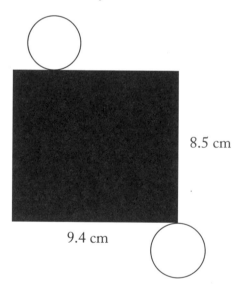

8.5 cm

9.4 cm

3. How can you find the radius of the cylinder you sketched?

© Portage & Main Press, 2011, *It's All About Thinking: Mathematics & Science*, BLM, ISBN: 978-1-55379-269-7

Figure 10.15 Cylinder Assessment, page 2

4. You have 140 cm² of paper. Which of the following cylinders could you construct?

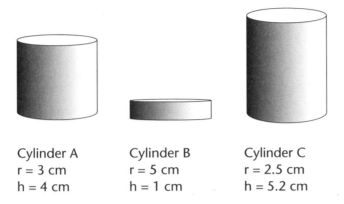

Cylinder A
r = 3 cm
h = 4 cm

Cylinder B
r = 5 cm
h = 1 cm

Cylinder C
r = 2.5 cm
h = 5.2 cm

5. Choose one of the following tasks:

   a. Which of the cylinders above would hold the most?

   or

   b. None of the cylinders above is large enough to hold 200 cm³ of material. What combination of these cylinders would you need to hold all 200 cm³ of material?

6. What's the most important thing to know when finding the area and volume of a cylinder?

Carole's Reflections

When originally planning these lessons, I had underestimated the need for students to interact with the objects and to deconstruct them. I had assumed that they would be able to visualize the nets of 3-D objects, but I was wrong. Working with actual objects (a tuna can, a chip can, a cereal box, a chocolate box) gave students real-life referents for the objects they were to deconstruct. Presenting online applets (lesson 2) to the group allowed us to model and predict the nets of far more complex shapes. Having a collection of objects on hand made it easy to meet the needs of a diverse group of learners. Keeping the big math ideas in the forefront helped to focus everyone's attention on the important concepts to be mastered and understood.

I also misjudged the students' buy-in for this unit's series of lessons. During lesson 3 and the class work on the surface area of different objects, one boy (judged to be "cool" by his peers) said quite excitedly to another student:

> "Oh you've got to know this stuff. It's really important if you want to build things."

And that's when I knew I had them. Students began to talk about situations where they could see applications for the math they were learning. I overheard one group engaged in a chat about a TV program called *Cake Boss*. They were discussing why the bakers and decorators on that show would need to know the surface area of cylinders and prisms.

Our students loved to explore and test their hypotheses around the cylinder task presented in lesson 5. This classic problem creates real cognitive dissonance and, with it, rich conversation. All students in this classroom had a voice as they reasoned through what they thought made sense. Debates—even heated discussions—sprang up between students as they worked toward a solution, and the deepest learning happened between students.

What I love best about the measurement and geometry units is opening up the math to a different set of learners. Students who might struggle with number-based tasks or with pure operations and procedures can shine most brightly in tasks that involve visualizing and the dynamic imagery essential to the task. When these students begin exploring the measurement and spatial sense strands, they are on their way to becoming successful in mathematics.

Chapter 11

Thinking about Data Management

Grade 5/6—Mathematics

Assessment FOR Learning
- Quick-writes
- Concept-mapping
- Peer-mediated conversations
- Midway check-in (performance task)

Open-ended strategies
- Connecting, processing, transforming/personalizing
- Critical thinking
- Problem prompts

Differentiation
- Adaptations to content, process, product
- Technology
- Digital manipulatives
- Diverse texts

Assessment OF Learning
- Portfolio assessment

The Collaboration

Catherine Ludwig is a gifted and caring teacher. She thrives on reaching all learners, stretches herself in implementing appropriate instructional techniques, and seeks the best in each child in her care. When outlining the year for her grade 5/6 students, she sought out support in planning and implementing a mathematics unit that would allow her students to stretch their capacity for learning and celebrate each student as an individual within the collective. This began an investigation into mathematical pedagogy, planning assessment for learning strategies, and ways of addressing diversity.

The 29 students in Catherine's grade 5/6 class represented the array of needs and abilities one would expect to find in any classroom in the lower mainland of British Columbia—ESL learners, students with learning disabilities, and gifted learners. We, Catherine and Carole, worked together to plan and implement a math unit that celebrated the diversity in the room, ensuring that all students in the class had an entry point into both the math concepts and the goals we had set for reading.

Tait Elementary, Catherine's K–7 school, had identified a school-wide goal for the year—to support students in "making connections and inferences" while reading. The school's staff members recognized that the skill of making inferences had application in all content areas, and we planned to make these skills explicit in math.

Our collaboration began in the third week of September and lasted seven weeks. We both believe that reading and math are interwoven, and we wanted to connect what students would be learning in other subject areas about making connections and inferences to the practice of reading in math. The math curriculum unit we chose was data management—the study of trends in the collection of data.

To make the math more accessible, we opted to pilot new data management software being considered by the district—a tool called TinkerPlots®. Like any data management software, this application supports students in thinking like a mathematician. It also prevents time-consuming computation and graph creation from overtaking the students' development of related math concepts. A variety of data management software can scaffold students' learning in this way.

The Context

Reading in math—making connections to literacy

A math textbook provides a rich opportunity for students to apply their reading strategies to nonfiction technical materials. Within the data management strand of mathematics, students must engage with information presented in a range of ways. Charts, graphs, and tables are the most common of these, and each one requires students to read and interpret the data presented. This is a complex task. Not only is the information dense, but it is coded in particular ways and can contain bias; students have to apply their background knowledge to access and make sense of the graphs or the patterns in the data. Any time we as readers use our background knowledge to formulate a new idea or to connect to prior knowledge, we are making inferences. In data management, this is a critically important skill—a reading skill that supports students in becoming fully numerate.

This is where the TinkerPlots Project began, with the reading and interpretation of data presented in a graph. However, Catherine and I wanted more for our students—we wanted them to learn to make sense of the information, to read critically in order to make predictions, and to establish relationships. To prepare our route, we outlined the big math ideas for the unit.

In some lessons, we add relevant big math ideas that evolve from the class work.

Big Math Ideas

- Mathematicians read and interpret the information on a graph. This information is called *data*.
- We can make true statements about data.
- We can draw inferences about data. When we make an inference from data, we must support our thinking with relevant data and explain why we think so.
- There are relationships between some aspects—or *attributes*—of data. Mathematicians describe these relationships as *trends*.
- Mathematicians use trends in data to make predictions.
- It's important to choose the right *format* when we present data. The format we choose (*line graph, bar graph, circle graph*) changes the "story" of the data and how it can be "told."
- We can organize data to answer questions.
- We can organize data to compare different attributes and to make true statements about them.
- Mathematicians know that the way we organize data changes the story it tells.
- When we survey a group, that group is known as a *population*. When the population changes, the results of the survey change as well.
- The predictions and inferences we make about a population come from making connections to what we already know. These connections are considered math-to-math, math-to-self, or math-to-world.

Key Structures

Open-Ended Strategies
- Use problem-prompts during each lesson:
    - *How can you…?*
    - *What can you find out about…?*
    - *What do you notice about…?*
- Focus on strategic competence, student thinking, and capacity.

Critical Thinking
- Accessing and applying background knowledge to unfamiliar situations
- Making reasoned judgments and sensible predictions based on data
- Extrapolating trends from the data

Connecting, Processing, Transforming
- Sort and predict
- Prior knowledge warm-up: Getting re-connected
- Math-to-math connections
- Sequences focused on big math ideas
- Summary discussions to connect and focus on transformation of learning
- Online e-connections that allow for immediate feedback

Assessment for Learning
- Quick-writes
- Concept-mapping
- Peer-mediated conversations (partner interviews)
- Midway check-in—performance task to demonstrate understanding
- Portfolio assessment (summative)

Differentiation
- Adaptations to content, process, product
- Technology used during lessons allows students to access the math in an efficient way (process, product)
- Digital manipulation and comparison of data (process)
- Diverse texts (student-created, picture books, websites, IM chat)

Overview of the Lessons

The lessons in this unit required between 45 and 90 minutes, depending on the big math idea being addressed. We structured the process to include lessons 2 or 3 times a week, which allowed students to become comfortable with the math concepts and to have time to practise the strategies featured between lessons.

The work of mathematics educator and author John Van de Walle (2001, 2006) framed not only the content of our lessons but also the three-part lesson model. We used this instructional sequence and the "understanding by design" framework to construct each lesson around one big math idea for the day—backward design. By doing so, we could focus our questions, our instruction, our assessments, and any necessary adaptations on connections to the intended enduring understandings.

Assumed prior knowledge

Because in prior grades, the students have had experiences reading bar graphs, line graphs, and pictographs, they should be able to recall these parts of a graph—the title, the axes, and the labels—and make true statements about the data represented there.

Catherine and Carole collectively shaped a unique educational story as they worked with rich mathematical concepts, intuitive user-friendly software, and a school-wide goal for students of developing the skill of making inferences from their reading across the content areas.

Lesson 1—Reading for Information: Data Management

BEFORE THE MATH: Get re-connected

Sort and Predict

- Put the following 15 words and phrases on the board, in no particular order.

    data, graph, plot, axis, inference, bar graph, scatter plot, attribute, connection, prediction, data set, survey, line, graph, relationship, trend

- Have students form groups of 3 or 4, and read the words, highlighting ones that are not familiar. Then, using what they know, sort the words/phrases into sets that make sense to them.
- Next, have each student group decide on a title or category for each of their sets of words.
- Then pair up the student groups and ask them to compare their sets and their titles or categories to see where they overlap.
- Last, have students make a prediction—given only these words and the categories they have created—about the content of the math unit they are about to begin.
- Confirm that the unit involves the study of data management—an important field of mathematics that is closely related to everyday life. Assure students that, even if they do not yet understand all the words or phrases, the meanings will become clear over time.
- Put the list of words on the Word Wall or in a pocket chart, and mark the words that students did not know.

- Explain that in doing the sort-and-predict task, each student has made inferences about the words on the board and the relationships between them. Emphasize that making inferences is what mathematicians do when they "read" or interpret data—they use their background knowledge and make math-to-math connections as they infer from graphs and tables.

DURING THE MATH: Learning math by doing math

- To begin the unit and establish what it means to make an inference from data, present the graph in Figure 11.1 to the students along with the Problem.

Thinking like a mathematician

Consider the graph yourself. What is involved in understanding this image? What inferences can you make from the graph? What information did you draw on in order to make the connection?

Figure 11.1 Making inferences from a graph

What can you infer from this graph?

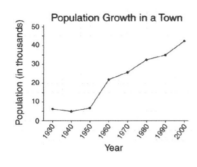

Problem: What do you notice about this graph? What true statements can you make? What inferences can you make?

- The questions about the graph are actually complex and multi-layered, requiring students to work through several tasks.
- Give students an opportunity to work independently before they share their ideas with others.
- Ask them to record their observations on paper before they turn to a partner.
- While students work, circulate and ask questions such as:
    - *What made you think that?*
    - *Where did your information come from?*
    - *How can you defend your thinking?*
    - *What connections did you make?*

A Window In: What the kids did

To sort out what the graph is describing, students had to read the title, the labels, and the units on both the horizontal and the vertical axes, and they had to understand that the line connecting the dots represents the growth in population over time.

> ### Key Vocabulary
>
> *Data* is information that is gathered about a population. Data can be organized into graphs that can, in turn, be interpreted.
>
> A *line graph* is a graph with data points joined by a line. It shows change over time.
>
> An *axis* is one of the numbered lines along the edges of a graph. They identify the names of the data being displayed.

Then, they had to pull in some of their background knowledge of the history surrounding the dates on the graph, and use that knowledge to make an inference about the changes in the population.

When we presented this graph to our grade 5/6 students, their initial reaction was not to make inferences, but rather to read facts from the graph. Overwhelmingly, we read and heard statements like the following:

> In 2000, the total population was 42,000.
>
> In 1950, the population started to get higher.
>
> The only time the population went down was from 1930 to 1940.

Although each of these statements is true, showing that the children are correctly reading some of the data, no statement is really an inference. Instead, they are very basic on-the-surface readings of the data.

To move toward our goal of having students make inferences, we needed to provide more scaffolding. Our students told us that making an inference was "reading between the lines"—an ironic thought when, in this case, it was the line on the graph that was telling the story. We agreed that their statements of what they had noticed showed that they had read and understood, but we suggested that, to infer from the data, they had to also consider the question *Why did it happen?*

We then set them to work again in partners, asking them to go back into their original statements and to qualify them with a response to the why question. The second time, we got a totally different set of results:

> There probably was a war between 1930 and 1940. That's why there was a population decrease.
>
> There was a big growth spurt from 1950 to 1960. I think there was a baby boom or a major immigration.
>
> The population got bigger every ten years. It might be the gold rush there, and it gets higher because more people are building and selling houses.

The students' new statements are, indeed, inferences. In exploring their initial responses mid-lesson, we challenged them to explain their thinking and say how they arrived at their ideas. An interesting discussion followed, in which the students began to make personal connections to their own experiences of moving to new places, and to ask questions about the data and its historical context. They had moved from reading data to making sense of it.

AFTER THE MATH: Highlighting and consolidating

- Bring students together and ask them to share their inferences and their reasoning. Focus on the big math ideas of the lesson.

Big Math Ideas

- Mathematicians read and interpret the information on a graph. This information is called data.
- We can make true statements about data.
- We can draw inferences about data. When we make an inference from data, we must support our thinking with relevant data and explain why we think so.

Assessment for Learning

Quick-write

- Allow students 2 or 3 minutes for a quick-write, recording individually what they learned about making inferences from data.

Lesson 2—Making Inferences from a Table

TinkerPlots® Dynamic Data Management software was used for this investigation. It, like other data management software, allows for the efficient manipulation of data and the translation of the data into various graphic forms—from a spreadsheet format to circle graphs, bar graphs, and scatter plots. Unlike other software, however, it is built on an intuitive, image-based framework. Each piece of information entered into the application is converted to a circle icon. These icons can be moved, dragged and sorted on-screen, according to their various attributes.

In entering the information, students need to define each attribute as either *numerical* or *non-numerical*. The software program then assigns a colour to each attribute (varying degrees of a single colour for numerical data; completely separate colours for non-numerical data). As students organize and classify their data by attribute, the colours or the range of colours make numerical and non-numerical attributes of the data explicit and easy to recognize. This is a critical aspect of the software, and supports students in making an appropriate choice of graph to display their findings (circle graphs for non-numerical data; scatter plots for comparing two types of numerical data, and so on).

Students can create multiple, overlapping and contrasting graphs in this software by using multiple attributes concurrently. That is, students might concurrently compare the age of respondents on a survey to the distance travelled to school with the type of transportation used, to see if younger children are driven to school more often than older children or whether the distance from school itself is the determiner in who gets a ride to school or not.

This feature of TinkerPlots software allows even very young learners the opportunity to take concurrent attributes of data into consideration and to make inferences between them. This software is a powerful tool. Screen captures of the data displayed when used by the students are embedded in this chapter. Their visual nature made the content accessible to all learners, in particular, to those who were learning English while the unit unfolded.

BEFORE THE MATH: Get re-connected

Remind students that in the previous lesson they read information in a line graph and made inferences from the changes over time. Tell them that they are going to use the same strategies for inferencing to make sense of data presented in a different way.

- Display the table in Figure 11.2 and ask:
  - *What do you notice?*
  - *What inferences can you make?*
  - *What questions do you have?*
- Explain that sometimes it is difficult to make inferences from data in a table format, and that it is helpful to organize the data in another graphic format in order to read it.

DURING THE MATH: Learning math by doing math

- Present the graph in Figure 11.3 to your students, and the screen shot of student work on TinkerPlots.
- Ask:
  - *What do you notice?*
  - *What does the graph tell you?*
  - *What patterns can you see?*

Figure 11.2 Collection I, Table of ages (in months) and heights (in cm)

	age	height
1	76	126
2	68	112
3	78	123
4	81	117
5	90	127
6	101	127
7	145	172
8	144	158
9	108	135
10	113	138
11	120	146
12	132	147
13	132	155
14	149	157
15	148	164

Collection 1

Figure 11.3 Collection I, Graph of ages (in months) and heights (in cm)

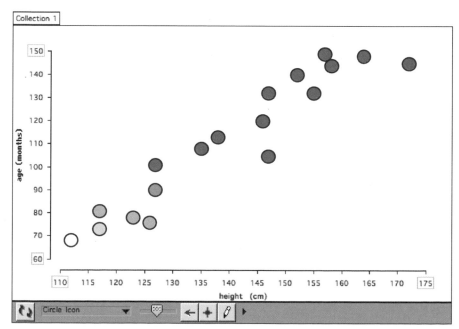

- Note that each dot on the graph represents a person. The attributes of age (in months) and height (in cm) are being compared.
- Have students read the graph to a partner and then share their interpretations.
- Ask whether seeing the data presented in this way helped them to make inferences—or to establish relationships between the data sets—more easily.

AFTER THE MATH: Highlighting and consolidating

- Working with the class as a whole, ask them to explain what inferences they could make from the graph.
- Tell them that the same data as in Figure 11.2 was used to create both graphic organizers, but that the scatter plot (Figure 11.3) is the tool that mathematicians use to highlight relationships between data sets. Ask:
  - *What relationship did you see between the data?*
- Support the students, leading them to craft causal statements, such as:

    The older you are, the taller you are.

    As we age, we tend to grow taller.

    There is a relationship between a person's age and their height.

Big Math Ideas

- Data tells a different story depending on how it's organized.
- We can compare different aspects—or attributes—of data.
- Mathematicians look for relationships between the attributes of data. They describe these relationships as trends.
- Sometimes these attributes are related (age and height). Sometimes they are not (age and eye colour).

Key Vocabulary

A *scatter plot* is a graph made up of data points. If there is a relationship within the data presented in this way, we say there is a *trend* in the data.

An *attribute* of data is a way of describing it. One piece of data can have several attributes; e.g., the data for one person in a survey can be classified into attributes of height, weight, eye colour, and gender.

Go Deep

Have students organize in groups to carry out the tasks below.

- Gather data from your classmates about the following attributes: height, arm span, age, eye colour.
- Predict which of these attributes might be related. Explain your thinking.

- Enter your data into TinkerPlots by creating a data set with the attributes listed.
- Organize your data into a scatter plot to show your results.
- Add similar data on your teacher or another adult to your data set. Include these data in your graph.
  - *What do you notice?*
  - *How does the new data affect your conclusions?*

Charvi wrote:

> Adding the adult affected the graph a lot because the adult is older and taller so, as you can see, it made a difference.

What Charvi has noticed but does not yet have the language to describe is the effect of an outlier on a data set.

Figure 11.4 Scatter plot of data set collected

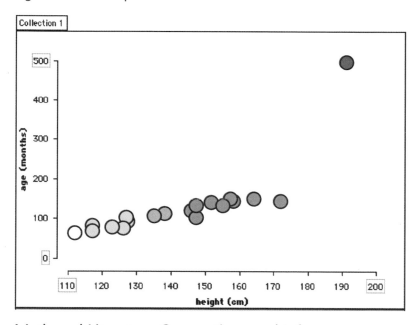

Math and Literature Connections and Inferences

Making connections for students means considering the data in terms of the students' experience. The chart in Figure 11.2, for example, might have made students think about the height chart at the doctor's office, or it might have reminded them of how their grandmother makes a mark on the wall to show how much they've grown between visits. They might have asked questions about the data, for example, "Are we really measuring the height of someone who is 76 or even 145 years old?", making connections to their background knowledge of what is a reasonable age for a human being. Inviting students to make connections encourages them to think more deeply and personally about the data, to engage with the numbers in order to situate them in a realistic context.

With the students, establish that making inferences goes one step further, that reading the information from the table, placing it in a context, and then telling the story surrounding it (i.e., what it means or what generalizations can be made from it) is inference-making.

Consider the graph in Figure 11.5. It shows the same data as in the chart, but it is sorted and organized visually, which makes it much easier to draw an inference.

Figure 11.5 Scatter plot being described

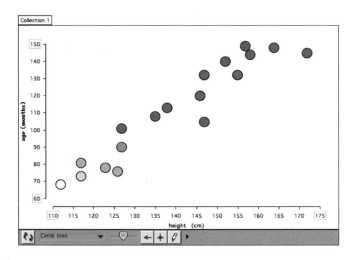

- First, the units for the data are explained in the *axes*—you can see that we're talking about age in months as compared to height in centimetres. Although there's no title on this graph, we can tell by the two axes that we are doing a comparison of these two numbers. When we compare sets of numerical data (like age and height, both expressed in numbers) on a graph, we're looking to identify a *relationship* between them. It is the relationship that allows us to make an inference. That is, if in reading the graph you can see a *pattern* emerging between the data sets, then a relationship exists—and that's the inference that can be made.
- In this graph (a scatter plot), one of the attributes of the data (height) depends on the other (age). The pattern of dependence can be read in the orientation of the plotted data—it forms a line, angled upward and to the right. This pattern in the data is called an *upward trend*. Students learn to identify upward trends when comparing numerical data and to draw inferences from them. In the case of the height and age graph, the inference was "The older you get, the taller you are." In mathematical terms, this is a *generalization*—one of the most powerful kinds of mathematical thinking that students can learn.

- To simplify the process of inference-making (from *decoding* to *context-setting* to *inferring*), prompt students with a key request: "*Tell me the story of your data.*" It helps the children to understand that there is meaning to be made from the data—whether it is presented in a graph, in a table, or in a stack of data cards—that is richer than the numbers themselves. Just like a story is more than the words on the page and has more depth when read carefully, data has a story to tell that only emerges when we sort and graph it, make connections, and infer what the trends mean.
- Consider the three-step process shown below:

Decoding	Context-setting	Inferring
I read...	It reminded me of... It made me think of...	What I think it really means...
The numbers say...	My connections were...	so the relationship is...

- Over time and with practice, students become more skilled at working through these steps—often without being aware of the transition from one to another.

Lesson 3—Looking at Attributes of Data

Creating Circle Graphs

Circle graphs are used to graphically represent data that together show parts of a whole. In using a circle graph, we use non-numerical data such as eye colour or country of origin. The individual bits of data are organized to show a fraction of the total circle, and are drawn within sections that match the fraction (or percentage) of the whole. For numerical data, we use other graphic forms. This lesson explores these important representations.

BEFORE THE MATH: Get re-connected

- Have a student come to the front of the room. Have the other students generate a list of attributes about their peer—hair colour, eye colour, height, age, favourite sport.
- As students offer ideas, record and sort the list of attributes into two groups—those that would be considered numerical attributes (age, weight, height) and those that would be considered non-numerical attributes (eye colour, hair colour, favourite sport).
- Do not put titles on the two groups, but ask your students what distinguishes one set from the other. If you like, insert actual data about that student beside each attribute to give students a hint.

- Ask:
  - *What can you observe about these sets of attributes?*
  - *What makes them the same?*
  - *How are they different?*
- Give the sets the appropriate titles (Numerical Attributes and Non-Numerical Attributes).
- Tell students that mathematicians make distinctions between these kinds of data because they determine the kinds of graphs to use.

> **Key Vocabulary**
>
> A *circle graph* is used to display data in sectors. Each *sector* shows a part of the whole.
>
> *Non-numerical attributes* describe aspects of data in words (breed of dog, mode of transportation, favourite food).
>
> *Numerical attributes* describe what can be measured in numbers (height, age, arm span, hours worked).

DURING THE MATH: Learning math by doing math

- Tell students you want them to conduct a survey to gather non-numerical data from their peers, and engage them in the problem:

Problem: How can you gather—and then represent—the results of a survey, when the information you gather is non-numerical?

- Watch carefully as your students problem-solve how they could gather the information needed. Some might need support with a class list or some other graphic organizer for recording information.
- If students have access to the TinkerPlots software, have them create a data card for each person in the class, with a field for the attribute they are exploring (hair colour, favourite sport, birth month). Next, they click to create a new plot, then drag the circle icons to separate and organize the data.
- By clicking on the fuse circular tool, they can transform the data into a circle graph and create a legend to match the colour of each section of the circle with the name of the data, as in Figure 11.6.
- If students do not have access to a data management system like TinkerPlots, have them create similar graphs by hand from their data, and provide an appropriate legend.

AFTER THE MATH: Highlighting and consolidating

- Bring students together and ask them to share their graphs and describe how they organized their data.
- Ask:
  - *What kind of graph did you choose for your non-numerical data?*
  - *What story does the data tell you?*

Figure 11.6 Hair Colour Survey

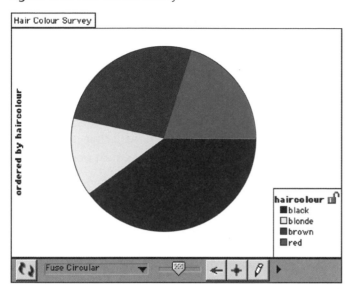
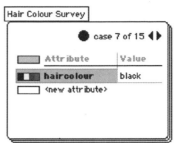

Note

Some students might organize their data into bar graphs or into a circle graph. Both types tell a valid story about the data. However, line graphs and scatter plots are not valid ways to represent this form of data; a line graph describes change over time, and a scatter plot describes a relationship between two numerical attributes of data. Students can self-correct by telling the story of the data.

Big Math Ideas

- A circle graph can be used to represent non-numerical data.
- A circle graph allows us to compare parts to the whole. The size of the parts, or sections, of a circle graph can be expressed as a percentage of the whole.
- A bar graph can be used to compare attributes.

Lesson 4—Non-Numerical Attributes and Circle Graphs

BEFORE THE MATH: Get re-connected

- Present the book *If the World Were a Village* by David J. Smith (2002) to your students.
- Explain that the author of the book uses numbers to describe aspects of the world's people—the languages they speak, the religions they practise, their access to fresh water and education.
- However, with 6.4 billion people on the planet, it is too complicated to use such

Tip

Go to the author's website <iftheworldwereavillage.org> to access videos and additional teaching ideas.

huge numbers. Instead, David Smith imagines that the world is a village of just 100 people, and uses that number as the whole in order to make his comparisons with the parts.

DURING THE MATH: Learning math by doing math

- Ask students to keep a record of the attributes that the author mentions while they listen to the story, noting which are numerical attributes and which are not.

    Note: All attributes mentioned are non-numerical, that is, they do not represent a range of values but rather give a count or tally for each part of the whole.

- Point out that because the data is present in a part/whole way within each of the attributes described (within nationality, we can compare the number of Asians to the population of the entire village of 100), we can use a circle graph to illustrate the data.

- Have pairs of students choose one of the attributes described by the author, then create a circle graph to represent the information and tell what they notice. If students have access to data management software, this task can be simplified.

Matt and Sam created the bar graph in Figure 11.7A to show the language data they had recorded, then created the corresponding circle graph in Figure 11.7B. They wrote what they noticed about the world's languages in the text box below the bar graph. Note how they described the data using fractions and percentages, both of which are used by mathematicians to describe part/whole relationships.

Figure 11.7A Bar graph of people, countries, and languages

Figure 11.7B Circle graph of same data

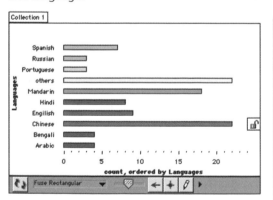

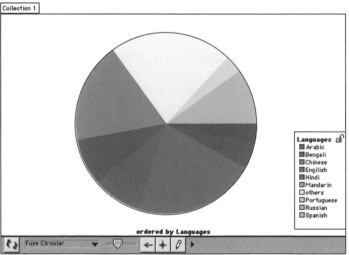

There are 22% of people speaking chinese in the circle graph. It looks like the amount of people speaking chinese is 1/4. The bar graph shows that there are the least amount of people speaking Russian and Portuguese. But the circle graph doesn't show clear enough.

AFTER THE MATH: Highlighting and consolidating
- Bring students together and ask them to explain what they discovered in creating their graphs.

Big Math Ideas
- A circle graph can be used to represent non-numerical data.
- A circle graph allows us to compare parts to the whole. The size of the sections of a circle graph can be expressed as a percentage or a fraction of the whole.

Assessment for Learning

Reflective writing
- Have students write examples of the kind of data they would display in a circle graph, then explain why they would choose to use such data, and sketch out their graph complete with labels.

Lesson 5—Creating a Class Survey

BEFORE THE MATH: Get re-connected

Figure 11.8

- Put a circle graph like Figure 11.8 on the board. Do not include a title.
- Ask students to read the graph and make inferences about the author of it. Ask:
  - *How was this information collected?*
  - *What question was asked to get this information?*
  - *How might the data be used?*
  - *Can you come up with a title that fits?*
- Remind students that a graph can give us information about a person or group of people. Mathematicians collect this information through surveys, a set of questions posed to many people to gain an overview of trends.

DURING THE MATH: Learning math by doing math

- Have students recall their circle graphs from the previous class and the attributes of the data they explored. Ask:
  - *How can you write a question to match the attribute you graphed?*
  - *What would it be?*
- Have students craft a question to match each of the attributes from the book they have been reading. Have students record these questions on the board. Explain that they will use this list of questions—or survey—to collect data about their classmates. The data will be sorted and organized to see if there are any trends.
- Add any new ideas to that list, including students' names and gender.

- Next, have students work in partners or small groups to answer the survey questions. They might use a chart or other organizer to gather the information.
- Alternatively, have students work with TinkerPlots. The students create a data card for their survey responses and then collate all their data cards into one stack to represent the entire class.

AFTER THE MATH: Highlighting and consolidating

Big Math Ideas

- We can gather data about a group of people by using a survey. The information gathered is called data. It can be sorted into numerical attributes and non-numerical attributes.

Assessment for Learning

Prediction

- Have students predict trends in the data they have just collected. Ask:
  - *What predictions can you make about your peers, without even seeing all the data?*
  - *What makes it hard—or easy—to do?*

A WINDOW IN: What the kids did

This group of grade 5/6 students were keenly interested in the issues raised in the book that they were reading—issues of equity, poverty, and diversity. They wanted more than anything to talk about themselves and their own backgrounds. As a group, we developed a survey to gather answers to their most pressing questions about themselves as "a classroom village of 29." Designing a survey and gathering data are important aspects of data management and, therefore, key outcomes in the math curriculum for elementary grades. Here are the questions they asked:

Survey Questions

1. What language do you speak at home?
2. What other language do you speak?
3. Where are your parents from?
4. Do you have a computer at home?
5. What is your religion?
6. How many people do you live with (including you)?
7. How old are you?
8. What kind of a home do you live in? (house, townhouse, apartment)
9. How long does it take you to get to school? (1–5, 5–10, 10–15, or 15–20 minutes)
10. How do you get to school? (walk, bike, scooter, car, bus)

11.   What do you like to do on the weekend? (play, read, shop, other)

12.   Are you a boy or a girl?

Each child in the class completed the set of survey questions. The data collected was transferred to a table and translated into data cards within TinkerPlots, in which each person's data was brought together on a single card as shown in Figure 11.9. This allowed the children to "see" themselves as individuals within the collected data set, and then to locate themselves within the collective when the data was represented visually.

Using the TinkerPlots software, the students were able to enter, organize, and manipulate the data about the languages that members of their class speak so that they could read it more easily. Figure 11.10 shows how students organized and compared aspects of the data while analyzing it.

The circle graph and the bar graph are examples of their work—both use the same data but tell the story differently. The circle graph illustrates fractions of the whole, the bar graph compares each of the parts. Reading and interpreting a

Figure 11.9 The corresponding TinkerPlots card stack

Attribute	Value	Unit	Formula
studentno	12		
gender	female		
language1	punjabi		
language2	english		
nationality	india		
computer	yes		
religion	sikh		
grade	5		
homepopulation	5	people	
age	10	years	
home	house		
distance_fro...	10 - 15	minutes	
transportation	car		
leisure	other		
school_name	Tait		

Division 4 Data — case 1 of 29

Figure 11.10 Students re-organize the data

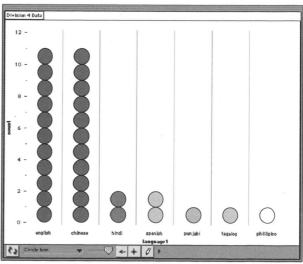

Students organized the data about the languages they speak in different ways – in a bar graph and a circle graph. They use the same data but tell the story differently; where the circle graph illustrates fractions of the whole, the bar graph compares each of the parts. Reading and interpreting a graph successfully means understanding how the structure affects the message. Like a poem or a piece of prose, there are different "genres" of graphs, each focusing on a different aspect of the intended message.

graph successfully means understanding how the structure of each type affects the message. Like words in different genres such as a poem or a piece of prose, graphs have different formats, each focusing on a different aspect of the intended message.

Making inferences from this data set was easy for our grade 5/6 students. The content was well known to them—they were, after all, writing about themselves—so bringing background knowledge into the conversation and making connections were natural outcomes. The students were really impressed by the diversity in their group. The data confirmed what they had predicted about the varied cultural backgrounds of their classmates, many of whom shared common experiences of immigrating to Canada or speaking a second language at home.

Figure 11.11 Math Word Wall

Our Math Word Wall

As shown in the photo, we recorded key words for discussing data management as they came up in our lessons. Students became quite fluent using them, both orally and in their written work.

Midway Assessment

A midway assessment gives feedback on the extent to which students are grasping the big math ideas and mastering the skills of graphing and representing data. Our assessment had two parts. First, the performance task asked students to create both a scatter plot and a circle graph from a sample data set in TinkerPlots, then answer questions to explain what they noticed on the graphs and what inferences they could make as a result.

Second, the students' ability to build a concept map and connect key terminology (Figure 11.11) learned in the data management chapter (words chosen from our Math Word Wall—*inference, relationship, scatter plot, numerical attribute, data,* and more) demonstrated their understanding of key math vocabulary and the relationships among the big ideas. This strategy had been presented by Faye Brownlie at a staff professional development day, and our students had already used it in other subjects. Preparing a concept map allowed students to delve into deeper understanding of the concepts we had been addressing. It also gave the students who had been less likely to contribute to a group conversation or a class debriefing an opportunity to express their understandings in print form.

Concept Map Instructions

1. Together, students and teacher brainstorm and list the concepts or key words to represent the text or the topic.

2. The teacher draws a number of circles on the overhead.

3. Students offer key ideas to be placed in the circles.

4. Students think of evidence from the text to link the two ideas. The teacher presses for words, phrases, and illustrations that reflect deep meaning.

5. The teacher and students continue connecting ideas, drawing lines to connect the concepts, explaining how the concepts are related, drawing from information in the text and from personal experience.

6. After working with the class, have students work alone or in partners to generate a concept map describing the important things to know about data management.

Figure 11.12 Student concept maps

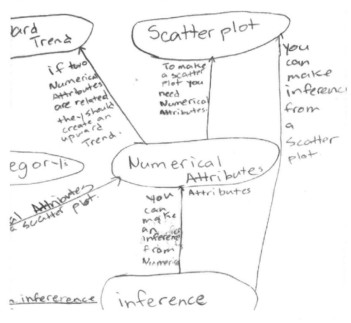

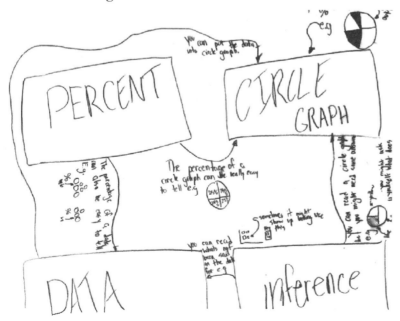

Lesson 6—Examining Our Data

BEFORE THE MATH: Get re-connected

- Invite students to work with a partner and share predictions about the class data.
- Have them justify their responses with a connection. Students should also share one question they have about the data.

DURING THE MATH: Learning math by doing math

- Ask:
  - *What can you find out about our class?*
  - *How can you organize the data to tell the story?*
- Students should manipulate and explore the data to answer their own questions.

Assessment for Learning

As students work, watch for those who use circle graphs or bar graphs for comparing non-numerical attributes of data, and scatter plots for determining relationships between numerical attributes. Ask questions and guide them to state the relationships in words.

AFTER THE MATH: Highlighting and Consolidating

- Bring students together and ask them to share their findings.
- Probe the different kinds of graphs they used to organize their thinking.

Big Math Ideas

- We can organize data to answer questions.
- It's important to choose the right *format* when we present data. The format we choose (*line graph, bar graph, circle graph*) changes the "story" of the data and how it can be "told."
- Mathematicians know that the way we organize data changes the story it tells.

Lesson 7—Surveying Another Population

BEFORE THE MATH: Get re-connected

- Select one aspect of the data you collected about your class (e.g., nationality).
- Ask :
  - *Would the survey data look similar if it were collected from a group of grade 2/3 students at your school?*
  - *Would it look similar if it were collected from a group of grade 5/6 students from a neighbouring school?*

> ♦ *What might survey data from a group of grade 5/6 students from another province or country look like?*

DURING THE MATH: Learning math by doing math

- Find another group to survey, either within or outside your school community. Collect data from that other *population* and add the results to those you've collected from your class. If the class has an e-pal class, the students might consider it as an additional population.
- Before they engage with the actual data, have students work in partners to make and record their predictions about the results.
- Pose the following problems to the whole class:
  - ♦ *What predictions can you make about the survey results of the new population?*
  - ♦ *Which attributes of the data do you predict will be similar? Which will be different? Why do you think so?*

AFTER THE MATH: Highlighting and consolidating

- Bring students together and ask them to share some of their predictions and reasoning.
- Explore any dramatic differences in opinion between students' predictions.
- Work with them to classify these responses as math-to-math (M-M), math-to-self (M-S), or math-to-world (M-W) as they debrief.
- Then, before students submit their own papers, have them code their predictions and inferences by including the initials M-M, M-S, or M-W in the margin beside each one.

Big Math Ideas
- When we survey a group, that group is known as the *population*. When the population changes, the results of the survey change as well.
- The predictions and inferences we make about a population come from making connections to what we already know—math-to-math (M-M), math-to-self (M-S), or math-to-world (M-W).

Assessment for Learning

Review students' predictions.
- Have they made reasonable math-to-self or math-to-world connections?
- Have any made math-to-math connections?
- Are students' predictions supported with justification— (I think... because...)?
- Are any of their inferences unusual or unique?

Lesson 8—Comparing Results

BEFORE THE MATH: Get re-connected

- Using TinkerPlots, display side-by-side graphs (a pair of circle graphs and a pair of scatter plots) for the two populations to be compared.
- Have students engage in a Think-Pair-Share about the data.
- Focus on the kinds of inferences made about each.
- Ask:
  - *What makes the data easy or hard to compare?*

DURING THE MATH: Learning math by doing math

- Ask:
  - *Compare the populations. What kind of graph will you use? (A scatter plot? A bar graph? A circle graph?)*
  - *What true statements can you make about the data?*
  - *What inferences can you make?*
  - *What questions do you still have?*
- While students work, observe carefully the ways in which they organize the data to answer their questions:
  - Are they using non-numerical data in their circle graphs?
  - Are they comparing numerical attributes in their scatter plots?
  - Are they able to identify relationships between attributes of the data?

AFTER THE MATH: Highlighting and consolidating

- Bring students together and ask them to share one true statement and an inference from their investigations.
- Make a list of student questions.
- Invite ideas on how those questions might be answered. Follow up on reasonable suggestions.
- If you have accessed an e-pal classroom for your data, consider an online chat with a focused topic (religion, language, nationality, type of home) to gather more data.

> **Assessing screen captures**
>
> When working with a software application like TinkerPlots, have students do a screen capture of their graphs to back up their statements and inferences. Organizing data in appropriate ways is a critical aspect of data literacy.

Big Math Ideas

- We can compare data to make inferences about a population.
- Not all questions can be answered by looking at a graph.

Assessment for Learning

- Review students' writing about the populations.
  - Are their comparisons sound?
  - Do their inferences draw on the available information?

 ◆ Were they able to organize their data into an appropriate graph to
   back up their statements?
 • Have students create a screen capture of their graphs as evidence — a
   digital image of what appears on screen while working in the software.

A WINDOW IN: What the kids did

The next step was to ask students to make predictions based on the data
and what they had learned about the world village from David Smith's book.
We had connected with Tom Fullerton, a colleague in Quebec to have his
grade 5/6 students answer our students' survey. We explained to our students
that the students from Montreal would be responding to their questions,
and we invited them to make predictions about how these new students
might respond.

Their predictions were based on their background knowledge, each
prediction an inference with supporting detail. Since we were working with
laptops and had access to the Internet during the lessons, students e-mailed
their reflections to us rather than printing them out and submitting them in
paper form. We responded electronically as well. Some examples follow:

Dennis wrote:

I think that most children will say English and French as their languages
because English and French are the two main languages of Canada.

*I think you have made an important point here, Dennis — English and French
are the two official languages of Canada, so we can make an inference about
how many people might have English or French as a language.*

Charlotte wrote:

I think that most adults would be from Paris, France, or Montreal because
I think most of them would speak french so the parents should be from
somewhere where people speak french.

*It's interesting that you have made a connection between the country of origin
and the language these children might speak. Nice idea!*

Avita wrote:

My prediction is on languages. I predict that students will speak mostly
french, some english and another language. Since they live in Montreal
and their main language is french and since their parents are probably
from another country, they probably speak another language.

*Avita, your inferring skills and your deep thinking amaze me. I think you
have made good connections between languages and nationalities. It will be
interesting to see the Montreal kids' data!*

Andy wrote:

My prediction is most kids live in single family houses because when I
looked at pictures of Montreal I didn't see many condos or complexes.

*Good thinking to look at a picture! That's another way to make connections
and inferences. Nice work!*

Jackie wrote:

For home population, I think there will be 4–7 people in a family. That includes mom, dad, children, maybe a little brother, grandma or grandpa.

Sounds like you are making comparisons to the families you know, Jackie. How many people live in your house?

You can see in their thinking that the students are applying their own personal background knowledge to make an inference about the data that will come from the Montreal students. One student went one step further when he said, "I think there will be some Chinese kids in the Montreal school, since in the world village most of the people are Chinese."

What's important to note here is that the data has been understood and is owned by the students, and they are beginning to make generalizations based on that data. This is another critically important aspect of mathematical thinking—the recognition and application of patterns (in this case, patterns in data) to new situations.

When the Montreal students' responses to the survey were e-mailed to us a day later, our Tait students couldn't wait to explore the data. After a quick lesson on how to separate the data into two sets, our students launched into an investigation to see how close they had been in their predictions.

To their surprise, the students from Montreal were not French-speaking; instead, most were anglophone although many were bilingual. There were very few who spoke anything other than English and French, save for a few Italian speakers. Most of their families were from Canada, and had not come from France. Also most of the Montreal students were not Christians as our students had predicted ("...because lots of us are Christian...")—they were Jewish.

The cognitive dissonance in the room was remarkable—and noisy! In viewing this new data, our Tait students were struck by their own cultural diversity, the range of languages spoken, and the religions practised. They reflected by e-mail, sharing what had surprised them in their initial analysis of the data:

Jerad wrote:

I was surprised that most of their parents were born in Canada and in our class most of our parents were born in China. What a difference!

Dramatic difference. What factors do you think influence the Chinese numbers, Jerad?

Arjay said:

I noticed that when they spoke the languages, Tait kids had 7 languages spoken and at Westpark they only had 2. It surprised me because the Westpark kids spoke mostly english then french.

That was weird, hey? I was really surprised at that, too!

Charvi wrote:

I was surprised by the languages. I thought that most of the kids would speak french in the school but they speak english. And another thing about the transportation is that most of the kids take car and bus to school.

Yes—I noticed that the kids take cars to school most often. What does that tell you about how far away they live?

The conversations as students worked in partners over the data were rich and varied. We pushed the students, encouraging them to make inferences about the other students through the data they were examining. One group wrote:

At Tait we are mostly Chinese and English because we are on the West Coast and its easier for Asians come to Canada through ships. Also because of the railroad building.

Another pair wrote:

The kids in Westpark have the home population of 5 or 4, so probably they have a bigger house. Lots of them live in houses. That means the bigger the population, the bigger the house. Here in Tait, we also live in houses mostly. I wonder if some of their houses are large?

We brought the whole group together for a debrief afterwards and asked what inferences they had been able to make about the students from Westpark school in Montreal. One student, Alvina, was adamant in her statement about their Montreal peers.

I think the students at Westpark are lazy, and they don't care about the environment.

Her data-based explanation (Figure 11.13) was that most of the students from Westpark school were driven to their school or took the bus; most of the kids at Tait walk.

Figure 11.13 Alvina's circle graphs on student transportation

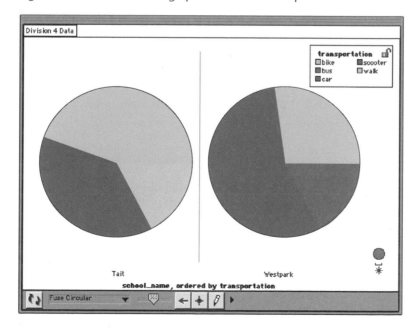

As often happens in open-ended lesson sequences, a new teaching point arose. We asked the students to consider what factors might influence Westpark students' choice of transportation to school. A reflective conversation ensued. Students wondered if maybe Westpark school was near a highway that made it unsafe for kids to walk. They suggested that there was too much snow or perhaps school started really early in the morning, making it hard to get there on time on foot. Dennis suggested, "Maybe we could just ask them why." And so we did.

A Window In: What the kids did

The next morning we set up an online instant message session between the students in Richmond, BC, and the students in Montreal, Quebec. After we calculated the 3-hour time difference, we realized that Catherine's students had to arrive at school before 8 a.m. to connect with the Montreal kids on their lunch hour. Their e-conversations (Figure 11.14) took place on the laptops we also used for the TinkerPlots pilot program, and they were monitored by an adult on each end. A snippet of the conversation follows (names marked with an asterisk are the students from Montreal).

Figure 11.14 E-conversations using laptops

Carole: *This morning we looked at the data about the time it takes you to get to school and how you get there. We wondered why so many people take a car.*

*Sarah: It is very convenient for my family.

*Kelsey: Some people live a bit too far to walk.

*Evan: Well, I walk to school.... because my parents work.

*Sarah: I found it odd that nobody in Tait took buses, considering Westpark does.

Tara: Because lots of people live close.

*Evan: Oo, that's also good.

*Sarah: That makes perfect sense. A lot of us cannot get to school by car and come in buses because of that reason.

*Tom: They noticed that no one there takes a bus.

*Kelsey: Is there a bus system?

Sydney: None of the schools in Richmond have buses.

Jackie: There isn't any bus system.

Dennis: No, I do not live close to school. It takes me more than 15 minutes to walk and 3 to 5 minutes to ride to school.

*Rebecca: A lot of people here bike to school

Matthew: Sometimes me too

Carole: *Do you bike all year???*

*Rebecca: No, we don't bike all year because there is snow in the winter.

Matthew: Wow!!!!

*Sarah: How is it that you're able to bike all year round? Is there no snow?

Sydney: Not that much

While some of the inferences they had made were confirmed by the students from Westpark, still other information entered into the conversation—things the students from Tait hadn't considered. In this live online forum, students in both regions of the country were reluctant to end the chat—questions about the languages they could speak and the religions they practised were fired over the e-chat. We agreed to reconnect the next day at lunch and continue the conversation.

For the next three days the students met online, sharing their first languages, recording their voices, and sending audio files back and forth to hear each other. They talked at length about their upcoming bar mitzvahs and bat mitzvahs, and children from Tait talked about Holi, the festival of the colours, each of them with great pride. The engagement level of the students was very high (Figure 11.15), and risk-taking was at its peak, as is evident from this ESL student's efforts during a chat on religions.

Charvi: I am a Hindu and i go to the Temple and Guruduara.

*Rebecca: What is guruduara?

Charvi: Guruduara is like a church.

*Kelsey: I'm a Reconstructionist Jew, i go to Synagogue almost every second week.

Regina: I pray before i sleep.

Gabriella: Me too.

Alex: My aunt and cousin were pray before the dinner!

Carole: *Alex came to Canada at the end of August from Macau. He is learning English as fast as he can!!*

Where's the Math?
Celebrating numeracy successes

Throughout this project, students had the opportunity to read graphs and make inferences about the data they read in those formats. Students were able to extract information from tables and data cards, connecting the raw data, classified by attribute, to people they knew. Grade 5/6 students were able to make true statements by connecting the numerical attributes to the non-numerical attributes of data (*time to school* as compared to *mode of transportation used*). They used their graphs to tell a story (*Westpark kids tend to drive to school because their school is far from their homes*) and could explain how the way they had organized their data confirmed or supported their inferences (time to school vs. *transportation to school*).

Figure 11.15 Faye Brownlie dropped into the classroom during one of the online chats between students.

Students went far beyond the grade 5/6 curriculum outcomes for data management by connecting three or four different attributes of their data to make and test their predictions. Some students, for example, investigated the connection between home population (large or small) and the type of home in which students lived (houses or apartments), and compared the data on this topic collected from the students at two different schools. Still others looked at languages, religions, and nationalities to make connections and draw inferences about where our parents come from and how that affects both the languages we speak, the religions we practise, and the parts of Canada in which we tend to settle. Beneath it all, students were driven to investigate the relationships between the attributes of their data to learn more about themselves and their newfound friends from Montreal. It led them not only to make deep connections and inferences from the data but also to ask questions about it and to seek answers to those questions, either in e-conversation with the students from Westpark or by using research tools like Google Earth to map out the roads and geography near Westpark school.

Figure 11.16 Data Management Project: Assessment Summary Sheet

Tinkerplots
Data Management Project

Dear:

We looked at your Tinkerplots work, and thought about how you worked with data and the questions you asked. Your work was assessed on the following criteria. Our comments are below.

Congratulations on your hard work!

Ms. Ludwig and Ms. Saundry

We assessed:

• Reading and interpreting survey data organized in a graph

  ☐ Could you tell what a graph was saying?

  ☐ Could you tell what you notice about the data?

  ☐ Were you able to pay attention to the axis labels, the key and the type of graph?

• Distinguishing numerical attributes from non-numerical attributes and creating appropriate graphs to display the data

  ☐ Could you figure out what attributes you needed to make a scatter plot?

  ☐ Could you use non-numerical attributes in creating a circle graph?

• Making a reasoned inferences from data

  ☐ Were you able to make connections to the information you collected?

  ☐ Could you make a prediction based on your connections?

  ☐ Could you see and describe a relationship between attributes?

  ☐ Were you able to ask questions about the data when you needed more information?

Assessment of Learning

The Portfolio

Our final assessment of student work was a review of the students' portfolios, which included writing samples, TinkerPlots graphs, and e-mailed reflections. Data from our observations was critical to making judgments about the students' learning—we both kept notes and recorded students' comments whenever possible. We had a great deal of video footage of the project as well, so we were well-armed with evidence when it came time to assess their work (Figure 11.16). Written as a letter to students, our assessment summary sheet, including specific comments, accompanied the students' portfolio. Students were very proud of their mathematical achievements and loved receiving comments on their portfolio letter.

English as a Second Language

The other part of the story

The students who were enrolled in this classroom were diverse both in first language and in national origin (as we discovered through the survey we designed) as well as in learning strengths and capacity. Throughout the unit, we put scaffolds in place to support student learning and to reinforce the big math ideas that were central to it.

Alex, as one example, had a remarkable story. Alex was new to Canada and totally unfamiliar with English at the beginning of the school year. Our data management unit started at the end of September, and the first task we gave the students was to read the population graph and make an inference. Not understanding the task at all, Alex dutifully—and cleverly, I think—copied the graph directly from the textbook, reproducing it with accuracy (Figure 11.17). Catherine spoke to him briefly about it, tracing her finger along the line graph to show the growth, using simple phrases like "more people" and "less people" to explain. He nodded and absorbed.

Accessing math vocabulary through the Word Wall

The Word Wall was one scaffold that all the students used daily because this unit of study had significant vocabulary demands. The power of having the right word to describe mathematical thinking was evident in student conversation. As they progressed through the unit, students added key words like *numerical attribute*, *scatter plot*, and *upward trend* to their oral and written lexicon. Alex, who had arrived in Canada two weeks before school started, was still so jet-lagged and over-taxed by the demands of learning English all day that he would fall asleep in class regularly, but still he learned and began to use this otherwise obscure terminology to describe his thinking.

Figure 11.17 Alex's reproduction of Figure 11.1

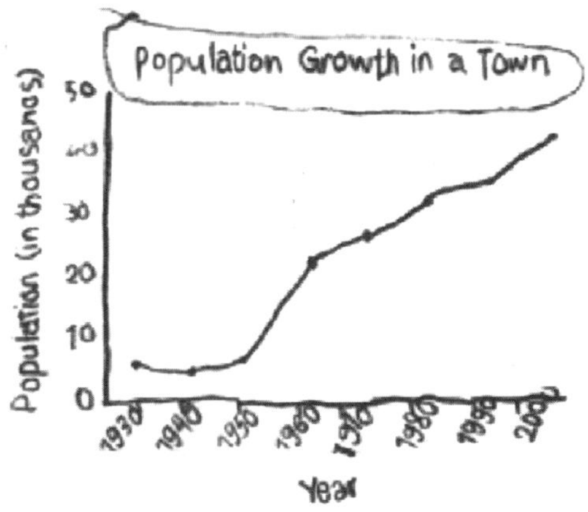

Accessing Mathematical Language

A-B partners, student interviews

We paired all the students for the online work, using the technology as a prompt for mathematical communication. Our scaffolding of the math talk was just what an English-language learner like Alex needed. The array of visuals and the dynamic nature of the TinkerPlots software supported all students as they described their graphs and experimented with different configurations of the data to answer questions. Students had to work hard to communicate meaning to their partner in order to answer the questions being asked of them.

We interviewed students every single day—often using a camcorder to record those assessment conversations. Having a camcorder on hand was a luxury most teachers do not enjoy, but, as a part of the project, it was invaluable for keeping track of student growth in making inferences. It also provided an alternative to writing for some students; Vincent, for example, was anxious about putting his thoughts on paper, but in front of the camera, he could communicate his developing capacity to infer what the data meant.

Alex also became more accomplished at inferring. His midway assessment results show how much he had absorbed from the lessons, the data, his conversations with peers, the whole-class debriefs, and the data that he himself had helped to create. When we asked students to create a concept map involving six of the key vocabulary words, Alex was given the option of choosing four and of adding pictures and examples to support his knowledge and understanding. The *language* for connecting one concept to another was somewhat lost (he repeated the phrase "goes into the" for each connection point), but his pictures clearly show that he understands the concepts and how they are connected. Note that in his concept map (Figure 11.18), his circle graphs show fractional parts, that they represent an attribute of the data, and that data is the number that represents each person's survey data. Alex's picture of "data" is an image of a TinkerPlots data card.

Alex was definitely getting it, and the video data of his performance task gave evidence of this growth. In the footage, Alex can be seen manipulating data to answer questions, pointing to the screen to show the aspects of the data that confirm his thinking, and using language to communicate understanding. The technology supported all students in growing understanding that data, organized thoughtfully, tells a story that can be read and interpreted.

Figure 11.18 Alex's Concept Map

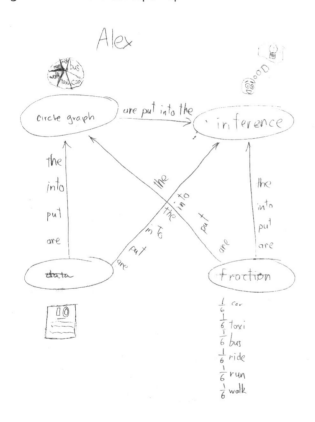

Alex's final written note (Figure 11.19) about the TinkerPlots Project was detailed and even includes in the text an inference about where the Montreal students live—that they "are not close the school"—drawn from his reading of the time it takes for them to get to school and their mode of transportation. The best part is that he ended his entry with a series of dots because, as he explained, he had so much more left to say. Note the date on the top of his page—he wrote this just eight weeks after arriving in Canada.

Figure 11.19 Alex describes his role in the project

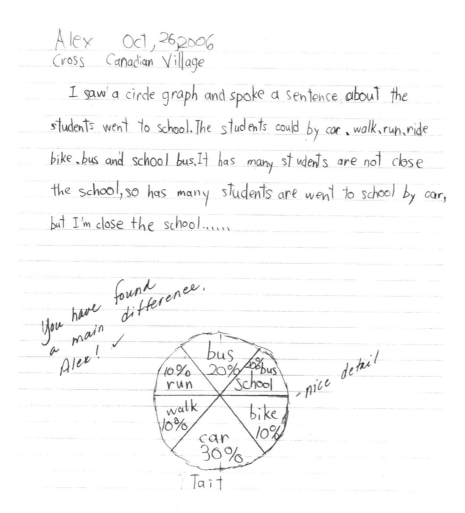

Alex   Oct, 26 2006
Cross   Canadian Village

I saw a circle graph and spoke a sentence about the students went to school. The students could by car, walk, run, ride bike, bus and school bus. It has many students are not close the school, so has many students are went to school by car, but I'm close the school......

You have found a main difference, Alex! ✓

bus 20%
10% run
10% bus School
nice detail
walk 10%
bike 10%
car 30%
Tait

Carole's Reflections

So often in studies of data management, students spend a lot of time constructing graphs, fussing with scale, plotting and re-plotting points on a grid. The mechanical aspects of graphing can easily detract from the important thinking outcomes around data management. Using TinkerPlots streamlined the act of graphing and highlighted the conceptual math, allowing the students to focus on connection-making, inferring, and predicting from the data. The software program's immediate graphic result meant that learners could read the data more quickly and derive more meaning. The students' rich mathematical conversations, the level of student engagement, the ease of including kids across the spectrum with the support of technology and self-directed inquiry made this project truly rewarding for all.

Catherine's Reflections

So many elements in the process made our TinkerPlots Project successful and rewarding. It taught me that listening to my students and encouraging conversation among them creates authentic learning opportunities that are rich with enthusiasm and growth. I remember asking one of the students "How do you know?" and she replied, "Because you are my teacher, and you and you and you!" as she pointed emphatically to her classmates who had gathered to chat about a graph we were interpreting. This young girl said it all—we must and can rely on each other to create an environment where learning takes place.

Our lessons were planned in response to the students, and the flow of each lesson was determined by the progress of all students. Diversity of instruction allowed each and every child to express his or her learning, and providing options was the norm, not a special adaptation. All students were always included. All students learned. Creating relationships, especially with my colleagues, is what has made my teaching and learning so rich and rewarding. My partnership with Carole did change my practice. Our role was to ask meaningful questions that would evoke a spirit of inquiry in the classroom. Together we discovered that honouring the students, making their connections and learning transparent, asking good questions evoke powerful learning opportunities. As in the scatter plot, there is a trend, a pattern, and a connection among and between all of us. Through the TinkerPlots Project, I learned how rewarding it is to take the time to uncover these connections, and want to make that a priority in my teaching.

Chapter 12

From Ratios to Trigonometry

Grade 10 — Mathematics

Assessment FOR Learning	• Student reflective writing • In-class observations • Learning task check-ins
Open-ended Strategies	• Open-ended questions and tasks • Concrete, pictorial, and abstract representations
Differentiation	• Open-ended strategies • Diverse texts • Extensions/adaptation provided
Assessment OF Learning	• Exit slips • Performance task

The Collaboration

With the implementation of the new mathematics curriculum for grade 10, Carole Fullerton has been working with teachers to design and select tasks that meet the new learning outcomes. Together, they have been looking for tasks that engage students in developing a deep understanding of trigonometry—the study of triangle measurement. Equally important, in the spirit of the new curriculum, is that these tasks embed the mathematical processes within the learning outcomes.

The lessons in this chapter offer investigations of similar triangles and applications of trigonometry. They offer an instructional flow to consider, and a way to present and explore important concepts in concrete and open-ended ways. Additional practice opportunities are suggested, but teachers may opt to supplement with other examples, depending on the needs of their classes.

What is unique about these lessons is their use of images and probing questions. The images and the questions present the content in a way that is accessible to all students. The problems posed relate to the big math ideas, eliciting students' curiosity and engagement with these important mathematical concepts.

In her work in Campbell River and Coquitlam, Carole collaborated with teachers to co-design tasks that would address the learning outcomes and focus on the mathematical processes. Teachers had many questions about how to embed communication, visualization, and reasoning within the grade 10 math content. They agreed that project-based learning provided an engaging way for students to apply what they had learned, but they worried about students' background knowledge and their willingness to take risks. They also agreed that the tasks would have to be presented differently, and would have to be designed not only to address key math concepts, but to do so in a way that would accommodate a wide range of learners.

Together they addressed the important things to know about the topics in grade 10, and they crafted open-ended lessons designed to motivate and engage. For creative direction, they accessed the work of Dan Meyer, a math teacher at secondary level whose educational blog has inspired teachers across North America to update their instructional practices for mathematics. (See <blog.mrmeyer.com>.) In 2010, Meyer was featured in a Technology, Entertainment, Design (TED) conference video presentation in which he discussed the necessity of updating—even overhauling—classroom techniques for teaching mathematics. Most notably, he advocated the use of multimedia in mathematics lessons—video, images, and applets that present important math concepts in visually appealing ways. As for math pedagogy, Meyer believes that, if we teachers want to develop mathematical thinkers, we need to "be less helpful." Textbooks, he argued, make for "impatient problem-solvers" because all the information needed is neatly packaged and presented. Students who engage with mathematics only through a textbook learn to seek out the formula to arrive at the correct answer quickly, rather than engaging fully with important mathematical ideas. They do not see the meaning—or the beauty—of the math.

The problems in this mini-unit demand thinking, connection-making, and reasoning on the part of the students. Although these lessons feature minimal technology, Dan Meyer's blog offers a treasure trove of ideas from which to draw and adapt. The kinds of questions asked—*What can you find out about…? What do you notice? How can you find…? What patterns can you see?*—are purposefully crafted to make students accountable for thinking about the math. By "being less helpful" as teachers, we enable students to "be more thought-full."

The Context

The *Common Curriculum Framework for Mathematics* (2008) developed by the Western and Northern Canadian Protocol (WNCP) for secondary schools has introduced new pathways for mathematics. Beginning at grade 10, students choose either a Foundations of Mathematics and Pre-Calculus course (FMP10) or an Apprenticeship and Workplace (AW 10) course. The content of these courses is very different from the previous pathways (Essentials of Math, Applications of Math, and Principles of Math) in terms of both content and philosophy.

In September 2010, implementation of both of the new Math 10 courses began—and some teachers began teaching both concurrently. They were looking for ways to overlap the content of the two courses, where possible, and to design challenging tasks for both courses. As well, they were searching for ways not reliant solely on textbooks to teach important concepts. Focused on postsecondary choices, the courses promote the application of important math ideas and the development of students' capacity to reason, visualize, and communicate their thinking while solving problems. They present a unique and exciting opportunity to explore mathematical ideas in such a way that no student need ask, "When am I ever going to use this?"

Notice that, in the lessons of this mini-unit, the learning intentions are not posted at the beginning of the lesson. Through their mathematical explorations, students are led to uncover the learning intentions as the big math ideas, which are highlighted and made explicit at the end of each lesson.

Big Math Ideas

- Scaling a shape changes it according to a ratio. These changes are multiplicative.
- The new shape is called a similar shape. The sides of similar shapes are related by a ratio. Their angles are all identical.
- We can identify ratios within and between shapes.
- There are ratios between similar triangles. The angles in similar triangles remain the same, even if the side lengths are different.

- We can confirm this relationship on a graph. The slope of the line shows the ratio of the height to the base.
- We can use ratios between and within similar triangles to solve problems.
- In a right triangle, there are ratios between the lengths of the sides and the angles within it. Mathematicians call these ratios *trigonometric ratios*.
- We can use trigonometric ratios to solve problems.

Key Structures

Open-Ended Strategies
- Open-ended questions and conceptual tasks
- Extensions and adaptations
- Concrete, pictorial, and abstract representations of concepts

Diverse Texts
- Digital images (photos)

Assessment for Learning
- Student reflective writing
- In-class observations (during the math)
- Learning task check-ins

Assessment of Learning
- Exit slips
- Tree Project (performance task)

Lesson 1—Scale Diagrams

BEFORE THE MATH: Get re-connected

- Prepare a handout of Trapezoid A (Figure 12.1) to the exact measures shown, but without the labels. Distribute the figure along with rulers, as needed, for the Scale it! activity.
- Ask:
  - *How can you increase this trapezoid shape by a factor of 2?*
  - *What does it look like now? Include your measures.*

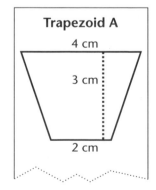

Figure 12.1 Scale It!

DURING THE MATH: Learning math by doing math

- Observe students while they engage with this task. Watch for those who use additive as opposed to multiplicative reasoning to enlarge the shape.
- To access students' thinking, ask metacognitive questions like:
  - *What are you doing?*
  - *Why are you doing it?*
  - *How does it help you?*

AFTER THE MATH: Highlighting and consolidating

Figure 12.2 Common strategies for enlarging the trapezoid

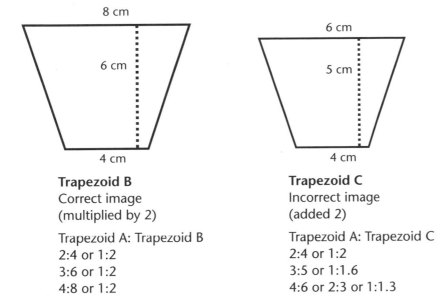

Trapezoid B
Correct image
(multiplied by 2)

Trapezoid A: Trapezoid B
2:4 or 1:2
3:6 or 1:2
4:8 or 1:2

Trapezoid C
Incorrect image
(added 2)

Trapezoid A: Trapezoid C
2:4 or 1:2
3:5 or 1:1.6
4:6 or 2:3 or 1:1.3

- Have students share their thinking with a partner. Take advantage of any student pairs who have created different images of the original shape like the ones below. Have them re-create their trapezoids on the board or an overhead, share their reasoning with the rest of the class, and compare their strategies for enlarging their trapezoid.
- Use ratios to explain the difference between the images. Compare the base and height of the original shape to the new bases and heights in each cases (Figure 12.2). In the correct image (Trapezoid B), students will see that each comparison creates a ratio equivalent to 1:2. In the incorrect image (Trapezoid C), the ratio varies by the measure of the side.
- Have students measure the sides that are not parallel, in both Trapezoid A and its image. Have them determine the ratio that exists between them.
- Ask:
  - *What can you find out about the angles in your shapes?*

- Encourage students to use a protractor to measure their angles. Have a student measure the angles in Trapezoid C and share what they find out.
- Tell students that they have discovered something important about shapes and their images. Mathematicians know that shapes can be enlarged according to a factor. The word *factor* suggests multiplication, which is how we find the new image—by applying the same factor to each side or height. Because we have used multiplication instead of addition this new image is related to the original by a ratio.
- Explain that these ideas will be very important as they explore the unit to come.

Big Math Ideas

- Scaling a shape changes it according to a ratio. These changes are multiplicative.
- The new shape is called a similar shape. The sides of similar shapes are related by a ratio. Their angles are all identical.

Go Deep

Challenge students to find other ratios—not just between Trapezoid A and its image, Trapezoid B, but within these shapes and their images. Ask:

What other ratios can you find within these shapes? How are they related?

Assessment for Learning

- Make and distribute copies of Figure 12.3.
- Have students follow the instructions on their copy to complete the task, and record both the *between ratio* and the *within ratio*.

Reflection

- As an exit slip, have students write about what they learned that day.
- Ask:
  - *What do you know so far about ratios and similar shapes? Include an example to show what you learned.*

Figure 12.3 Similar Sailboats

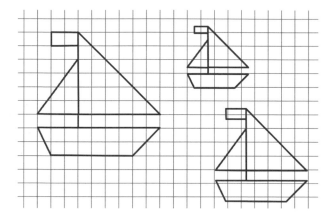

Drawn from John Van de Walle, *Teaching Student-Centered Mathematics, Grades 5–8* (2006)

1. Choose 2 boats. Measure the same part on both boats and form a ratio. Measure another part and form a ratio. Compare these ratios. What do you notice?

2. Choose 2 lengths on one boat and form a ratio. *(within ratio)* Compare the ratio of the same parts of the other boats. *(between ratio)* What do you notice?

3. Compare the area of the big sails with the length of the bottom side. What can you find out?

© Portage & Main Press, 2011, *It's All About Thinking: Mathematics & Science*, BLM, ISBN: 978-1-55379-269-7

Lesson 2—Sorting Similar Triangles

BEFORE THE MATH: Get re-connected

- Project shapes like those in Figure 12.4 for students and discuss the three shapes.
- Ask students which ones are related, and how they know.

Figure 12.4 Three shapes

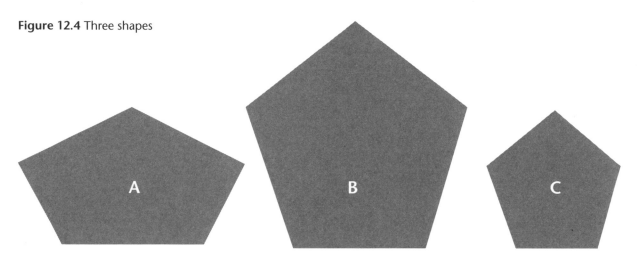

- Remind students of what they learned about scale and similar shapes during the last lesson:
    - When we apply a scale factor to a shape, the old and new shapes are related in a ratio. Their side lengths change, but the angles remain the same.

DURING THE MATH: Learning math by doing math

- Make copies of Figure 12.5, Triangle Sort. Then pass out scissors and a copy to the students.
- Ask:
    - *What can you find out about these triangles?*
    - *How would you sort them?*
- Watch and listen for students who group triangles according to their angles. Ask them to share their reasoning:
    - *Why are you grouping those triangles together?*
    - *How are they alike?*
    - *How are they different?*
- Confirm for students that there are 2 sets of triangles that go together on the page. Have students share their explanations of how the triangles in each set are the same and how they are different.

> **Teaching tip**
>
> Ask students to keep their cut-out triangles for the next lessons.

Figure 12.5 Triangle Sort

Triangle Sort

How can you sort these triangles?
What do you notice?

AFTER THE MATH: Highlighting and consolidating

- Focus the conversation on the kinds of angles found in both sets of triangles. Even without protractors, students will be able to compare these angles by overlaying one triangle on top of another, confirming they are identical.

Big Math Idea

- There are ratios between similar triangles. The angles in similar triangles remain the same, even if the side lengths are different.

Assessment for Learning

- Use the Frayer Diagram (Figure 12.7) to prepare a full-page graphic organizer. Make copies and distribute them. Have students complete the graphic organizer to describe what they know about the concept of similar triangles. This conceptual tool focuses students' attention on the enduring understandings of the lesson.

Comments on student work

This student was able to define and give examples of similar triangles—both separate and embedded, including right angles and without. He focuses on both the angle measures and the side lengths in his description.

Figure 12.6 Student's completed conceptual diagram

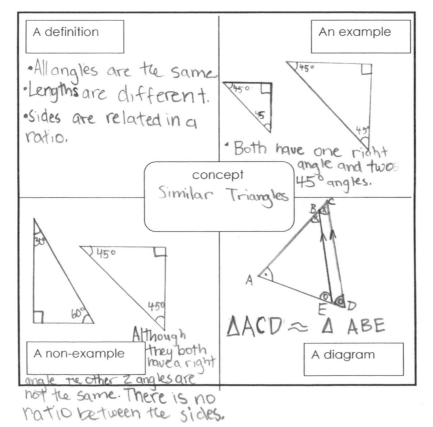

Figure 12.7 Illustrating a concept

Frayer Diagram

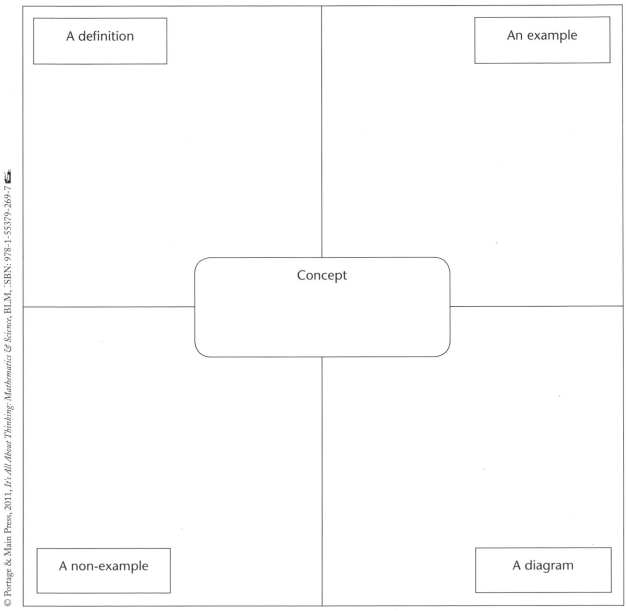

A definition

An example

Concept

A non-example

A diagram

Lesson 3—Using Similar Triangles to Solve Problems

BEFORE THE MATH: Get re-connected

- Recall with students that similar triangles not only share the same angles, but their sides are related according to a ratio.

DURING THE MATH: Learning math by doing math

- Place a small mirror on the floor. Stand 24" away from the mirror.

Figure 12.8A Calculating relative height

- Invite a student (preferably one considerably shorter or taller than you) to join you at the front of the room. Ask the student to stand on the opposite side of the mirror, positioned so that, when looking into the mirror, he or she can just see the top of your head.
- Have a second student measure the distance from the middle of the student's feet to the centre of the mirror.
- On a calculator, use ratios to calculate the student's height.

$$\frac{\text{Teacher height in inches x student's distance to mirror}}{\text{Distance to mirror (24")}} = \text{Student's height in inches}$$

- Without telling what you did, share the student's height, and confirm it by measuring.
- Ask:
  - *How did I calculate the student's height?*
  - *Why does it work?*

AFTER THE MATH: Highlighting and consolidating

- Confirm that you used ratios to solve this problem. Ratios work because the triangles created between the teacher and the mirror and the student and the mirror have the same angles. When we look into a mirror, the angle of reflection between the object and its image is the same.

Figure 12.8B Angles and triangles of solution by ratios

- In their notebooks, have students sketch the triangles created between people and mark the equal angles created.
- Have students work in pairs to try the same experiment. Have them record their findings and their calculations.

Big Math Idea

- We can use ratios between and within similar triangles to solve problems.

Task for practice

Use the overhead to project a transparency of Figure 12.9, a photo of Bao Xishun, who was one of the world's tallest men, and his wife, Xia Shujuan. Ask:

Bao is 7' 9" tall. If he stands 24" from the mirror, about where will his wife Xia have to stand? How do you know?

Extension Problem

Bao Xishun is 7'9" tall. He stands 24" from a mirror. What angle does he make with the mirror? Which trigonometric ratios help you to find the measure of the angle?

Figure 12.9 Angles to determine ratio of heights

A WINDOW IN: What the kids did

Students enjoyed this task. While they were initially stumped on how the teacher was able to quickly calculate the second person's height, they could intuitively see that there was something related in the task. This alone was a coup—classroom teachers commented on how engaged their students were in puzzling through the "trick." Students of all abilities shared equally in their wondering. The task became a great leveller—although it was clearly mathematical, there was something distinctly accessible about the task that made more students want to engage.

In thinking about the angle of the mirror's reflection, one student made connections to the game of pool. He knew from playing the game that, when a billiard ball rebounds off a wall, it does so at the same angle at which it hit. Although he didn't have the language to describe the *angle of reflection* and the *angle of incidence*, his classmates immediately understood what he was talking about, and nodded.

Once they sorted out where the equal angles were in the scenario, students were able to sketch and label similar triangles easily. What was more fun, however, was watching students pair up and predict how far away from the mirror the second person would have to stand to make a similar triangle with their peer. A pair of identical twins had a clear advantage.

Assessment for Learning

- Have students do a quick-write within 2 to 3 minutes, in response to the following:
    - *How can you use ratios in similar triangles to solve problems?*
    - *How much information do you need?*

Lesson 4—Graphing Similar Triangles: Making Connections to Algebra

BEFORE THE MATH: Get re-connected

- Cut out a large right-angle triangle from a sheet of letter-size paper.
- Show it to students and ask them to note what they see. Use scissors to cut a new height for the triangle—a line parallel to the original height.
- Ask students to say what is true about the new triangle compared to the old.
- Continue to cut pieces off the original triangle, creating smaller and smaller—but similar—triangles with each cut.
- Remind students that similar triangles have the same angles and sides that are related in a ratio. Explain that this information can be used to solve problems.

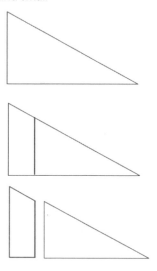

Figure 12.10 Triangles, large and small

DURING THE MATH: Learning math by doing math

- Have students re-use the triangles they cut out for lesson 2 to explore the bases and heights of the set of right triangles. Some might begin by overlapping their triangles, matching up identical angles. Draw their attention to these matching parts, and encourage them to use a T-chart to organize their information systematically.
- Pass out 0.5 cm grid paper. Ask students to create a graph to explore relationships within and between select triangles.

Math-to-world connection

In examining his similar triangles, Cam made a connection to a drawing program. He said that when he lined up his triangles on the grid paper, it reminded him of clicking the "lock aspect ratio" button on the computer. Each triangle was exactly the same, he said, except it had been enlarged with all the aspect ratios maintained.

- Have students compare the base of each triangle to its height, and record the heights on the y-axis and the bases on the x-axis (See Figure 12.11).
- Ask:
  - *What do you notice about your graph?*
  - *What do you notice about the slope of the line joining each of the heights?*
- Have students share what they learned with others.

AFTER THE MATH: Highlighting and consolidating

Confirm for students that the slope of the line between the points is the same. This means the rate of growth of the triangles is proportional—that is, each triangle in this set is related to all the others by a ratio. This is what mathematicians call a *between ratio*.

Figure 12.11 Similar triangle graph

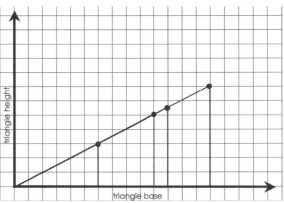

Big Math Ideas

- There are ratios between similar triangles. The angles in similar triangles remain the same, even if the side lengths are different.
- We can confirm this relationship on a graph. The slope of the line shows the ratio of the height to the base.

Teaching Tip

In the set of triangles on Figure 12.5, the ratio of the height to the base of the right angle triangle is 0.52:1. Therefore, the slope of the line connecting the origin to the height of each triangle in the set is 0.52.

Go Deep

- Have students use their graph to generalize the formula for the linear function created. This is an excellent way to connect to an algebraic representation of the proportionality of the shapes.
- Have them use their expression to calculate the dimensions of three new triangles that fit the linear function.

A WINDOW IN: What the kids did

Jeffrey and Marlon were ready for a challenge. As the other students worked with rulers to locate points on the graph that would satisfy the ratio, Carole pulled these students aside. Their conversation follows:

Carole: *What do you notice about your graph?*

Marlon: The whole thing is the same. It's just bigger.

Carole: *Marlon says the whole thing is the same. What do you suppose that means, Jeffrey?*

Jeffrey: (pointing) He's talking about this line, It's the same angle all along. Right from here (indicating the origin).

Carole: *So you're saying it rises at the same angle?*

Jeffrey & Marlon: (nodding) Ya. It's constant.

Carole: *Interesting word, constant. So, what predictions can you make beyond this last point on the line?*

Marlon: It's going to continue in the same way. You could just draw the line along the same path.

Carole: *Mathematicians have a way of describing what you've noticed about that line. They say that the line has a slope—a constant slope. The angle of inclination doesn't change at all. It just rises at exactly the same rate all the way along. Now—it's pretty obvious that some points would never fall on the line.*

Jeffrey: Ya—like something over here (pointing to the space well above the line).

Carole: *How do you know?*

Jeffrey: Because the height would be way too big for the base.

Marlon: Ya—the ratio would be all wrong. The triangle wouldn't be similar.

Carole: *OK. So only points with the same ratio of height to base would lie on this line? Hm… So would this point (3, 3) be on the line?*

Marlon: No.

Jeffrey: That would be a totally different looking triangle. The slope would be way steeper.

Carole: *I think you're onto something, when you talk about the slope (the angle) of the line. And Marlon, you've hit on something important, too, when you talk about ratios of base to height. I'd like you to look at the graph and see if you can come up with a mathematical way to predict what points will be on this line, no matter what. Test your ideas, and let me know what you figure out.*

After some time, Marlon and Jeffrey returned to say that as long as the ratio of height to base was 0.52:1, the points would fall on the line. They had generalized the formula below and included a table to show their thinking:

Height = 0.52 (base)

base	height
10 cm	5.2 cm
20 cm	10.4 cm
5 cm	2.6 cm

Carole took their chart one step further, and created *ordered pairs* for each set of height and base. She explained that the factor they had named (0.52) was the number that mathematicians give to *the slope*, the line that passes through and joins each of the ordered pairs they listed.

In the debriefing conversation, Jeffrey and Marlon shared how their formula worked for every one of the triangle dimensions suggested by their peers.

Task for practice

- Have students create and name the height and base for at least 3 more right-angle triangles that share the same ratio and that would also fall along the same line on the graph.
- Have them use what they know about the Pythagorean theorem to find the length of the hypotenuse in each case.

Assessment for Learning

Cam identified a triangle with a height of 7.28 cm and a base of 14 cm. Is his triangle similar to the others? How can you use the graph to prove whether this is true or false?

- Have students submit their response to you as a ticket out the door.

Lesson 5 — From Similar Triangles to Trig

BEFORE THE MATH: Get re-connected

- Present the graph of similar triangles from lesson 3. Have students hypothesize why the heights and bases are related in these triangles (e.g., the angles in each are the same).
- Ask students if they believe this might be true for all right triangles. Explain that mathematicians asked the same questions.

DURING THE MATH: Learning math by doing math

- Ask:
  - *What can you find out about the angles and sides of your triangles?*
  - *What other ratios can you find?*
- Give students the language to describe the sides of their triangles relative to its angles. Students will be familiar with the word *hypotenuse* when describing right triangles. Introduce the terms *adjacent* and *opposite*.
- Circulate in the classroom, asking students to describe their thinking and confirming what they see. For example, confirm that the longest side of the triangle in each case is the hypotenuse, and that the hypotenuse is opposite the right angle of the triangle each time.
- Bring students together and ask them to describe their findings.
- Use the graph. Focus attention on the angle at the origin — the common angle in all the triangles. Note that the smallest angle in each of these right triangles measures approximately 27.5°.
- Explain that mathematicians know that there is a relationship between the measure of this angle and the ratio of the height to the base.

Trig, simplified

The term trigonometry means "triangle measurement." Trigonometric ratios (sine, cosine, and tangent) simply describe relationships within angle and side measures of a triangle.

Mathematicians have a name for this ratio. They call it the *tangent ratio*. Finding the tangent of this angle tells us the ratio of the height (the opposite side) to the base (the adjacent side).

• Demonstrate using an overhead calculator. Use the measure of the height and base from several different triangles in the set to confirm the ratio (0.52:1). Then use the calculator keypad to calculate the tangent of 27.5°.

• Both the ratio of the height to the base and the tangent of 27.5° is 0.52.

AFTER THE MATH: Highlighting and consolidating

• Post the trig ratios for student use.
• Have groups of students choose one triangle in their set and measure each side with a ruler.
• Have them explore the sine and cosine ratios for the 27.5° angle, (comparing the ratios they find among the opposite and adjacent sides and hypotenuse) and share their findings.

Big Math Idea

• In a right triangle, there are ratios between the lengths of the sides and the angles within it. Mathematicians call these ratios the *trigonometric ratios*.

Tasks for practice

• Have students apply the trigonometric ratios to the other— complementary—angle in the right triangle (62.5°), and record their results.
• Consider assigning additional tasks drawn from your text or other resources.

Assessment for Learning

• Ask:
  ◆ *How can you explain trigonometric ratios to a friend?*
  ◆ *What's the important thing to know?*
• Students may consider using a Frayer diagram for this task.

Lesson 6—Using Trig Ratios to Solve Problems

BEFORE THE MATH: Get re-connected

• Draw a simple 3-4-5 right triangle on the board.

- Have students record the sine, cosine, and tangent ratios for this triangle:

$$\sin x = \frac{3}{5}$$

$$\cos x = \frac{4}{5}$$

$$\tan x = \frac{3}{4}$$

Figure 12.12 Simple 3-4-5 right angle

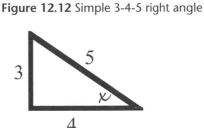

- Demonstrate how to use the inverse function on the calculator to determine the value of *x*. Students should find that angle *x* measures 36.87°, regardless of whether they use sine, cosine, or tangent.

DURING THE MATH: Learning math by doing math

To set up the problem, show Figure 12.13, the image of the world's tallest man, Sultan Kosen, and the world's shortest man, Pingping He. Sultan is 8'1" tall. Pingping is 2'5" tall. Together they do the mirror task from lesson 3. Pingping stands 2' from the mirror. Sultan backs up until he makes a similar triangle. Ask:

- *How far away from the mirror will Sultan stand?*
- *What angle of reflection exists between Pingping, the mirror, and the image of Sultan's head?*
- *Which trig ratios help you to find the measure of the angle?*

Taking the terror out of trig

While working on the problem to find the angle of reflection between Sultan and Pingping, one pair of students sat huddled in a corner, seemingly lost. When asked what they were doing, they answered they were trying to use their calculators to find the missing angles, but that it wasn't helping them. "I don't think I get trigonometry," one student said. "It freaks me out."

Figure 12.13 The world's tallest and shortest men

Carole had heard comments like this before. Too often, trigonometry is built up by peers and parents to be a frightening and complex topic, and she set out to calm the emotion—in effect, the most powerful thing standing in the way of success—by presenting a simpler problem and making connections to prior knowledge. Their conversation follows:

Carole: *In any triangle, there are relationships we know.(Sketching a right isosceles triangle). In this triangle, what do you know for sure?*

Jessa: This angle is 90°, and these are 45°.

Carole: *Mei? Do you agree?*

Mei: Yes. It's because the sum of the angles is 180°. 45 and 45 and 90 make 180.

Carole: *True. That's one relationship we know about any triangle. The sum of the angles is always 180°. Is there anything else you notice about this triangle?*

Mei: These sides are equal to each other. (pointing)

Carole: *They are equal to one another, because this is an isosceles triangle. But what if I told you that any right-angled triangle with one angle of 45° was isosceles? Why don't you sketch one?*

The students began to draw triangles with an angle of 45°, and quickly figured out the point.

Jessa: The other angle is always going to be a 45° angle, so the triangle will have 2 equal sides.

Mei: It's always going to make an isosceles triangle.

Carole: *So what's the ratio between the sides of your triangle?*

Mei: 3 cm to 3 cm or 1.

Jessa: Mine's also 1—both short sides are 4.5 cm.

Carole: *Mathematicians figured out the same thing. When the ratio of the opposite side to the adjacent side is 1, the angle is always 45 degrees. Now that's a mouthful, so they gave it another name. They call this a tangent ratio, and they write it like this:*

$$\tan(45°) = 1$$

Try it on your calculator to be sure. (Students punch 45, then the tangent button and the display shows 1.

Jessa: Cool.

Mei: Oh, I get it. The calculator tells the ratio of the sides when you hit tangent.

Carole: *Well, it tells you the ratio of the opposite to the adjacent side, yes. Let's try just one more. OK, so say I change the length of one side... like this. (extending Mei's triangle by one cm on the base—a 3,4, 5 triangle). What do you notice about the angles now?*

Jessa: Obviously they're not the same.

Mei: This one is much smaller. (pointing)

Carole: *What would you estimate for a measure for that small angle now?*

Jessa: About 30°? 25°?

Carole: *Let's use trigonometry to figure it out. What measure is opposite this side? (3) What measure is adjacent? (4). So the ratio is 0.75. Because we started with the ratio, you'll have to work backwards to find the angle.*

Mei: (punching keys on her calculator) 0.75 and then inverse tangent because it's opposite over adjacent... that's 30°!

Jessa: Oh... cool.

Carole: *When we talk about trigonometry, we're really just talking about the relationships that exist within triangles. It's not scary, it's just cool.*

AFTER THE MATH: Highlighting and consolidating

Big Math Ideas
- In a right triangle, there are ratios between the lengths of the sides and the angles within it. Mathematicians call these ratios *trigonometric ratios*.
- We can use trigonometric ratios to solve problems.

Assessment for Learning

Have students do a quick-write (in 2 or 3 minutes) in response to the question.

How can you use trig ratios in to solve problems? How much information do you need? Give an example to show how you know.

Performance Task

Setting the stage
- Give students a right triangle cut from cardboard, with angles of 30° and 60°.
- Model how to hold the cardboard triangle with the 30° angle at your eye, and with the base parallel to the ground.

- Close one eye and sight along the hypotenuse until the top of an object (a poster or clock on the wall) comes into view.
- Measure the distance along the floor to the base of the object you sighted.
- Ask:
  - *How can you use what you know about similar triangles and trig ratios to determine the height of the object?*"
- Have students sketch their thinking and share strategies.
- Next, challenge students to apply this technique out of doors.

> **Teaching Tip**
>
> Consider showing the video found at <www.youtube.com/watch?v=F6fltSqlmFM> for different ways to find the height of a tree (including an Aboriginal technique). While the demonstration makes use of principles of isosceles triangles rather than trigonometric ratios, it may jump-start students' thinking about this problem, and they can use trigonometry to confirm it.

Problem: Find a tall tree, a building, or a flagpole outside. Use what you know about similar triangles and trigonometric ratios to assess the height of the object. Be sure to share all your calculations.

Figure 12.14 Assessing height of an object

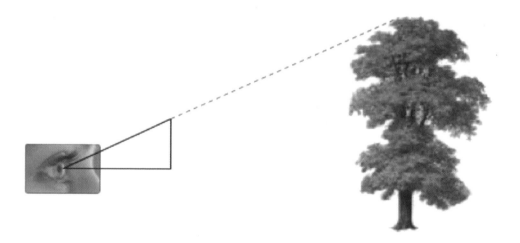

Go Deep

Consider having students complete the same task, with a more complex right triangle—one with angles *not* equal to 30°, 60°, or 45°.

Assessment of Learning

- Give students a copy of the assignment (Figure 12.15) and the assessment checklist (Figure 12.16) to ensure they understand the demands of this assignment before they begin.

How Tall Is It? Taking Trig Outside!

Find a large tree, a building, or a flagpole outside. Use what you know about
similar triangles and trigonometric ratios to assess the height of the object.
Be sure to share all your calculations.

Key vocabulary:	
Tangent	Trigonometric ratio
Sine	Similar triangles
Cosine	Angle
Ratio	

A sketch:

What I measured:

Why I measured it:

My calculations:

How I know it works:

Figure 12.16 Assessment Checklist for Figure 12.15

How Tall Is It? Assessment Checklist

What I measured:		
Assignment Components	**Mark**	**Comments**
A Sketch: A diagram with all known measures and angles marked on it.	5	
What I measured and why I measured it: Description of the aspects (angles and measures) that were critical to solving the problem. Key vocabulary included in response.	5	
My calculations: Complete calcuations including all possible trigonometric ratios to show the missing height.	5	
How I know it works: Justification (with examples) of why the math I used works in this example. Key vocabulary included in response.	5	
Total	20	

Key vocabulary:

Tangent	Trigonometric ratio
Sine	Similar triangles
Cosine	Angle
Ratio	

© Portage & Main Press, 2011, *It's All About Thinking: Mathematics & Science*, BLM, ISBN: 978-1-55379-269-7

Carole's Reflections

Students enjoy the tasks assigned in this unit, and engage with them eagerly. Early in the unit, they are invited to sort and to reason through the big math ideas of similarity. Exploring these ideas in concrete ways is important, and allows all learners to access the concepts.

The task of measuring their peers in lesson 3 gives students the opportunity to apply what they are learning about similar triangles to real situations—and to test the validity of the mathematics. The startling images from the media (the tallest and shortest people) are a great hook, and they provide another context in which to apply student reasoning. The final performance task is just that—a performance. It asks that students consolidate the big math ideas of the unit by applying them to a real-world context.

Trigonometry is a most useful concept, used widely in engineering, surveying, and design, which makes it only logical that students are introduced to these ideas in a concrete way. Instead of asking "When am I ever going to use this?" students see the application to real-life problems.

Professional References

Allington, Richard L. 2001. *What really matters for struggling readers: Designing research-based programs*. Glenview, IL: Addison-Wesley/Pearson Education.

Alvermann, Donna E. 2001. "Effective literacy instruction for adolescents." Executive summary and paper commissioned by the National Reading Conference. Chicago, IL: National Reading Conference.

Bereiter, Carl, and Marlene Scardamalia. 1993. *Surpassing ourselves: An inquiry into the nature and implications of expertise*. La Salle, IL: Open Court.

Biancarosa, Gina, and Catherine E. Snow. 2004, 2006. *Reading next: A vision for action and research in middle and high school literacy: A report to Carnegie Corporation of New York, 2nd ed*. Washington, DC: Alliance for Excellent Education.

Black, Paul, and Dylan Wiliam. 1998. "Assessment and classroom learning." Assessment Research Group: *Assessment in Education*, 5 (1), 7–74. British Columbia Ministry of Education. 2002.

Black, Paul, Chris Harrison, Clara Lee, Bethan Marshall, and Dylan Wiliam. 2003. *Assessment for learning: Putting it into practice*. Maidenhead, UK: Open University Press/McGraw Hill Education International.

Bransford, John D., Ann L. Brown, and Rodney R. Cocking, eds. 2000. *How people learn: Brain, mind, experience, and school*. Washington, DC: National Academy Press.

British Columbia Ministry of Education. 2008. *Mathematics: 8 and 9; 10 to 12*. Victoria, BC: British Columbia Ministry of Education. Available from: <www.bced.gov.bc.ca/irp/subject.php?lang=en&subject=Mathematics>.

BC Performance Standards: Reading Literature, Reading for Information; Writing. Revisions 2009 and ongoing. Victoria, BC: Student Assessment and Program Evaluation Branch. Retrieved February 2, 2009, from <http://www.bced.gov.bc.ca/perf_stands/>.

Brownlie, Faye, and C. Feniak. 1998. *Student diversity: Addressing the needs of all learners in inclusive classrooms.* Markham, ON: Pembroke Publishers Ltd.

Brownlie, Faye. 2005. *Grand conversations, thoughtful responses: A unique approach to literature circles.* Winnipeg, MB: Portage & Main Press.

Brownlie, Faye, C. Feniak, and Leyton Schnellert. 2006. *Student diversity: Classroom strategies to meet the learning needs of all students, 2nd ed.* Markham, ON. Pembroke Publishers Ltd.

Brownlie, Faye. 2009. "Adolescent literacy assessment: Finding out what you need to know." In *Adolescent literacy, field tested,* 117–125, by S.R. Parris, D. Fisher, and K. Headley, eds. Newark, DE: International Reading Association.

Brownlie, Faye, and Leyton Schnellert. 2009. *It's all about thinking: Collaborating to support all learners — in English, social studies, and humanities.* Winnipeg, MB: Portage & Main Press.

Buehl, Doug. 2009. *Classroom strategies for interactive learning.* Newark, DE: International Reading Association.

Butler, D. L., L. Schnellert, and S. C. Cartier. 2005. Adolescents' engagement in "reading to learn": Bridging from assessment to instruction. *BC Educational Leadership Research,* 2. Retrieved December 2, 2005, from: <http://slc.educ.ubc.ca/eJournal/index.htm>http://slc.educ.ubc.ca/eJournal/index.htm>.

Butler, D. L., and Leyton Schnellert. 2008. "Teachers working to achieve valued outcomes for students: Making meaningful links between research and practice." *Education Canada* 48 (5) 36–40.

Cameron, C., C. Politano, J. Paquin, and K. Gregory. 2004. *Practical ideas to spark up the year, 4-8.* Winnipeg: Portage & Main Press.

Cameron, Caren. 2007. "Informed assessment practices." Webcast # 3 of 6. Retrieved January 18, 2009, from: <bcelc.insinc.com/webcastseries/20080116/>.

Carnegie Corporation of New York. 2004, 2006. *Reading next: A vision for action and research in middle and high school literacy: A report.* Gina Biancarosa, and Catherine E. Snow. Washington, DC: Alliance for Excellent Education.

Chapin, Suzanne, Nancy Canavan Anderson, and Catherine O'Connor. 2003. *Classroom discussions: Using math talk to help students learn*: Math Solutions, Sausalito, CA.

Clarke, Pauline, Thompson Owens, and Ruth Sutton. 2006. *Creating independent learners: A practical guide to assessment for learners, 7–9.* Winnipeg, MB: Portage & Main Press.

Darling-Hammond, Linda, Brigid Barron, P. David Pearson, Alan H. Schoenfeld, Elizabeth K. Stage, Timothy D. Zimmerman, Gina N. Cervetti, and Jennifer L. Tilson. 2008. *Powerful learning: What we know about teaching for understanding.* Mississauga, ON: Jossey-Bass/Wiley Canada.

Earl, Lorna. 2001. "Assessment as learning." In *The keys to effective schools,* Willis D. Hawley, ed. National Education Association. Thousand Oaks, CA: Corwin Press.

Fullan, Michael. 2004. *Leadership and sustainability: System thinkers in action.* Thousand Oaks, CA: Corwin Press/Sage Publications.

Fullan, Michael. 2010. *All systems go: The change imperative for whole system reform.* Thousand Oaks, CA: Corwin Press/Sage Publications.

Gladwell, Malcolm. 2008. *Outliers.* New York, NY: Little, Brown and Company.

Hakkarainen, Kai, and Matti Sintonen. 2002. "Interrogative model of inquiry and computer-supported collaborative learning." *Science & Education,* 11, 25–43.

Harvey, Stephanie, and Anne Goudvis. 2000. *Strategies that work: Teaching comprehension to enhance understanding.* Portland, ME: Stenhouse.

Hattie, John, and Helen Timperley. 2007. "The power of feedback." *Review of Educational Research,* 77(1), 81–112.

Helin, Calvin. 2008. "Surfing the demographic tsunami: Indigenous education in the 21st century." Presented at the 3rd annual Rural Schools Conference, Richmond, BC.

Hiebert, James, and James W. Stigler. 2009. *The teaching gap: Best ideas from the world's teachers for improving education in the classroom.* New York, NY: Simon & Schuster.

Hourcade, Jack, and Jeanne Bauwens. 2003. *Cooperative teaching: Re-building and sharing the schoolhouse,* 2nd ed. Austin, TX: Pro-Ed.

Kilpatrick, J., J. Swafford, and B. Findell, eds. National Research Council. 2001. *Adding it up: Helping children learn mathematics.* Mathematics Learning Study Committee, Center for Education, Division of Behavioral and Social Sciences and Education. Washington, DC: National Academy Press.

Lenz, B. Keith, and Don D. Deshler with Brenda R. Kissam. 2004. *Teaching content to all: Evidenced practices for middle and high school settings.* New York: Allyn & Bacon/Pearson Education.

Liston, Daniel P. 2004. "The lure of learning in teaching." *Teachers' College Record* 106 (3) pp. 459–486.

McKinsey & Company. 2010. *How the world's most improved school systems keep getting better.* Author. Information available at <Mckinsey.com>.

National Council of Teachers of Mathematics (NCTM). 2000. *Principles and Standards for School Mathematics*. Available from:<standards.nctm.org/document/chapter2/learn.htm>.

National Research Council (NRC). 2001. *Adding it up: Helping children learn mathematics*. J. Kilpatrick, J. Swafford, and B. Findell, eds. Mathematics Learning Study Committee, Center for Education, Division of Behavioral and Social Sciences and Education. Washington, DC: National Academy Press.

National Science Education Standards (NSES), National Academy of Sciences, NRC. 1996. Washington, DC: National Academy Press. Available from: <www.nap.edu/openbook.php?record_id=4962> and from the National Science Teachers Association (NSTA) <www.nsta.org/>.

Novakowski, J., and Saundry, C. 2005. *Intermediate investigations to inspire: A numeracy resource for grades 4-8 classrooms.* Self-published: Vancouver, BC.

Papert, Seymour. 2002. "Hard fun." *Bangor Daily News*, Bangor, ME. <www.papert.org/articles/HardFun.html>.

Pearson. P. David, and Margaret C. Gallagher. 1983. "The instruction of reading comprehension." *Contemporary Educational Psychology*, 8(3) July 1983, 317–344.

Reading Next. 2004, 2006. Biancarosa, Gina, and Catherine E. Snow. *A report to Carnegie Corporation of New York, 2nd ed.* Washington, DC: Alliance for Excellent Education.

Robinson, Viviane M. J. 2007. "School leadership and student outcomes: What works?" Australian Council for Educational Leaders (ACEL), #41, October 2007.

Rose, David H., and Anne Meyer. 2002. *Teaching every student in the Digital Age: Universal Design for Learning.* Alexandria, VA: Association for Supervision and Curriculum Development.

Scardamalia, Marlene, and Carl Bereiter. 2008. "Pedagogical biases in educational technologies." *Educational Technology*, XLVIII (3): 3–11.

Schnellert, Leyton, and N. Widdess. 2005. "Student-generated criteria, free verse poetry, and residential schools." *Update: The Journal of BC Teachers of English Language Arts,* 47 (2), 19–28.

Schnellert, Leyton, D. L. Butler, and S. Higginson. 2008. "Co-constructors of data, co-constructors of meaning: Teacher professional development in an age of accountability." *Teaching and Teacher Education*, 24(3), 725–750.

Schnellert, Leyton, M. Datoo, K. Ediger, and J. Panas. 2009. *Pulling together: How to integrate inquiry, assessment and instruction in today's English classroom.* Markham, ON: Pembroke Publishers Ltd.

Smith, Frank. 1978. *Understanding reading: A psycholinguistic analysis of reading and learning to read.* New York: Holt, Rinehart, and Winston.

Smith, Michael W., and Jeff D. Wilhelm. 2002. *Reading don't fix no chevys: The role of literacy in the lives of young men.* Portsmouth, NH: Heinemann.

Smith, Michael W., and Jeff D. Wilhelm. 2006. *Going with the flow: How to engage boys (and girls) in their literacy learning.* Portsmouth, NH: Heinemann.

Statistics Canada. 2006 Census. Website accessed March 28, 2011: <www.statcan.gc.ca>.

Stigler, James W., and James Hiebert. 2009. *The teaching gap: Best ideas from the world's teachers for improving education in the classroom.* Re-issue as trade pb of edition drawing on 1999 TIMSS. New York, NY: Free Press, A Division of Simon & Schuster.

Tovani, Cris. 2000. *I read it, but I don't get it: Comprehension strategies for adolescent readers.* Portland, ME: Stenhouse.

Turpel-Lafond, Mary Ellen (BC Representative for Children and Youth.) Making Connections Conference, November 2008. Richmond, BC.

Van de Walle, John. 2001. *Elementary and middle school mathematics: Teaching developmentally*, 4th ed. Boston, MA: Addison-Wesley Longman/ Pearson Education.

Van de Walle, John A. and LouAnn H. Lovin. 2006. *Teaching student-centered mathematics, grades 5-8.* Boston, MA: Allyn & Bacon/Pearson Education.

Villa, Richard, Jacqueline Thousand, and Ann Nevin. 2004. *A guide to co-teaching: Practical tips for facilitating student learning.* Thousand Oaks, CA: Corwin Press.

Western and Northern Canadian Protocol (WNCP) for collaboration in education. 2006. *Common Curriculum Framework for K–9 Mathematics.* Contact information available from: <www.wncp.ca/>.

Wiggins, Grant, and Jay McTighe. 2001. *Understanding by design.* New Jersey: Prentice Hall Inc./Pearson Education.

Wilhelm, Jeffrey D., Tanya Baker, and Julie Dube. 2001. *Strategic reading: Guiding adolescents to lifelong literacy.* Portsmouth, NH: Heinemann.

Wilhelm, Jeffrey. 2007. *Engaging readers and writers with inquiry.* New York: Scholastic.

Willms, Doug. 2002. *Vulnerable children.* Edmonton, AB: University of Alberta Press.

Student Texts and Related Resources

Carmichael, Allan, William Shaw, Kirsten Farquhar, Sarah Marshall, and Joy Reid. 2006. *BC Science Probe 8*. Toronto, ON: Nelson Education.

Crossroads 10. 2000. Toronto ON: Gage Education Publishing/Nelson Education.

Doyle, Susan, Jean Bowman, and Darlene Vissers. 2005. *BC Science Probe 6*. Toronto, ON: Nelson Education.

Morrow, Peggy, Don Jones, and Bryn Keyes. *Math Makes Sense 6*. 2006. WNCP Edition, Pearson Education Canada.

Ondaatje, Michael. 1982. "To Colombo," p. 72. In *Running in the Family*. Toronto, ON: McClelland and Stewart.

Pratt, E. J. "The Shark" in *E. J. Pratt: Complete Poems. Vols. I and II*. Ed. Sandra Djwa and R. G. Moyles. 1989. Toronto: University of Toronto Press.

Saki [pseud.]. "The Interlopers" by H. H. Munro. In *SightLines 9*, p. 33. Toronto, ON: Prentice-Hall/Pearson Education. Also available from: <haytom.us/showarticle.php?id=97>.

Smith, David J. 2002. *If the world were a village: A book about the world's people*. Toronto, ON: Kids Can Press.

Stead, Tony. 2000. *Should there be zoos?* New York: Mondo.

Strauss, Rochelle; illustr. Margot Thompson. 2004. *The tree of life: The incredible biodiversity of life on Earth*. Toronto, ON: Kids Can Press.

Suzuki, David. "Why we grow insensitive to dangers." In "Encounters with Nature," a unit in *Crossroads 10*. Toronto, ON: Nelson Education. From The David Suzuki Foundation, a science-based and solutions-oriented Canadian environmental organization: <www.davidsuzuki.org/#>.

TinkerPlots® Dynamic Data Exploration software. Key Curriculum Press.

Vieth, Ken. 1999. Family Tree assignment. In *From Ordinary to Extraordinary*. New York, NY: Sterling Publishing.

Websites

<bubbl.us> a web application for brainstorming online.

How to Measure a Tree: <www.youtube.com/watch?v=F6fltSqImFM>.

Math Open Reference: <www.mathopenref.com/>.

Meyer, Dan: <blog.mrmeyer.com> A mathematics blog.

National Geographic Explorer: <magma.nationalgeographic.com/ngexplorer/index.html>.

National Geographic Kids: <kids.nationalgeographic.com/kids/>.

National Library of Virtual Manipulatives <www.nlvm.usu.edu>.

A Plethora of Polyhedra — Exploring 3-D objects and their nets: <www.uff.br/cdme/pdp/pdp-html/pdp-en.html>.

Prezi: a web-based application for both building and sharing a presentation.

Index of Frameworks, Structures, Approaches, and Strategies